The Computer Contradictionary

The Computer Contradictionary

second edition

Stan Kelly-Bootle

The MIT Press
Cambridge, Massachusetts
London, England

The first edition of this book was entitled *The Devil's DP Dictionary*, published by McGraw-Hill.

© 1995 Massachusetts Institute of Technology

This book was set in Times and Helvetica by The MIT Press and printed and bound in the United States of America.

Library of Congress Cataloging-in-Publication Data

Kelly-Bootle, Stan.
  The computer contradictionary / Stan Kelly-Bootle.
    p. cm.
  Originally published: The devil's DP dictionary. New York: McGraw-Hill, 1981.
  ISBN 0-262-11202-7.—ISBN 0-262-61112-0 (pbk.)
    1. Electronic data processing—Dictionaries. 2. Electronic data processing—Anecdotes, facetiae, satire, etc. I. Kelly-Bootle, Stan. Devil's DP dictionary. II. Title.
QA76.15.K44   1995
004'.0207—dc20   94-44186
                                                                          CIP

To my wife Iwonka,
Ukochana, na zawsze,
à plus finir . . .
and
In memoriam Anna Clare (1954–1985)

Acknowledgments

I have been exposed to computing (and vice versa) since the EDSAC I 1950s, and it would not be easy to list all those who have, knowingly or innocently, influenced the entries and diatribes in my *Computer Contradictionary*. With numbing magnanimity I have acknowledged many known and suspected sources in the ensuing text, but the data processing whirligig has generated such a rich and volatile folklore that some errors and omissions must be expected. I invite proofs of violent injustices, so that future editions might dilute my claims to originality and reduce my exposure to litigation.

Entries marked [from JARGON FILE] are reproduced, with permission and minor changes, from a computerized glossary maintained at SAIL and MIT by Mark R. Crispin, Raphael A. Finkel, Guy L. Steele Jr., Richard M. Stallman, and Donald A. Woods, with the assistance of colleagues from other AI communities. I am grateful to El Don, the Mighty Knuth for directing me circa 1979 toward this definitive source of DP wordage, not to mention the nondenumerable blessings of his three-going-on-four gospels.

Since the original DDPD (*Devil's DP Dictionary*) appeared (McGraw-Hill, 1981), the Jargon File has been edited and annotated by Guy L. Steele Jr. (et ses amis) and published to wild acclaim as THD (*The Hacker's Dictionary*, Harper & Row, 1983). TNHD (*The New Hacker's Dictionary*, The MIT Press, 1990), recompiled and relinked by Eric S. Raymond and Guy L. Steele Jr., expanded on THD chiefly reflecting the UNIX pandemic and its new generation of Hackersprecherin. A second edition of TNHD appeared in 1993, and it is to this edition that this edition makes reverent cross references (*See* THIS). My debt to the original Jargon File, its parents and diverse progeny is hereby reaffirmed.

To further clarify this publicational and referential morass, my entries marked *See also* TNHD or *More at* TNHD direct you to the entry TNHD, which in turn invites you to examine complementary exegeses in the *second* edition of TNHD. Prior exposure to POINTERS, HANDLES and INDIRECTION will prove useful.

In 1984 I started writing a monthly column, The Devil's Advocate, for UNIX Review. With hardly-ever a DEADLINE missed, the column rumbles on, and I feel compelled to thank the UNIX Review publishers, Miller-Freeman Inc., my current editor-in-chief, St. Andrew Binstock, his current managing editor, Lea Anne Bantsari, and the hordes of percipient readers who have encouraged me in this endeavor. My dictionary incorporates their feedback with locally explicit nods wherever possible. I have also reused material from my columns in *Computer Language* (now renamed *Software Development)* and *OS/2 Magazine,* and wish to thank their respective editors, Larry O'Brien and Alan Zeichick, for their support, which I wear daily.

At extremely odd and awkward moments during my compilation, in both the informal-osmotic, ceilidh-driven, drunken-walkthrough and structured-discoursed environments, I have been helped and hindered by Fritz Spiegl; Michael, Ilse and Christa Godfrey; Carver Mead; Romuald Szramkiewicz; Peter and Mary Felgett; Doreen Ada Godoy; Margaret Rose, Edmund Paul, Tim, Toni, David Russell, Peggy and Anna Bootle; Steve and Jane Bourne; Peter Wegner; Barry Smiler; Bob Fowler; Charles Ackerman; Anton and Natasha Leof; Allison Wegner; Bertrand Meyer; Michael Marcotty; Anne Mellinger; Tim Neely; Oleg and Pavel Luksha; Michael Howard; Katharine Snyder; Patrick Brennan; Melissa Clemens; Judith Williams; Ken Iverson; Alexander Antoniades; David Crystal; Peter H. Salus; Ed Cherlin; Judith Williams; Stuart Yarus; Samuel P. Harbison; Pavel and Nina Machotka; Stan Hey; Kate Mitchell; Richard Nelson; Laura Grenyo; Kelly Rich; Rod Lehman; Shabbir Khan; Pete Becker; Carolyn André; Peter van der Linden; Michele, Crispin and Samuel Coxon; James, Carol and Luke Bailey; Wesley Walton; Rudolph Langer; Gary Zoller; The Dean of Westminster; Bjarne Stroustrup; Joan Smith; Chris Hipwell; Ken Hertzler; Gary Masters; Bob and Jean Toxen; David Hartley; Maurice Wilkes; the Liverpool Football Club; John Smart; Karen Rogers; Joe Celco; David Intersimone; Nicole Freeman; P. J. (Bill) Plauger; Bert Speelpenning; Dave Chandler; Mark Halpern; John Barry; Paul Ceruzzi; Martin Campbell-Kelly; Henry G. Baker; Eric Allman; Peter, Roz, Kerry and Lyndsey Hazelwood; Kirk McKusick; the Baltimore Consort; Julia Reisz; Richard Werthimer; David Hendry; Scott Taylor; Kevin Keegan; la famille Sitter; Ken Arnold; Mark Compton; Crispin Littlehales; Frederick and Anne Butzen; Cosima Sakapuśkaia Kelly; Lill Adolfsen; Fred and Lisa Avolio; Nathan Myers; Pandu Rudruraju; Robert and Donna Ward; Ron Burk; Henry G. Nimble; Michael and Tania Marcotty; Marie-France Plassard; Doug Fraser; Robert DeShetler; Ibrahim and Amal Omar; and the mysterious Dr. Ellipsis...*See also* SPACE PRECLUDES.

A nonlinear salute goes to Barry Richman, Mr. B. R., onlie begetter of the 1981 McGrUr-Hill text. He it was who pushed the DDPD and breeched my baby. Si parientinas requiris, circumspice! But never look back.

A transcendent appreciation is demanded for those who were acknowledged in, but have died since, the original DDPD. I see no direct cause-effect here, but a sad guilt pervades: "Y'a des petit's fleurs, y'a des copains au, au bois de mon coeur..." (Georges Brassens). For example, did Peter Davies, who guided me through the maze of proper lexicographical usages, and (O Schmerz!) caught my typo *logomarchy* (shades of *malarkey*?), ever know how much his loving help would be missed. Likewise, UCB-UNIX pioneer Jim Joyce (no relation except in Celtic exuberance), a rare bigraduate in Anglo-Saxon and Computer Science, is no longer here to hone my **vi** skills or guzzle my Laphroig.

I must also thank the custodians of the Ambrose Bierce House in St. Helena, California, where I browsed for bitter imbuement, including two nights spent in Lillie Langtry's bed (she was elsewhere, alas).

In addition to my obvious debt to the Ambrose Bierce corpus (I suspect that El Gringo is still alive, boozing in Tijuana, confirming that wit survives humor), I should acknowledge the influence of three other sources of off-beat lexicography: Gustave Flaubert's *Dictionnaire des Idées Reçues;* Georges Elgozy's *Le Contradictionnaire—ou L'esprit des mots;* and Jonathon Green's *The Cynic's Lexicon.*

I am also greatly indebted to Managing Editor Michael Sims, whose stakhanovite interceptions have spared you my grosser stylistic and typographical solecisms.

Finally, it's an unsettling honor that child of the *Devil's DP Dictionary* has been nursed into life by The MIT Press, imprint of my deepest linguistic hero, Noam Chomsky, and the hot-throbbing center of Steven Pinker's "language as instinct." My unbounded gratitude is therefore declared for Teresa Ehling, MIT's Acquisitive Editor, Computer Science and Engineering, who initiated the rebirth and patiently coaxed the delivery.

Permission to quote, adapt, or parody material from the following sources is gratefully acknowledged.

abacus Cartoon by Michele Coxon.

algorithm Parody based on Ira Gershwin (lyrics) and George Gershwin (music). "I Got Rhythm," Chappell Music Company, New York.

console and **nest** Parodies based on Richard Rodgers and Oscar Hammerstein II, "My Favorite Things," Williamson Music Inc., Chappell Music Company, New york.

decade counter From H. Lukoff, *From Dits to Bits*, Robotics Press, Portland, 1979.

hexadecimal From William Barden, Jr., *TRS-80 Assembly Language Programming*, Radio Shack Publications, 1979.

Jargon file See entry.

lemma three Parody based on Will Holt, "The Lemon Tree," Dolfi Music Inc., Chappell Music Company, New York.

numerology From D. E. Knuth, *The Art of Computer Programming: Fundamental Algorithms*, vol. 1 (Reading, Mass.: Addison-Wesley, 1979).

Ogam From *America BC*, by Harry Fell © 1970 Quadrangle Books. Reprinted by permission of Times Books, a division of Quadrangle—The New York Times Book Company.

reality Parody based on Betty Comden, Jule Styne, and Adolph Green, "The Party's Over," Chappel Music Company, New York.

Introduction to *The Computer Contradictionary*

"**Publish** *v.* In literary affairs, to become the fundamental element in a cone of critics."—Ambrose Bierce.

"Tell it not on the sidewalks of New York; publish it not in the Avenues of the Americas..." (2 Samuel 1:20, SKBRV)

Thirteen years and untold computer "generations" have passed since my DDPD (*The Devil's DP Dictionary* [New York: McGraw-Hill, 1981]) was first exposed to conical, nay, hyperbolic dissection. *Malgré tout,* the book survived "in print" for over ten years and, I believe, fulfilled its original satirical aim of "increasing the dearth of useful data processing glossaries."

The ould DDPD eventually achieved its predestined *épuisage,* but at least it remained unremaindered to the bitter end, sparing me the authors' ultimate indignity: snapping up job lots at tuppence a gross.

Since its demise, I have been occasionally reminded, especially by readers of my UNIX Review "Devil's Advocate" column, that a new DDPD is long overdue, exploiting both the catastrophic decline of our fair trade ("the laxicon was never laxer") and the steady increase in my omniscience since 1981.

After much coaxing and ridicule, therefore, I now offer this update under a fresh title and a more fertile imprimatur. My initial working title was the gender-free *Child of Devil's DP Dictionary* until an informal poll revealed that DP was no longer associated with computing. Those interviewed suggested "displaced person" (56%), "double play" (33%), "deferred payment" (7%), "directione propria" (5%), and "data processing" (−1%). Clearly, the locus of computing has moved from the manipulation of information to the painting of icons and the tracking of mouse balls.

The new title tips *mon vieux chapeau* to Georges Elgozy (*Le Contradictionnaire* [Paris: Éditions Denoël, 1967]), yet another underappreciated cynical lexicographer. In addition to taking the obvious interpretation of Elgozy's portmanteau, you are invited to consider the transition from bassoon to contrabassoon.

I have added over 500 new headwords, doubling the original target domain, but need to stress that wit resists a uniform distribution. Dip away until, if ever, an entry tickles your fancy. Ignore or forgive the rest.

Introduction to the First Edition

This book is aimed at the dearth of useful data processing glossaries. It may well increase this dearth, but nevertheless I hope that it casts an amusing glare on the many linguistic opacities which bedevil the computing trade.

Ambrose Bierce (1842–1914?), the underappreciated inventor of cynical lexicography, defined the dictionary as "a malevolent device for cramping the growth of a language and making it hard and inelastic."[1] Whether we like it or not, language has never paid the slightest attention to such crampage—not once since that almighty cock-up at Babel (Genesis 11:1–9)—nor to the countless Academic-type crusades mounted to enforce goodspeak and proper usage. Indeed, the dictionary has recently been blamed for endorsing "shanty-town constructions" and lending authority to "how a sufficiently large number of half-literate immigrants talk."[2]

The computer revolution is still "too much with us" to justify a dogmatic "naming of parts"—or even a positive taxonomical posture—but we can learn from similar crises in the history of science. Linnaeus (1735) and Lavoisier (1787), for example, were faced with the problem of assigning new names to new and old objects (organisms and chemicals, respectively); their choice of "neutral" roots from the "dead" Latin and Greek established a trend followed by most scientific disciplines. The precision of the new appellations compared with the vernacular (e.g., not all cats are *Felix domesticus*, and there are salts other than sodium chloride) has had the negative side effect of alienating the nonscientist.

The DP vocabulary is still very much based on Anglo-Saxon roots, reflecting the informality of the English-American pioneers, and underlining the fact that computer science is not yet ready for Linnaean classifications.

---

1. Bierce's aphorisms, masquerading as definitions, first appeared in various California newspaper and magazine columns between 1881 and 1906. They were collated and issued "in covers" as the *Cynic's Word Book* (1906). A more complete edition emerged in 1911 as *The Devil's Dictionary* (New York: Neale Publishing Company). Bierce avoided the horrors of a conventional demise by disappearing in Mexico during the 1913–1914 revolution.
2. Lancelot Hogben, *The Vocabulary of Science* (London: Heinemann, 1969).

In the meantime, we survive merrily with our anthropomorphic *memory*, our medical *bug*, our sexual *random access*, our homely *address*, our gastronomic *chip*, our sportive *jump*, our ornithological *nest*, our narcotic *hash*, our thespian *mask*, our law's *delay*, our daily *queue*, and our slum's *degradation*.

Stan Kelly-Bootle
San Francisco, California, and Bargemon, Provence

Guide

Main entries (headwords), arranged in alphabetical order, are set in boldface type.

The meaning of an entry should always be ascertained *before* consulting this dictionary.

Parts of speech are shown in italics: *n.* (noun); *v.* (verb); *v. intrans.* (intransitive verb); *v. trans.* (transitive verb); *adj.* (adjective); *adv.* (adverb); *interj.* (interjection).

Pronunciations are indicated, rarely, between reversed virgules: \glass titty\

Etymologies are suggested between squarish brackets: [From Latin *aboriri* "to miscarry."]

Cross-references (implicit and explicit) are signaled by the typographical nuance of small-capital letters.

Diatribes following the so-called definition are offset in a minuscule font—beyond the reach of legal beagality.

A

AA *See* AUTO-ANTONYM.

abacus *n.* [From Latin *abacus* "a back up."] A reliable solid-state biquinary computing device now partly superseded by the Intel PENTIUM.

⇒The venerable bead still has many champions, but most attempts to refine the technology have proved self-defeating, to say the least. The Irish Business Machines megabead frame with gravity-assisted multisliding, for example, failed to catch on even in the lucrative Russian point-of-sale market. Some blame the excessive miniaturization adopted to provide 64 K beads per wire; others point to the bewildering array of color schemes used to distinguish mantissa and exponent in the various floating-bead sections. The original, time-honored abacus (see the illustration on p. 2), which can be manipulated without tweezers and microscopes, survives as a useful standby for the PC XT. *ISO Maintenance Bulletin* 2, covering the monthly greasing of cross wires, should be strictly observed to achieve maximum bead rates. Looking ahead to the inevitable disappearance of real abaci, we should mention that virtual substitutes are being mooted. In the Macintosh version, you will be able to mouse-drag the beads while a small window displays totals and error messages.

abbreviation *n.* The shortened form of a word or phrase. *See also* ACRONYM, CURTATION, IDENTIFIER.

⇒Abbreviated phrases carry little weight in the DP LAXICON unless generated with acronymic cuteness. Ironically, some abbreviations are syllabically longer than their roots: the TV show "That Was The Week That Was" was vocally doubled to TWTWTW until TW-cubed was coined. Worse fates attended the trisyllabic "When, Where, Why" (a time-management package) and "World Wide Web" (an Internet hypertext system) each of which moved to WWW (9 syllables) and thence to W-cubed (4 syllables).

abend *n.* [From German *guten Abend* "good evening."] A system ABORT deliberately induced (usually on Fridays) to allow the third-shift staff to leave early.

ABM *n.* [Arab Business Machines.] A shadowy consortium rumored to be poised for an IBM takeover bid in the mid 1960s.

⇒Critics have claimed that ABM was a Zionist plot intended to flood the Arab world with early versions of OS 360. Others believed that it was a genuine Arab attempt to switch from oil to a more profitable enterprise. Yet others postulated that the Judeo-Christian exploitation of the ALGORITHM, an Islamic invention (patents pending since 825 C.E.), had gone a little too far without proper dues. A rhymster of the period captured the excitement:

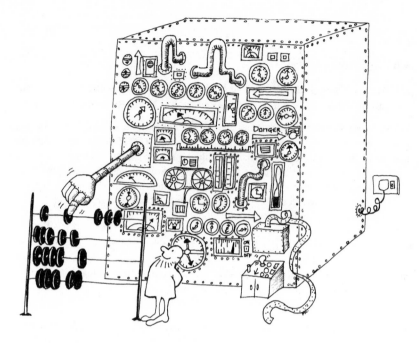

Haroun al-Raschid (may his revenues increase)
Awoke one night from a dream of peace;
He called his guards with eastern phlegm
And said, "Go buy me IBM!
Here's fifty billion on the nail;
If there's any change, get me ICL!

A muezzin to call the compilers,
Mecca bureaux for service divine;
We'll remove the golf ball from the printers
And have UNIX protecting each line."

abort *n. & v. trans.* [From Latin *aboiri* "to miscarry."] **1** *n.* The rather heavy interruption of a process or system, usually self-induced, but sometimes invoked by the user. *See also* ABEND. **2** *v. trans.* To conclude (a salesperson's visitation) by producing a loaded firearm of sufficient caliber.

ACATA *n.* [Acronym for the Association for Computer-Assisted Text Analysis.] An international organization working to establish an interuniversity network of machine-readable corpora. This will, for example, allow scholars in Canterbury to access the Chaucerian database at the University of

California at Berkeley, while researchers in St. Louis are online to the T. S. Eliot disk at Oxford University.

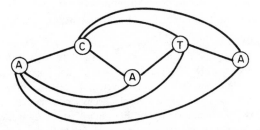

A rare example of acronymic graph theory.

Access™ *n.* [From Latin *accedere* "to come near."] The Microsoft DATABASE named with an optimistic abandon not uncommon in the DP ONOMASTICON.

⇒Francophone cynics, having survived Ingres as a possible corruption of "ingress," tend to interpret *accès* as "l'arrivée ou le retour d'un phénomène pathologique."

accountant *n.* One engaged in the regular verification of *assets* = *liabilities* + *(assets − liabilities)* and similar identities.

ack *n.* [Origin: back-formed negation of NAK.] A signal indicating that the error-detection circuits have failed.

acronym *n.* [Acronym for Alphabetic Collocation Reducing Or Numbing Your Memory.] A memorable word from which a non-memorable phrase is acrostically generated; a circumlocutory abbreviation often confused with its antonym, MNEMONIC.

⇒Devising an acronym is the first step in systems design. Contrary to common belief, most acronyms are really RETRONYMS, created by mapping initial letters onto words rather than the reverse. The former mapping, is 1-many and therefore easier. This also explains the antimnemonicity of most acronyms. Many design teams manage without a resident full-time acronymist. This is fatal penny-pinching and explains the current low standards in DP acronymity.

David Harris has suggested an alternative self-acronym: Absurdly Contrived Reduction of Nomenclature Yielding Mnemonic.

acuracy *n.* An absence of erors. "The computer offers both speed and acuracy, but the greatest of these is acuracy" (Anon. doctoral thesis on automation, 1980).

Ada *n.* [Named for Augusta Ada (Byron), Countess of Lovelace (1815–1852), programming pioneer.] The DoD-sponsored language often

3

confused with ADA (American Dental Association; American Diabetes Association; Americans for Democratic Action; and adenosine deaminase). In particular, ADA deficiency is a severe immune system disorder not yet proved to be related to the Ada language. *See also* BABBAGE.

⇒William A. Whitaker's "Ada—The Project" lecture at HOPL-II (*ACM SIGPLAN Notices* 28, no. 3 [March 1993]) dispelled many of the Ada myths before a traditionally dubious audience. Yes, the language *is* big, bloated, and Pascalian, but so are the needs of U.S. military computing. The latter covers a range of hardware and software in size, complexity, and legacity beyond normal secular commercial comprehension, from Bawston Abba T-distributions in proto-Fortran to Gettysburg battle plans in pre-JOVIAL. The new "common" language is already saving billions just in code maintenance. Ada was, in fact, the first major high-order-language design project subjected to open, international tender. The French won! The Russians were close runners-up (only joking, Bill!) Further, "The language product was on time and within budget, and of very high quality" (ibid., p. 327). The biggest lie about Ada calls it "a language designed by a committee." The truth is that the procurement committee and the winning design team were each dominated by a single person.

ADD *n.* [Acronym for Attention Deficit/Deficiency Disorder.] **1** *Children* An affliction that is best treated with a sudden blow to the head or by a prolonged matrix of indepth psychocognitive evaluations depending on the sociodemographics of the parents. **2** *Computers* An affliction that is best treated by pushing in the boards or replacing the chips depending on the current service contract. *Compare* DYSLEXIA.

ad hoc *adj.* [Of a STANDARD] established for a particular purpose, namely, after suitable bullying, to become *de facto* and, after further bullying, *de jure*.

adjective *n.* (*esp.* DP usage) any noun. *See also* NOUNS, MARCH OF.

⇒Jacques Barzun in "An Essay on French Verse," notes the "vive la difference" between English and French grammatical attitudes. The English "say toothbrush and driving license; French must have *brosse à dents* and *permis de conduire.*"

adjectival chain *n.* (DP usage) any sequence of nouns used cumulatively to modify the terminator, "system." As in: Front End Object SQL Link Run Time Database Management C++ Class Library System.

⇒Young, budding writers who employ tired, two-adjective modifiers in their first, rejected novels before taking on potboiling, technical assignments must learn to adjust their antiquated, predicational METHODOLOGY.

ad ROMinem *adj.* Relating to a personal attack on your BIOS.

aerosol spray *n.* A container holding a pressurized panacea that can be released in a series of unskilled squirts. *See* the table on pp. 5–6.

Table of Errosol Inc.™ Aerosol Sprays

Trade Name	Function	Mode d'Emploi
Smegma	Emits cheap, stale, personalized tobacco fumes, old coffee aromas, and the smell of busy peripherals	Before quitting prematurely, spray the computer room or data prep area for 30 seconds. Smegma persists for at least 8 hours, reassuring the next shift arrivals that they have just missed you
Writ-guard	Antilitigant. Repels 99% of all known attorneys, high court judges, monopolies, commissions, federal consumer protection agencies, more	Spray lightly and evenly over all write, subpoenas, juries, Das, exhibits, and sub-judice software. Caution: Avoid the innocent or guilty, whichever the case may be
Thesis	Imparts a scholarly gloss to your doctoral susmission; adds donnish wit and waspish innuendo	Apply liberally to your ms and assessors. Double-spray the first and last pages and all footnotes and references
Compat	An effective general conversion aid. Gives instant compatibility with alien systems, both hardware and software. used and recommended by both SHA members	Hold spray 3 inches from your target tape, card, compiler, DBMS, DPM, or CPU. Squirt and rotate to ensure an even covering of all bits, links, code holes, and subschemas. Caution: Do not spray the source environment
Walpurge	The sure-fire file and database purging and initiation remedy! Tried and tested with all media: ROM, PROM, EPROM (beats the most ultra UV!), core, mag'n'paper tape, hard'n'soft disks, paper'n'mag cards, bubbles, mercury delay lines, William's tubes, Brunsvigas, more	Save hours cleaning those old files! One quick squelch nullifies all but patterns (overflow areas, too!). For ivory abacus beads, a second application may be needed. Caution: Do not inhale! Your cellular DNA code may disappear
Launch	Ensures a smooth new model release. Impacts the market, not your old range!	Spray with abandon on your PR department, brochures, existing user base, and Press Day sandwiches

Shoo-bug	Instantly fixes all detectable BUGS! Soothes the undetectables! Ends your endless loops, supplies missing declarations, takes pounds off your flabby syntax while you sleep! Guaranteed effective, all languages, all levels! Why wait for that new compiler release? Save $$$$ NOW! Prof. Knuth writes: "My secret is no more. Thanks to Shoo-bug, the era of the People's Algorithm has dawned."	Treat your suspect code before and after compilation. If the condition persists, treat the compiler. Very high-level languages may require repeated applications. Will not harm or stain error-free modules. Use only as directed
New Improved Shoo-bug	Incredibly, the omnipotent, infallible Shoo-bug plus the added, secret ingredient FOO!	Spray freely, as before. But now Shoo-bug works on your OS and on all documentation. Caution: Keep away from domestic animals and AI departments
Prop-Rite	Protects your software instantly. Prevents unauthorized copying of source or object code, whatever the medium	Apply sparingly to disks, tapes, and listings. Protection lasts 12 hours. Will not harm the most delicate programs
Steal	The essential spray for timeshare freaks and software thieves. Will break down the tightest security barriers. Converts all passwords to FOOBAR! and all files to public! Even overcomes Prop-Rite. Used by Control and Chaos agents the world over	For the best results, spray the target system. If this is not possible, spray the terminal and modem. Prop-Rited systems may need several applications to remove protection

affordable *adj.* Marketing weaselese meaning "It's never been easier to raise a second mortgage."

⇒Beware of computer adverts listing the price as $CALL which equals $404,149 in TURING's base-32 notation. Likewise, ignore such specious enticements as "Limit 2 per family," and "No dealers, please." *Compare* "**Price** *n.* Value, plus a reasonable sum for the wear and tear of conscience in demanding it" (Bierce, *The Devil's Dictionary*).

AI *n.* **1** A cry of pain. **2** A three-toed, trumpet-tree-chewing sloth that squeals when disturbed. **3** Overloaded *abbrev.* Artificial Insemination; ARTIFICIAL INTELLIGENCE; Amnesty International. *Warning* Often resists contextual disambiguation.

AI, strong *n.* AI funded by the Department of Defense. *Compare* AI, WEAK.

⇒Professor R. Schank writes: "My work has required a significant amount of financial support, which has come for the main part from the U.S. givernment [sic], specifically the Department of Defence. When one mentions the DoD in a research funding context, there is the usual groan of how scientists are helping make more weapons and such. In fact, the DoD, through the Advanced Research Projects Agency, the Office of Naval Research, and more recently, the Air Force, have been some of the most enlightened supporters of real scientific research in this country. I thank the people who have made those agencies as sensible and significant as they are. I also thank the National Science Foundation for its support over the years" (*The Cognitive Computer*, Reading, Mass.: Addison-Wesley, 1984).

Non-machine translation: "Keep them funds a-rolling."

A strong AI supporter is one who would drag John Searle and Hubert Dreyfus into a dark alley and beat the shit out of them. A strong AI opponent is one who refuses to buy any product with the words "Thinking," "Smart," "Expert," "Knowledge," or "Intelligent" in or near it or its vendor's name.

AI, weak *n.* AI funded by the private sector. *Compare* AI, STRONG.

aibohphobia *n.* The fear of palindromes.

⇒Sufferers who wish to succeed in the DP field should bend over backward to overcome this disability. It is not unknown for some stacks to push in when they should have popped out, and vice versa. It is, therefore, sound programming strategy to ensure that *all* strings and sgnirts are made palindromic, and therefore immune from any trivial reversal-type transformations.

A DP doctor writes: "Aibohphobia *can* be cured with a little cooperation from the patient. Those with mild attacks, characterized by a brief, passing irritation with palindromes, are usually taken through a gentle verbal therapy. I get them to repeat such phrases as 'Madam, I am Fred,' 'Able was I ere I saw Josephine,' and 'A man, a plan, a canal, Suez!' In more severe cases, for example, with patients who shake uncontrollably at the sight of a radar, I often perform a rather pretty little hippocampectomy."

Don Hoey's enormous, computer-generated palindrome (based on a Jim Saxe template) can be examined in *Expert C Programming*, Peter van der Linden, SunSoft Press, Prentice-Hall, 1994. It starts "A man, a plan, a caret, a ban, a myriad,..." and ends a page or two later with "...a dairyman, a bater, a canal—Panama."

ALGOL 84 *n.* [Acronym for ALGOrithmic Language 84.] An extension of ALOGOL being formulated by 84 dissidents from various user groups. The original target date of 1984 has been advanced to 2084 to avoid renaming the language.

algorasm *n.* [Origin: blend of *algorism* + *orgasm*.] A sudden, short-lived moment of pleasure enjoyed by the programmer (and, for all we know, by the system) when the final KLUDGE rings the bell.

⇒A DP psychiatrist writes: "However brief the thrill, and however many disillusions lie ahead, one's first algorasm is long remembered and savored. Many programmers, alas, in spite of years spent sweating over a hot terminal, have never attained this summit. Perhaps they try too hard. Learning to relax while the system recompiles successive VERSIONS is a good habit to acquire. And then one day, after a series of FLEEPs, when least expected, the magic 'No detected errors' message will fill your screen. In their classic, *The Algorasm Dissected: A Prolonged Study of Person-Machine Intercourse in the Climactic Environment*, Masters and Thumps have described a variety of algorasmic step functions, the many different tumescent plateaus possible before the final, massive tintinnabulation, or the 'real McCoy' as we psychiatrists prefer to call it. After the Holy Grail has come home to roost in the ballpark, expect a period of deflation, or perhaps even self-doubt and guilt.

"Some of my patients, disregarding the mural caveats, light up a cigarette and ask themselves, 'O God, do I really *deserve* so much happiness?' This is such a crazy attitude I could scream. Relish that moment, I say, feel good and comfortable, even though the algorasm may signal a project completed and the need to seek employment elsewhere! Fresh fields and postures new lie ahead. The frequency and intensity of your algorasms will certainly improve with a change of system, and who knows, maybe a coarser language and a less inhibiting development environment await you. A log of your previous climaxes with date, place, language, OS, etc., can spice the weakest résumé, but keep the narrative crisp and objective. Your prospective employer cannot be expected to wade through a forum of boastful confessionals: 'As I stroked the keyboard, I felt my patellae stiffening; *yes, yes* implored the screen, just one line more, escape...' and similar hyperbole are unlikely to impress a bank seeking some RPG fixes in the School Savings package. Simple entries such as '03/15/94:2:00A.M.; made it with Win32; all the way; wow; three days to recover' are infinitely more effective.

"Patients often ask me what the *normal* algorasmic frequency is—a typically misguided attempt to quantify the unquantifiable. If you are content to write and run furtive FACTORIAL N routines in FORTRAN, a meaningless masturbatory exercise, there is, of course, no limit to your daily emission rate. Similarly, there are voyeurs and kibitzers who achieve dauntingly high climactical averages by invading someone else's interactive space. So there is, and I stress this regularly at $150 per stress, no conceivable pattern of algorasmic activity or inactivity that can be in any way characterized as *abnormal*. As DP involvement sinks downward into socioeconomic groups unaware of the cost-effectiveness of psychiatry, our profession and fee scales will maintain their traditional integrity. The humblest of personal computer owners will be treated no differently from our major mainframe victims."

algorism *n.* A pre-LISP ALGORITHM devised by abu-Ja'far Mohammed ibn-Mūsa al-Khuwārizmi (Persian mathematician fl. C.E. 825) who wrote the first BASIC substring modifier in a vain attempt to shorten his name.

⇒There is much unexplored and spurious evidence that he cooperated with his poet-mathematician friend Omar Khayyâm in many other areas of anachronistic computer science. Alas, the demon drink then (as now) clearly interrupted the study of stacks and Boolean algebra.

For 'IS' and 'IS-NOT' though with Rule and Line,
And 'UP-and DOWN' by Logic I define,
Of all that one should care to fathom, I
Was never deep in anything but—Wine.
                                    (Tetrasich #58, *Rubâiyât,* tr. E. Fitzgerald)

Omar's entire output reflects that poignant, calvinistic despair common to all programmers. Then (as now) progress was stultified by the lack of effective text-editing
facilities:

The Moving Finger writes; and, having writ,
Moves on: Nor all your Piety nor Wit
Shall lure it back to cancel half a Line,
Nor all your Tears wash out a Word of it.
                                    (Tetrasich #76. Op. cit.)

algorithm *n.* [Origin: ALGORISM with a pronounced LISP.] A rare species
endangered by the industry's cavalier pursuit and gauche attempts at domes-
tication.

⇒The current plight of the unspotted algorithm, *Algorithmus accuratus,* can be traced
back to overculling in the 1960s. It will be recalled that the previous decade had wit-
nessed an uncontrolled population growth, indeed a plague of the creatures in diverse
academic terrains. Their pernicious invasion of the commercial environment in the late
1950s prompted IBM to offer the controversial $4.98 bounty per pelt. Hordes of
greedy and unskilled people from all walks of life deserted their jobs and families, sold
their possessions, and flocked to dubious, fly-by-night programming schools.
Overarmed with high-level weapons, these roaming bands of bounty seekers hunted
down and massacred the poor algorithm around the clock. The inevitable reaction
occurred, but almost too late, in the form of an ecological "Save the Algorithm" lobby,
replete with badges, bumper stickers, and fund-raising algorithms. Public opinion was
aroused, in particular, by the future vice-president's catchy campaign song:

Al Gore-ithm, Al Gore-ithm, Al Gore-ithm,
Who could ask for anything more?

The 1970s have brought some hope to the preservationists. Two reasonably hardy variants appear to have evolved, the *Algorithmus pascalia* and the *Algorithmus heuristi-
cus,* which in their different ways are proving more resistant to the grosser exploita-
tions of the unstructured. The new strains are partly the result of neo-Darwinian survival (the fitter code overcomes an antagonistic environment) and partly the outgrowth
of patient, prolonged interbreeding in areas protected by bagbiters, chompers, diddlers,
users, and other anathematic influences. Wirth and Knuth deserve praise in this context. The hybrid *A. seminumericalis,* for example, gently nurtured by Prof. Donald
Knuth, can be spotted regularly cavorting on the sylvan campi of Stanford University,

California. Its sweet, anthropomorphically cuddlesome disposition attracts weekend crowds of panda proportions. The feeding signs state quite clearly that the hybrid will not perform for peanuts; indeed, the *A. seminumericalis* needs a substantial bunch of greenery before it will embark on its dazzling repertoire of parlor tricks, delighting all age groups and both cultures. Perhaps not all, for some killjoys liken these displays of mock intelligence to the exploitation of circus animals or the chimpanzee tea party. Also, there remains the fear that, however amusing and superficially sycophantic we breed our algorithmic pets, they will prove to be feline, superior, inscrutable, and the ultimate victor.

ALLC *n.* [Association for Literary and Linguistic Computing.] An international association founded by Prof. Roy Wisbey (King's College, London) and Mrs. Joan Smith (Regional Computing Centre, University of Manchester) to promote the use of SNOBOL.

⇒Literary computing is where you can drop names as well as digits.

alpha *adj.* (Of a VERSION) being the first (and invariably the best) of a series expected to converge to a usable product.

⇒Owing, *inter alia*, to the sad decline in classical language skills, the series never progresses to the Johannine limit of perfection at *omega*. Indeed, versions beyond *gamma* are rarely encountered since Marketing traditionally loses patience with QA and ships the BETA.

ALU *n.* [Arthritic Logic Unit *or* (rare) Arithmetic Logic Unit.] A random-number generator supplied as standard with all computer systems.

ambiguity *n.* **1** That which resists disambiguation. **2** [From Latin *ambi* "both sides" + GUI.] The nagging uncertainty as to whether your application is running under Windows, Motif, PM, Open Desktop, or Open Look. *See also* GRAND GUIGNOL.

⇒I proclaim the "pessimistic" rule for disambiguation. When the anti-viral package says "These programs contain viruses," it is safer to assume "include" than "suppress."

ancillary *adj.* [From Latin *ancilla* "maid."] *Preferred DP spelling:* **ancilliary**. Essential.

⇒As with most gadgetary acquisitions, the primary purchase is designed to generate a growing list of essential adjuncts. Familiar domestic examples include those shown in the accompanying table.

Table of Ancillaries

Primary purchase	Ancillaries
Movie camera	Projector, screen, splicer, splicing cement, projector stand, books of various thicknesses to adjust projector height, tolerant neighbors
VideoCam	VCR, TV, tapes, Japlais-English dictionary, offline rewinder, converters to/from U.S./European standards, tolerant neighbors
Fish tank	Fish, water, heater, thermostat, thermometer(s), pebbles, filter, charcoal, antichlor, replacement fish, plants, snails, lamps, more fish, fish food

The corresponding list for computers varies considerably according to type, size, and application. The environmental ancillaries are still extensive for the larger mainframes (air conditioning, false floors, tacky mats, standby generators, and so on), whereas the newer breeds of mini- and microsystems can be plugged in like toasters in the greasiest of kitchens. The set of ancillaries common to all DP installations contains:

A THINK SIGN

A warning sign such as the much-reproduced deterrent posted on the walls of the London University ATLAS site in the 1960s:

> ACHTUNG!!   ALLES LOOKENPEEPERS!!
> Das computermaschine ist nich für gefingerpoken und mitten-grabben. Ist easy schnappen der springenwerk, blowenfusen und poppencorken mit spitzensparken. Ist nich für gewerken bei das dumpkopfen. Das rubbernecken sichtseeren keepen hans in das pockets muss; relaxen und watch das blinkenlichten.

A large receptacle for discarded printouts

Sticky Post-It™ pads for recording passwords and vital operating instructions

Several Errosol Inc.™ sprays

With the advent of the PC pricing wars, the list of ancillaries now includes keyboard, monitor, RAM, and CPU. To disguise such deficiencies, machines are positively advertised as keyboard-ready, monitor-ready, and so on.

AND *v. trans. & adj.* **1** *v. trans.* To conjunct (several binary victims) in the Boolean environment. **2** *adj.* (Of a GATE) being able to and. *Compare* NAND; NOR; OR.

ANSI *n.* [Origin: Corruption of French *ainsi*, "thus," as in *ainsi soit-il* "so be it," whence "ordained, obligatory." Now the presumed acronym for American National Standards Institute.] One of many national and supranational bodies devoted to establishing standards, i.e., dedicated to changing those rules that have already been universally adopted. *See also* ASCII; IBM; ISO.

any key *n.* As in "Hit any key to continue..."

⇒Having suffered the early, unforgiving precisions, newcomers are completely dazzled by their first "any key" command. Their fingers hover, frozen in suspicion and disbelief...

apiphobia *n.* [From API, Applications Programming Interface + Greek *phobia*.] The fear of being stung by a large collection of unrelated functions with indistinguishable prototypes.

⇒JAX has pointed out that the Microsoft NT function modifier APIENTRY correctly indicates the point where bugs swarm in through your window.

APL *n.* [A Programming Language.] *Also called* **The Un-COBOL.** A WORS (Write-once, read seldom) language, devised by K. Iverson (1961), so compacted that the source code can be freely disseminated without revealing the programmer's intentions or jeopardizing proprietary rights. *See also* J.

⇒ There are three things a man must do
   Before his life is done;
   Write two lines in APL,
   And make the buggers run.

Some linguists have noted similarities between APL and Basque. Both languages have supporters low in number but fierce in loyalty, and both present incredible challenges to the learner. Also, in spite of their limited distribution, both APL and Basque have developed into many annoyingly incompatible dialects.

The APL cause has suffered several setbacks over the years. First, IBM decided to fill the gaps in the PC Extended ASCII character set with miscellaneous grinning glyphs rather than provide the special APL characters. Next, two much heralded applications failed to convince a cynical world: the Soviet nuclear safety system and the IBM's sales strategy suite, both written in APL.

The APL community's good-humored patience amid all these slings and arrows seems to be paying off: APL is emerging as the ideal language for the rapid-prototyping of parallel-processing algorithms. The arrival of Unicode will also help solve the APL character-set problem. To some, an added bonus is that APL has, so far, resisted all attempts at object-orienteering.

app *n.* [Diminutive of "application."] The irrelevant 10 percent of your code lurking beneath, and well-nigh inaccessible from, the glamorous, marketable GUI layer. *More at* WINDOW, APPLET.

⇒There is much to be said for the whole gooey, *klicken und schleppen*, mouse-ridden maze of playful PULL-DOWN MENUs, undecipherable SPEEDBARs, ICONs, popup DIALOG BOXes, and HYPERTEXTual HELP screens. These can all be assembled effortlessly from standard WIDGETs and serve to delay, indefinitely if possible, the user's confrontation with profit-centered drudgery.

"The interface must compliment the system" (Sigsoft, SEN, April 1993). So let's try `msgbox("Hello, pretty system");`

Apple *n.* A popular personal computer (made by Apple Computer Inc., Cupertino, California) with a refreshingly nonnumeric, non-acronymic apple-ation.

⇒ I gave my love an Apple, that had no core;
I gave my love a platform, that had no floor;
I wrote my love a program, that had no end;
I gave my love an upgrade, with no cryin'.

How can there be an Apple, that has no core?
How can there be a platform, that has no floor?
How can there be a program, that has no end?
How can there be an upgrade, with no cryin'?

An apple's MOS memory don't use no core!
A platform that's perfect, it has no flaw!
A program with GOTOs, it has no end!
And I lied about the upgrade, with no cryin'!

See also MAC.

applet, applette *n.* [Diminutive of APP.] An empty, provably correct statement immediately returning control to the calling GUI.

appliance computing *n.* The successful attempt to make your PC as USER-FRIENDLY as your VCR.

architecture *n.* **1** The layout or structure of a hardware or software artifact, carrying the spurious claim that prior *planning* was involved. **2** A useful phrase terminator *esp.* when SYSTEM alone fails to provide an attractive line justification or page layout, as in "Scalable Client/Server Distributed Multidatabase System Architecture." **3** *v. trans.* To design up to the highest billing standards possible.

⇒*Pace* John Barry and other critics of current jargon, the verbal form has an impeccable heritage, including such babblers as John Keats ("This was architectur'd thus By the great Oceanus").

archaism *n.* A word or phrase inadvertently pointing back to an earlier, inappropriate technology. *More at* HANGUP; BEL; CR; CORE; LEADING.

⇒Young MacUsers are often puzzled by the ICONs for disk files and directories since they have never seen manilla folders or Victorian filing cabinets.

argument *n.* [*diminutive* **arg.**] A disputatious variable given to wrestling with fractious FUNCTIONS. *See also* CALL.

⇒It is surely time to recover the original sense of "argument" (via Latin *arguere*, to put in a clear light) as "clarification, proof." The depressing confusion over name/value calling, between real/formal arguments and/or parameters, and how/when/where they are initialized and/or assigned *must* be resolved here and now. Remember: if you pass by name, the function can corrupt your actual argument, but if you pass by value, the function can only corrupt a *copy* of your argument. Some sophisticated languages let you pass explicit pointers, pointers-to-pointers, references, references-to-pointers, pointers-to-references, and so on to any depth (whence the phrase "beyond fathomage"), allowing the function to corrupt not only your arguments *and* their copies, but also those of your erstwhile friends running in distant parts of the system. It's your call, as they say.

ARM *n.* Acronym for *The Annotated C++ Reference Manual*, Margaret A. Ellis and Bjarne Stroustrup, Addison-Wesley, 1990. The ANSI C++ base [sic] document, more perused and exegeted than John 1:1.

⇒Overloaded: Adjustable Rate Mortgage, Master of Architecture, Armenian, Armorican, escutcheon, and weapon. *Warning* Often resists contextual disambiguation.

armadillo *n.* [Portmanteau: ARM + "peccadillo."] A piquant error in the ANSI C++ specifications.

ARPA *n.* [Acronym for Advanced Research Projects Agency.] An agency of the U.S. Department of Defense established in 1968 to test its defenses against misuse and piracy in the large-scale distributed processing environment.

⇒Currently, more than 10,000 disparate host computers at government, academic, and commercial sites are linked acronymically into the worldwide INTERNET (formerly ARPANET and later DARPANET). The results of the experiment are somewhat obscured by the fact that a few nodes slavishly observe protocol, while others have not yet learned how to pirate.

artificial intelligence *n. abbrev.* AI **1** The area researched by the artificial intelligentsia (attributed to Christopher Strachey [1916–1975]) **2** The misguided search for a lower-unit-cost *Homo sapiens* at a time when a majority of the species remains critically underexploited [unemployed]. **3** The construction of algorithms for the blackleg assembly of wooden building-block motor cars. *See also* AI, STRONG; AI, WEAK; SHRDLU.

⇒One emerging truth from the ups and downs of AI is that AI researchers and their machines seem equally incapable of *learning*.

The Bible has the first and last word: "See, I have given into thy hand the king of AI…And there was not a man left in AI…And Joshua burnt AI and made it a heap for ever…and the king of AI he hanged on a tree until eventide" (Joshua 8:1–28). "Howl, O Heshbon, for AI is spoiled…" (Jeremiah 49:3) [Ruler James Version]).

as is *adv. & adj.* (Of or as a) sleazy disclaimer formerly confined to pre-abused-car salespersons, now mandatory in all hardware and software legal preambles.

⇒But before we semanticize, let's morphologize. Consider the amusing CONST of "as is" with respect to tense, number, and mood: "The vehicle was sold as is," "The man pages come as is," "Chicago will be released as is," and so on.

The "as is" idiom carries, how can I say this without offending Chuck at the Name-Your-Deal Motorama (Se Habla Tagalog, Bad Credit OK), a distinctly damaged-goods, *caveat unusquisque* resonance. You might, however, view "as is" as Chuck's *only* honest predicate in his traditional flood of misrepresentation, an essential but reluctant footnote to dilute the local Lemon Law. Even so, it's sad to see this seedy disclaimer shamelessly pushed by the most uprighteous of DP vendors.

Thus IBM and other fine suppliers regularly submit their hard-, soft- and be-wares, including the so-called supporting documentation, not just "as is" but "strictly as is." How "as is" can you get? Further, these escape clauses are no longer rendered in the traditional, legalistic "small print." Rather, ALL CAPS are defiantly spouted as in the Ziff Computer Select preamble, kindly forwarded by Ted Jerome via TJJerome@tallysys.com:

EXCEPT AS SPECIFICALLY PROVIDED ABOVE, THE ISSUE AND DOC-UMENTATION ARE PROVIDED TO YOU "AS IS" WITHOUT WARRANTY OF ANY KIND. ZIFF AND THE THIRD PARTY SUPPLIERS MAKE NO WARRANTY OR REPRESENTATION, EITHER EXPRESS OR IMPLIED, WITH RESPECT TO THE ISSUE, THE SUBSCRIPTION, THE PRODUCT OR THE DOCUMENTATION, INCLUDING, BUT NOT LIMITED TO, THEIR QUALITY, PERFORMANCE, MERCHANTABILITY, OR FITNESS FOR A PARTICULAR PURPOSE, AND ASSUME NO RESPONSIBILITY FOR THE ACCURACY OR APPLICATION OF OR ERRORS OR OMIS-SIONS IN ANY DATA OR SOFTWARE CONTAINED IN THE ISSUE OR DOCUMENTATION. FURTHER, NEITHER ZIFF OR ANY OF THE THIRD PARTY SUPPLIERS WARRANTS, GUARANTEES, OR MAKES ANY REP-RESENTATIONS REGARDING THE USE, OR THE RESULTS OF THE USE, OF THE ISSUE OR THE DOCUMENTATION IN TERMS OF COR-RECTNESS, ACCURACY, RELIABILITY, CURRENTNESS OR OTHER-WISE. THE ENTIRE RISK AS TO THE RESULTS AND PERFORMANCE OF THE ISSUE OR SOFTWARE IS ASSUMED BY YOU AND SUCH ARE PRICED ACCORDINGLY…

How can marketing and masochistic self-effacement be so majestically entwined?

Prof. Michael Godfrey (ISL, Stanford) points out (private communication until now) that the people who say "as is" are inveterate, Cretan-type liars, which gets us into Deep Smullyan Country. We need to ask if an "as is" statement is a claimer, disclaimer, neither, or both, and whether an "as is" statement should itself be treated "as is," or its presumed negation, "as isn't." But at this lowest level of philosophical, copulative altercation, it is hard to envision a "meaningful anything" that is other than "as is." When I raised these points with Chuck while haggling over a Porsche/Mercedes trade, he referred me to Heidegger's phenomenological analysis of being-toward-death, the mysteries of *Dasein* and *Ek-sistenz*, and the essential finitude of the $/Dm exchange rate. The conclusion was that his manager would meet me halfway.

ASCII *n.* [Acronym for American Standard Code for Information Interchange? Possibly from English Comedian Arthur Askey.] A 7- or 8-bit code forced upon the free world by vicious anti-IBM rebels, led by the U.S. Government, who held 16 card-carrying EBCDIC hostages at gunpoint in a Washington committee compound for two years.

⇒The ASCII code, now with us like death and taxes, provides lexicographers with much-needed diversion and fun in order that "abacus," for example, can be made to precede "ZETA" in their tabulations. Some of the descriptive tokens assigned to each ASCII code help preserve quaint archaisms: *See* BEL; CR.

ASL *n.* [American Sign Language.] A formal system of body signs for use in the non-verbal, interpersonal communications environment.

⇒The DP industry offers many new employment opportunities for the disabled; indeed, computing has forced a fundamental re-examination of the traditional criteria for job discrimination on the basis of facultative impediments. Applicants with, say, chronic logismus or persistent numeriosis have always been welcomed, but we are now seeing fresh openings for those with deficiencies in the audioglottal departments. Total deafmutes, in fact, have consistently achieved top marks in the Sperry Univac "Shut-up-and-Listen" test. Recent ASCII extensions to ASL (see the illustrations on pp. 18 and 19) offer a graceful nonlinear fluency to all who are deafened by DP noise (see CRASH), or numbed by the semantic vacuity of a typical computer listing.

assembler *n.* A program that converts ASSEMBLY language statements into machine code.

⇒The confusion between "assembler" and "assembly" is beyond undoing in the laxicon.

assembly *adj.* (Of a language) DP's first mollycoddling disaster whereby the simple, unambiguous bit patterns of the CPU's instruction set were granted alphanumeric MNEMONICS. And this was done that the run-time errors be as prophesied: "But his sons shall be stirred up, and shall Assemble a multitude of great forces; and one shall certainly come, and overflow, and pass through; then shall he return..." Dan 11:10.

assertion *n.* **1** A non-deductive proof, beyond refutation unless the assertor is physically weaker than the assertee.

⇒It is unlikely that AI will ever be able to cope with Aristotle's *eristic* mode of argument, where, as opposed to rational truth-seeking, the goal is simply victory in disputation.

ATM *n.* Overloaded *abbrev.* Automatic Teller Machine, Asynchronous Transfer Model, Adobe Type Manager. *Warning* Often resists contextual disambiguation. As in "The ATM on each ATM in our bank's ATM network can now print your transaction in microGothic italics."

AUGRATIN *n.* [Acronym for Amalgamated Union of General Rewriters, Amenders, Tinkerers, and INterpolators.] *See* PAYROLL.

auto-antonym *n. Also called* **self-antonym, antilogy.** A word or phrase that carries two contrary meanings. *More at* REGULAR; BROWSE.

⇒Jack Train is the doyen collector of these NatLang quiddities, for which he resurrected the word "antilogy." However, Galenus (2 C.E.) used "antilogy" as a synonym for "contradiction," and this does not quite capture the flavor of the auto-antonym.

apparent / clearly so; an illusion
buckle / fasten; fall apart (collapse)
cleft / joined; separated
continue / proceed; (legal) put off proceeding
critical / opposed; essential support
downhill / getting easier; getting worse
dust / remove dust; add dust (crops)
engagement / loving tie; battle
enjoin / command doing; forbid doing
expansive / generous; acquisitive
fast / speedy; immobile
fix / repair; destroy
flop / (theatrical) failure; (non-Pentium math coprocessor) success
handicap / disadvantage; advantage (golf)
horned / with horns; without horns
knockout / collapse; triumph
let / allow; hinder
minimum / no less than; no more than
moot / under consideration; not under consideration
pinch hitter / superior substitute (baseball); inferior sub
overlook / watch over; ignore
oversight / guidance; neglect
quite / slightly; exceedingly
qualified / just right ; not quite right (accountant's report)

Reverse pinkie notation

Floating thumb

Unit increments in the base are indicated by clenching the fist. Touching the left ear with the right forefinger restores to binary. Tapping the Adam's apple with the left thumb signals a switch to octal. Sinistral users should add or subtract (base) ↑4 as the case may be, unless performing with mirrors. For IBM card messages, remember the simple rule: Nine edge leading, palms facing.

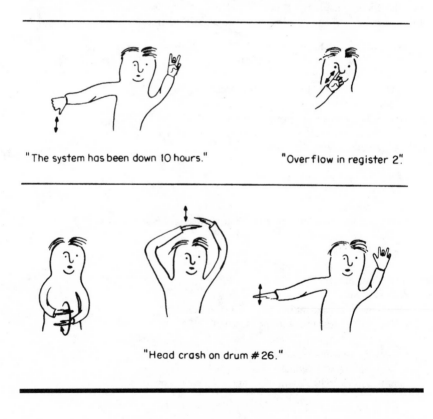

"The system has been down 10 hours."

"Overflow in register 2."

"Head crash on drum #26."

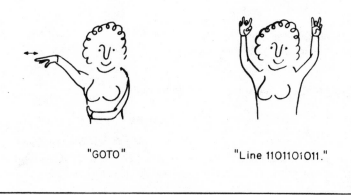

"GOTO"   "Line 1101101011."

"Logging off... see you tomorrow!"

And now, a few simple exercises:

Did you spot the syntax error ?

ravel / tangle; untangle
temper / harden;soften
terrific / repellent; attractive
trim / cut down; embellishing (Christmas tree)
untouchable / eminent ; bottom of heap
vegetate / burst forth, germinate; stagnate
zap / delete, erase; add spice

autoepistemic *adj.* (Of a logic) self-knowingly and consistently smug. *See also* SW5.

⇒There are, as I write, a growing number of concurrent enigmata in the multiprocessing environment where A needs to know the state of B, and vice versa, and where B needs to know whether A knows the state of B and vice versa. A's knowledge of its own state calls for YET ANOTHER set of flags, and so on, until RAM and/or funding is exhausted.

autoeroticism *n.* The computer generation of best-selling novels.

⇒The Playgol package, for example, ensures the correct distribution of marketable events by line, paragraph, page, and chapter. The author simply inputs the quotas of rape, incest, bestiality, necrophilia, uralgomania, bestial rape, necrophilic incest, and so on, together with the target age group (e.g., "Under 9," "9–12 years," "Light Parental Guidance").

The ETHELRED OS was the first to promote itself via a self-generated Robbinsesque novella called "The Ethel," of which the following extract must suffice.

Joe Spanasky stubbed out his cigarette. Another late night, he thought. Damn these Labor-saving devices. His mother had been right. He should have followed his brother Antonio into his Godfather's drug pushing syndicate in the Bronx. "Software is no kind of a job for a *man*," Momma had cried as he boarded her private jet for London two months ago. Still, things had worked out real good, he thought. He had gained control of the British Computer Society, and his henchmen were beginning to put the screws on the members. That ballot-rigging expert from the Longshoremen's Union had done a great job....His next move was to quadruple the BCS dues, then the IBM UK takeover plan could move forward.

Joe lit a cigarette and glanced at the E13B numerals on his 24-carat gold Alpha wrist watch. 23 hundred hours. The computer room downstairs would be emptying soon. All except Ethel, who would be working late. At the thought of Ethel he felt the heat surging in his loins. What a doll. A Ph.D in statistics, and she knew all the standard deviations...plus a few not in the textbook. Joe stubbed out his cigarette and turned to the sleek VDU on his desk. He keyed in his secret account number and paused while the soft-green characters flashed in acknowledgement. "Tell Ethel I love her," he typed. "Sod off, don't interrupt," came the reply, almost instantaneously. Joe smiled at the low-level language and stubbed out his cigarette on the keyboard. He lit a cigarette and swivelled round to the remote air conditioning control panel. He shut down the cooling system in the computer room and gradually increased the ambient temperature rheostat. He stubbed out his cigarette and strolled to the elevator. Ignoring the signs, he lit a cigarette and stepped into the glass-walled corridors, breathing in the satisfying smoke.

He stubbed out his cigarette viciously on the Tacky Mat and strode into the computer room. Ethel was leaning over the throbbing line printer. The heat was overpowering. His ploy had worked. Ethel had removed her skirt and sweater. She was straining forward on tiptoe, joggling some cards. The vibrating panels of the 401 sent cascades of ripples down her ample buttocks. Joe felt the heat surging through his loins. He took her brutally from behind, a million Think signs spinning round his head. A juicy dizziness consumed them both and a row of asterisks clattered out serially on the monitor printer. * * * * * * * * * * * *

autoexec.bat *n.* What you get when you cross Lee Iaccoca with a vampire (Light Bits, *ComputerWorld,* July 26, 1993).

-aware *suffix Largely* spurious as in *data-aware. See also* -READY.

B

BA [Origin: Egyptian "divine soul" or possibly *abbrevs.*] **1** Bachelor of Arts. **2** Brain-assisted: a natural reaction to the pandemic of CA (Computer-assisted) acronyms. *See* BASE.

Babbage *n.* A language mooted by Tony Karp in the early 1980s as a macho challenge to the then nascent Ada.

⇒In the event, Ada turned out to be a sturdy, nay, hairy, affair beyond further enmasculation. The speed of Babbage, according to Karp, is revealed by the fact that in the place of "call by reference" and "call by value" we find "call by 'phone."

Babbage, Charles (1792–1871) English polymath and inventor of CAC (Cog Assisted Computing). *See also* OEM COGS; ADA.

⇒Babbage's pioneering contributions to computing go far beyond the program-as-data concept found in his Analytical Engine. He also invented the concept of demonstrating a series of working but non-scalable prototypes in order to attract government funding. Further, the influence of Babbage's non-Victorian friendship with Lord Byron's married daughter, Augusta Ada, Countess of Lovelace (1815–1852) clearly reaches forward to urban 20th century Afro-American music:

> My baby's got somethin' like a grinding mill;
> My baby she's got somethin' like a grinding mill;
> Every time she touch me, O Lord, I can't keep still.
> ("Grinding Mill Blues," Johnny Temple, Chicago, 1939)

There is no "rosebud" mystery about Babbage's dying words: "Vive la difference! Vive l'engin!"

Babble *n.* A rare, honestly named text-generation package devised by Korenthal Associates.

⇒Babble deconstructs thirty or so canned texts in different genres, ranging from Beatles to Zola by way of Bible, DickJane, Insults, and Robbins. There is even a John C. Dvorak mode, but no mention of his bestselling coauthors! A pleasant screen lets you set mix ratios to generate a randomly risible stream of "sentences" from three chosen modes. A choice of 30 percent Bible, 30 percent Robbins, and 40 percent Insult, for instance, gives such fragments as "Lo you nerdfaced toad silk gown rustling unto death…" and so on. Yes, it palls quite quickly. There are other tricks to jazz up the action. Using every possible function key, Ctrl, and Alt combination, you can select any number of dialectal overlays and typographical templates: Pig Latin, Jewish, Brooklyn, Rasta, Mirror, Ransom Note, and so on (BEV is noticeably absent, though). These throw in the occasional "Oy" and "choiping boids" as well as some amusing display variations. The spooky Censor overlay blacks out words at random, for example, while Whisper and Shout switch to dim and bold-caps. Apart from selling Babble to the late William Burroughs, I do see a market. I refer to the party conversation piece market. What do you show your visitors when they say "Oh, you have a computer!"? Entering your guests names with an 80 percent dose of Insult and several cocktails can add much hilarity to your party. More fun than showing your latest spreadsheets or those tired revolving beach balls.

BABOL *n.* [© Irish Business Machines.] A common language proposed to heal the endless, bloody logomachic schisms which fragment the industry. BABOL combines the compactness of COBOL and the legibility of J with the portable brick-shit-house safety of C and the ancient get-it-done wisdom of JCL.

backtracking *n.* The rare admission that an impasse has been reached or a DEADLINE exceeded.

backup *n. & v. & adj.* **1** *n.* Any file, device, or person that results from backing up; the total deviance from the original is directly proportional to the number and scale of the catastrophes resulting from each copying or matching error. **2** *v. intrans.* To compound errors while merely trying to perpetuate them. **3** *v. trans.* To risk (a file, program) by attempting to copy it. **4** *v. trans.* (Of a programmer, engineer) to specify someone unacquainted with the system, job, and user. *See also* STANDBY. **5** *adv.* Annoyingly, as: "That salesman got my backup."

backward *adj.* (Of a reasoning chain) **1** Primitive. **2** Taking the truth of an implied proposition as verification of its antecedents (*see also* SYLLOGISM) as in

    IF "You are overdrawn" THEN PRINT BALANCE<0

Compare FORWARD.

ballpark *adj.* [Origin: U.S. branch of measure theory known as baseball.] **1** Deliberately underquoted, as: "The ballpark price is $25K." **2** Deliberately overquoted, as: "The printer speed varies with layout, buffer size, font repertoire, form depth, urgency, and humidity, but a ballpark figure is 500 characters per minute."

⇒The basis of baseball measure theory is the analysis of input data from a series of fiscal, ballistic, gymnastic, and altercatory experiments held at ballparks each summer. The game space is divided into discrete *plays*, each of which can be reduced to about 250 numerical parameters. The definition of the measure μ on this set can be varied to produce any desired ordering of the players, teams, managers, owners, fans, conforming streaks, and hotdog sales, e.g., player X has struck out more often than any other left-handed third-base Jewish Cardinal in the eighth inning of an Easter Friday road game played on Astro turf.

The Stan Kelly-James Baseball Bible is the only publication that stat-tracks the plight of home-run balls and in-the-seats fouls (hit-by; caught-by [including assists] with name and seat number; whether retained or thrown back in disgust). It also maintains statistics on celebrity game-start pitches, e.g., President Ford's record is: 4 balls, 0 strikes, 2 passed balls, 5 wild pitches, 3 hit umpires, and 6 balks. To those who doubt our credentials, it should be noted that Kelly-James has struck out less often than Barry Bonds, has walked fewer players than Sandy Koufax, and has been caught stealing less often than Ricky Henderson.

bandwidth *n.* **1** (During the Big Band era) between fifty and sixty feet depending on the orientation of Count Basie's piano. **2** (Of a computer bus) an upper limit to the error-transfer rate.

BASE *n.* [Acronym for Brain-assisted Software Engineering (Tom Lister).] *See also* BA; CA; CASE.

base address *n.* Low-rent accommodation of the kind frequented by operators, programmers, and other no-collar workers.

⇒Even cheaper accommodation is possible—*a relative address*—if you have an aunt or uncle living in the area.

base class *n.* (C++) No less respected than its specialized derivations:

"...Why bastard? wherefore base?
"...Why brand they us
"With base? with baseness? bastardy? base, base?"
(King Lear, act 1, scene 2)

BASIC *n.* [Origin: *Either* acronym for Beginner's All-purpose Symbolic Instruction Code *or* Geology: *basic* "containing relatively little silica."] Originally, a simple mid-level language used to test the student's ability to increment line numbers, but now available only in complex, extended versions. *See* EXTENDED BASIC, VISUAL BASIC.

⇒To determine the amount of silica in your code, use

```
INSTR(1,X$,"SILICA")
```

on all your strings. Scores below 5 are reassuring; scores over, say, 10 mean that you are probably using FORTRAN by mistake. Consult your supervisor at once.

Batch, Elsie *See* DANGLING ELSE.

Bayesianism *n.* [Origin: *Either* the Reverend Thomas Bayes (1701–1761) or French *baiser* "to kiss or swive."] The application of theology to statistics, or vice versa.

⇒Bayes' formulae can be used to calculate the conditional probability that FUZZY Logic will succeed given the prior certainty that Lotfi ZADEH is stark, raving mad.

BBC [Acronym for Bjarne's Better C.] *See* C++.

BEL [*abbrev.* Bell] The ASCII 07 code. *See also* FLEEP.

⇒A communications ARCHAISM recalling the days when your attention was solicited by electromechanical tintinnabulation.

benchmark *v. trans.* To subject (a system) to a series of tests in order to obtain prearranged results not available on competitive systems. *See also* MENDACITY SEQUENCY.

bends *n. pl.* [Origin: Borrowed from sailors' slang for caisson disease.] A painful, paralyzing, sometimes fatal dizziness caused by unseemly haste in implementing a BOTTOM-UP programming project.

besack *v. intrans.* [Origin uncertain: possibly Russian *bez* "lacking" + ACK "a feedback signal during communications indicating acceptance."] To engage in a prolonged monologue on diverse subjects beyond the speaker's competence and the listener's interest. *Also called* (Brit.) **malik.**

best-last search *n.* Known in Ireland as the Polish search; and in Poland as the Irish search. *See also* ETHNOLOGY.

beta *adj.* (Of a software version) the one that ships.

⇒Originally, beta software was sent only to volumteer testers who had signed a nondisclosure agreement (NDA). Unfortunately, most such volunteers had previously signed disclosure agreements with a competitor. *See also* ALPHA.

better *adj. & adv.* Originally intended to indicate a later version, as in "requires DOS 2.0 or better." Now ambiguous: e.g., "DOS 4.0 or better" includes *all* DOS versions with the possible exception of DOS 6.0.

bidirectional *adj.* **1** (Of a printer) boustrophedonic. **2** (Of a system) being down or up. **3** (Of a consultant) able to move *toward* a prospect and *away* from a client. **4** (Of a paper- or magnetic-tape drive) able to wrench the medium from both the right- and left-hand reels.

bin *n.* [Origin dubious: *abbrev.* binary *or* dustbin (U.S. trash can).] A suitable receptacle for your compiler/linker output. *See also* GARBAGE.

binary *adj.* **1** Offering little choice; maximizing the chance of error. **2** Relating to the 20th century's boring challenge to the Babylonians. **3** Relating to a numbering system introduced to protect children from parental help during math homework assignments. **4** Reflecting the quintessential dichotomy of the universe. *See also* BIT.

binary search *n.* A locational strategy devised by J. W. R. Dedekind (1831–1916) which worked perfectly until the advent of the file-oriented digital computer. The search is, in fact, misnamed since there are three possible outcomes: *not-there, wrong-find, find*. The rarity of the last explains the misnomer.

binding time *n.* The moment when the hash table becomes corrupted.

⇒Advances in computing can be mapped against the "lateness of binding," which has me thinking about my own so-called CS so-called career: golden past, gray present, and rosy future. This is my version of Synge's optimism: the grass is greener except at t = 0. On EDSAC I, my functions (5ch paper-tape subroutines) were punched, spliced, and bound about two weeks before input. This is known as *premature* binding and calls for deftness with elastic bands. FORTRAN came next with a new kind of binding: soggy decks of cards that refused to be shuffled. Then with Algol and C, I enjoyed static (compile-time) binding, until C++ brought the numbing joys of dynamic (run-time) binding. My current research aims at delaying the binding until well after execution. I call this *end-time* binding, as prophesied in St. Matthew's Gospel: "…and whatsoever thou shalt bind on earth shall be bound in heaven.…" (Matthew 16:19 KJV).

BIOS *n.* **1** A chip offering Basic I/O Support. **2** Biographical summaries in job-application CVs.

⇒Which can claim the higher density of misinformation? Close call. *See also* SOCIAL CLIMBERS.

bistable *adj.* Pertaining or relating to an above-average system which is stable approximately 50 percent of the time.

bit *n. & adj.* [Origin: *Either* Old English *bita* "something small or unimportant," *or* engineering *bit* "a boring tool."] **1** *n.* The quantum of misinformation. **2** *n.* One-half of the fee needed to carry out a threat, as: "For two bits I'd ram this board down your stupid throat." **3** *n.* A BINARY digit: a boringly dichotomic entity which precludes rational discussion. "Avoid situations which offer only two courses of action" (S. Murphy). **4** *adj.* (Of a programmer) inadequate; versed only in FORTRAN or RPG. **5** *adj.* (Of a map) many-1 and many-0. The 1s in an AlphaMicro bit map indicate to the system those sectors of mass memory which are immune from further corruption.

bit bucket *n.* [Origin: possibly (vulg.) Cockney rhyming slang.] **1** A binary spittoon. **2** A digital cuspidor.

⇒Bit buckets are analogous to the receptacles fitted in the back of high-priced television sets to catch the corpses of cowboys and indians. Without a well-placed bit bucket to collect overflow characters as they are coughed up from stretched stacks and raucous registers, an offensive GRUNGE accumulates beneath the computer cabinets. This binary detritus, if left to fester, can be a hazard to operational health and efficiency.

bitmap *n.* **1** The ultimate in painting-by-numbers. **2** The very large, but never quite large enough, set of bytes representing the PIXEL positions and colors of a tasteless image. **3** The memory vendors' best friend.

bitomancy *n. also* **flagomancy**. Dubious predictions based on the state of your registers. *See also* -MANCY.

blank card *n. Also called* **spacer card**. An unpunched card placed in an input deck at 10,000-card intervals. Since electromechanical devices enjoy a consistent $1 \cdot 10^4$ error rate, the blank-card trick minimizes the impact of card-reader malfunctions.

⇒The Zen representative at the ISO (International Standards Organization) has proposed that certain card punching conventions be observed to avoid the present confusion between space, blank, null, and "not there." It does seem helpful to have a positive "not there" column code so that *missing* columns and cards—the erstwhile bane of unit recorders—can be punched and verified before input. Perforatricial productivity payment schemes, which traditionally penalize columnar oversights, would reward sins of omission and commission with equal severity. The Zen convention demands that each blank card be punched and verified (a total of 160 keystrokes), but whether a missing blank card requires this effort or not is still subject to intense mootation.

bloat, code *n. See* CODE BLOAT.

blob, BLOb *n.* Acronym for Binary Large Object. Codd'n'Date's scifi nightmare in which huge unstructured thingies attack the relational integrity of all we love.

block *n. & v. trans.* **1** *n.* The place of execution. **2** *v. trans.* To hinder (a user, job, program) by changing the password or improving the operating system. **3** *v. trans.* To interject control characters at arbitrary points (in a message) prior to transmission.

blockhead *n.* The first character foolish enough to venture into a VTAM applications program.

blyb *n.* (ISO GUI unit) An 8×8 fuzzy PIXEL matrix, or 16 SEURATS.

BO Overloaded *abbrev.* Board of Ordinance; Box Office; Back Order; Branch Office; Brought Over; Best Offer; Broker's Order; Buyer's Option; Bugger Off; Body Odor…but the greatest of these is Bugger Off.

body *n.* The defining bulk of a FUNCTION.

bonus *n. Usually called* **added bonus**. [Latin *bonus* "good."] **1** *n. Payroll* A random amount added to your net pay to compensate for random withholding errors. **2** Any unexpected, additional benefit encountered or offered when all seems to be going well.

⇒The superstitious, i.e., experienced, DP person dreads and shuns all added bonuses. They are known as portents of 12th-hour revenge and disaster in nonadjacent modules. Thus:

> "Finishing the stock update by 3:00 P.M. provides the *added bonus* of two extra hours on the Fixed Asset Depreciation Schedule."

> "If you order the additional 16K RAM, you get the *added bonus* of three days free tuition in BASIC from one of our extended counselors."

> "Our book club will save you up to 40 percent off normal retail price, and as a *bonus*, your name will be passed to 98 carefully selected mailing lists."

books, computer *n. See* COMPUTER BOOKS.

books for the baffled *n. See* LOW-SELF-ESTEEM BOOKS.

Boole, Fred (1810–1884) George Boole's older, unheralded logical brother, also self-taught, who stuck to his father's cobbling trade from first to last, having early decided that the best Boolean was two watertight wellies, left *and* right, and that the true table of truth should hold the harvest home. And, to the *avec-tes-sabots* of Lincolnshire, wasn't Fred the super Boole?

bootstrap *n. & v. trans.* [Origin: from the fictional attempts by Baron Münchhausen (described by Rudolf Raspe, 1785) to refute Newton's third law. Subsequent real bids at self-levitation led to the disappearance of straps from the footwear environment.] **1** *n.* The first straw that breaks the system's back. **2** *v. trans. Also called* **boot** To ensnare (an operating system or program) in a sneaky, cumulative manner.

⇒The thought that a cold system needs to read in the read-in subroutine before it can read in anything has kept countless amateur ontogenists and etiologists from the arms of Morpheus since the dawn of cybernetic consciousness. The practical DP pioneers chickened out of this infinite regress by laying a golden egg, to wit, a bootstrap.

A Dead Sea scroll fragment from Cave 2 seems to indicate that "A time to boot and a time to kick" belongs in Ecclesiastes 3:1–8 to further emphasize the absurdity of everything.

bottom-down *adj.* [© Irish Business Machines.] Relating to a pessimistic and discredited programming METHODOLOGY.

⇒Bottom-down projects are characterized by deep-rooted doubts as to where to start, and by a signal lack of progress once started. *Compare* BOTTOM-UP; MIDDLE-OUT; TOP-DOWN.

bottom-line *n.* The 25th line on a typical monitor screen, reserved for error messages. This convention is also used on balance sheets and other financial reports.

bottom-up *adj.* Relating to a programming methodology in which the finer details are coded before any study of the overall needs of the system has been made.

⇒Historically, the bottom-up approach replaced the less optimistic BOTTOM-DOWN strategy, only to be challenged by the TOP-DOWN philosophy. A recent Taoist revolution bids fair to replace all three with the MIDDLE-OUT credo. Project coordinators still working in the bottom-up environment face the happy task of blending a cornucopia of well-written but mutually contradictory submodules. The ideal bottom-up coordinator should be a top-downer at heart, able to dive in before any of the team have surfaced, meet them at three fathoms or less, and gain control of their oxygen control valves. *See also* BENDS.

Bourbaki, Nicolas (?–?) **1** Mythical Poldavian hiding the identities of a set of leading but shy French mathematicians engaged in endless axiomatic groupware. **2** Real columnist for *AI Expert* magazine.

Bourne shell *n.* [Named for Dr. Stephen R. Bourne.] The first and best of the UNIX shells, the hard currency of which is characterized by the $ PROMPT.

⇒The old UNIX joke, "If you don't like the Bourne shell, write your own," was unfortunately taken seriously by several M'AS-TU-VUS, adding further to the pains of Unicial VERSIONITIS.

Brady Gooch The spooneristic doyen of OBJECT ORIENTEERING often confused with Crad Box.

Brain-assisted *See* BA.

breakpoint *n.* **1** A situation in which the system and the programmer are tied after a certain number of runs and the winner is decided by a sudden-death series of DUMPS. **2** The delightful but self-defeating moment when the DPM dismisses the entire systems/programming team, the user rejects the supplier, and four overextended legal partnerships meet to berate the litigious fervor of their respective clients. **3** (Debugging) A line in a program highlighted by the clairvoyant and dubious.

broket *n.* [Origin: by analogy with "bracket," a broken bracket. From JARGON FILE.] *Also called* **angle bracket**. Either of the characters "<" and ">."

⇒Dirac also broke the bracket, giving us the quantumously mysterious *bra* <x| and *ket* |y>.

browse *v.* 1 (Of a book) to read leisurely. 2 (Of an object-hierarchy) to chain frantically in all directions. *See also* AUTO-ANTONYM.

BTFFHT [*Abbrev.* BROWSE the Fine Friendly HyperText.] The GUI equivalent of RTFM.

bubble memory *n.* A storage device developed by South Sea Memory Products Inc.

⇒The chief advantage of bubbles over floppies is that they cannot be folded by the mailperson. Whether bubbles will ever replace the hard disk (which is also beyond the bending power of most postal workers) depends on the relative strength of the semiconductor and metallurgical lobbies.

bubble sort *n.* A program for arranging memory bubbles in any desired sequence (by diameter, mass, viscosity, manufacturer, cost, etc.).

buffer *n.* [Origin obscure: *possibly* Italian *buffo* "farcical, comic" *or* Latin *bufo* "a toad."] 1 A region between two devices designed to distort or, if possible, prevent the flow of data in either direction. 2 An old, greasy, and abrasive rag used to clean tape heads and floppy drives.

bug *n.* [Entomology obscure.] 1 An undocumented feature. 2 A mythical scapegoat invoked by all sections of the DP industry: "A pox on the bug and a bug on the pox, for one or t'other plagues my TOS" (Sir John Thumpstaff).

⇒The word implies that "things go wrong" because of some infection from outside. The *gremlin* which caused all malfunctions during World War II was an openly fictitious imp, blamed in jest; the DP bug, however, has assumed the unfunny proportions of an infestation. Putting things right, or DEBUGGING, therefore, requires the equivalent of fumigation, chlorination, swabbing, or, to use the proper chemotherapeutic terminology, "nailing the little bastards." That the epidemic persists would indicate that there are terminal diseases beyond the remedial arts of computer science. The ailing user is often advised to "keep taking the tablets and see how you feel in the morning." The patient must accept the palliative KLUDGE or the placebo of a MAJOR NEW-LEVEL RELEASE. Since, in truth, most DP errors arise from sins of omission, rather than commission, the appropriate medical analogy to the DP bug is not infection but metabolic disorder or vitamin deficiency.

bundled *adj.* [From the verb *bundle* "to throw together in haphazard fashion."] Of or relating to an arbitrary collection of software items offered AS IS, without charge or warranty, to certain prospects in a competitive environment.

⇒Of interest to sociolinguists is the fact that the DP usage of *bundled* was triggered by the prior introduction of the antonym *unbundled* by IBM the previous day. *See also* UNBUNDLING.

bus *n*. A ponderous vehicle for transporting people or data at irregular intervals.

⇒Note, however, that "missing the bus" has opposite connotations in the people and data environments: a failure for folk, but a blessing for bits. Of the contending mini- and microbus formats ("You say ISA and I say EISA…"), the ruthless, teutonic SS-100 standard is certain to dominate. As the name suggests, a task force of highly motivated "standards specialists" regularly descends upon non-conforming stockists, outside of normal trading hours, and throws some rather exegetical pitches. Few can resist the board-crunching logic of these visits.

C

\$CALL *n. or interj.* **1** An outrageous price that the advertiser dare not reveal in print. **2** \$404,149 (Turing base-32).

C *n.* A brilliant mix of low high-level and high low-level languages devised *chiefly* by Dennis M. Ritchie at AT&T Bell Laboratories in the early 1970s. *See also* C++; NATURAL C; UNIX.

⇒C was named as the successor to Ken Thompson's B, which in turn was derived from Martin Richard's BCPL. This oversimplified history at least explains the in-joke: Will C be enhanced to D or to P? The answer seems to be "Neither." For some, known as the "No Power Without Danger" gang, C is the ultimate portable peril and needs just an occasional ANSI tweak to maintain its supremacy. Others are betting on C++ as the source of even more exciting obfuscation for the upper classes.

The rapid, some say insidious, growth of C is no surprise to those sharing the programmer's dream: a dizzy pointer-powered access to the silicon innards without the irksome sweat of ASSEMBLER. The C industry has reached the point where there is now a C book devoted to each extant line of code, and a C pun for every keyword.

C++ *Also called* **BBC: Bjarne's Better C.** A version of the C language post-fix-incremented with ideas from Simula by Bjarne Stroustrup at AT&T Bell Laboratories in the early 1980s.

⇒The original 1980 version was called "C with Classes," until the catchy C++ designation was suggested by Rick Mascitti in 1983. This name caught on irreversibly before more careful syntactical and semantic analyses indicated that the prefix-incremental ++C would have provided a more appropriate appellation. Misguided DORYPHOREs insist that C++ figuratively says "enhance (increment) the C language, then use the unenhanced version" (see e.g., *The C++ Programming Language,* Bjarne Stroustrup, Addison-Wesley, 1987, p. 4, and Randall Bart's letter to the *C Users Journal,* December 1991). The difference between C++ and ++C (where C is a waxable variable) is best seen in the following snippet:

```
int x=0, C=0;
x = ++C;    // both x and C now equal 1
x = C++;    // x still equals 1 but C equals 2
x = C++;    // x now equals 2 but C equals 3...
x = C++;    // x now equals 3 but C equals 4...
...
```

So, there is no doubt that C++ (figuratively) does eventually "improve" C, but you have to keep at it!

One can also, possibly, defend the term C++ from general, descriptive linguistic considerations: meanings are derived from current and evolving usage not from "etymology." Thus, Jerusalem Artichokes are neither artichokes nor from David's City.

A more credible defense of C++ rests on the fact that in post-2.1 versions of C++ (such as the current ANSI C++) the prefix and postfix ++ operators can be separately overloaded for user-defined types. Thus, following Christopher Hecker, we can define a class Language and overload the prefix and postfix Language::operator++:

```
Language& Language::operator++() // prefix
{
     BetterSelf( );
     return(*this);
}
     . . .
inline Language& Language::operator++(int dummy)
// postfix
{
     return(++(*this));
}
     . . .
Language C, X;    // declare Language objects C and X
     . . .
X = C++;    // X is enhanced C and Bjarne's your Uncle!
```

Hecker has therefore proposed, without high hopes of general acceptance, that the language be called **C.operator++(dummy)**.

See also C; C+—; CLASS; OBJECT.

C+— *n. \pronounced* C more or less\ A language devised for the AI community by Richard Nelson and Dr. Michael Hirsch, with extensions by Marina Michaels, Tom Clune, and THIS writer.

⇒Unlike C++, C+— is a subject-oriented language. Each C+— class instance (or *subject*) holds *hidden* (or *superprivate*) data members, known as *prejudices* or *undeclared preferences*, that are impervious to all messages, as well as public members known as *boasts* or *claims*. The following C operators are overridden as shown:

> better than

< worse than

>> much better than

<< forget it

! not on your life

= = comparable, other things being equal

C+— is a strongly-typed language based on stereotyping and self-righteous logic.

The Boolean variables TRUE and FALSE (known as constants in less realistic languages) are supplemented with CREDIBLE and DUBIOUS, which are fuzzier than ZADEH's traditional FUZZY categories. All Booleans can be declared with the modifiers *strong* and *weak*. Weak implication is said to "preserve deniability," and was added at the request of the DoD to ensure compatibility with future versions of Ada. WFF's (well-formed falsehoods) are assignment-compatible with all Booleans.

WHAT IF and WHY NOT tests are aided by the special conditional

```
evenifnot (X) {Y};
```

C+– supports information hiding and, among FRIEND classes only, rumor sharing. Borrowing from the Eiffel lexicon, non-friend classes can be *killed* by arranging *contracts*. Note that friendships are intransitive, volatile and non-Abelian. The *locale* mechanism is enhanced by a series of *calumnies* of type *ethnic*.

Single and multiple inheritance mechanisms are implemented with random mutations. Disinheritance rules are covered by a complex *probate protocol*. In addition to *base* classes, *derived* classes, and *abstract* classes, C+– supports *gut* classes. In certain *locales* polygamous derivations and *bastard* classes are permitted. Elsewhere, loose coupling between classes is illegal so the *marriage* and *divorce* operators may be needed as follows:

```
marriage (MParent1, FParent1);
// child classes can now be derived
sclass MySclass: public MParent1, FParent1
{ ... }
sclass YourSclass: public MParent1, FParent2
// illegitimate
divorce (MParent1, FParent1);
marriage (MParent1, FParent2);
sclass YourSclass: public MParent1, FParent2
{ ... // legal!
}
```

Operator precedence and other rules can be suspended with the DWIM (Do What I Mean) pragma.

ANSIfication will be firmly resisted. C+–'s slogan is "Raise High Your Own Standard!"

CA- [Acronymical prefix.] Computer-aided X or Computer-assisted X.

⇒The flood of CA-prefixed acronyms (CASE, CAD, CAI, CAL,...) does not yet include the vital one: CAC (Computer-aided Computing) and the potentially infinite regress (CA(CA(...)))C.

Borrowing this format, Tom Lister has suggested the prefix BA- (Brain-assisted-), as in BASE for Brain-assisted Software Engineering and other endeavours unencumbered by yet another bug-ridden layer. Meilir Page-Jones prefers HA- (Human-assisted-), proving again that METHODOLOGISTS love to major in the minors ("Mine arrows are more pointed than thine").

cache *n. & v. \pronounced* cash.\ **1** *n.* A secret hiding place for data and instructions. **2** *v.* To hide in a cache. *See also* OUBLIETTE.

⇒Cache memory is usually faster and more expensive than standard RAM, leading to much puerile wordplay (*esp.* cache cow, "cache in your chips," and so on). *See also* PUN MORATORIUM.

CAD *n.* [Acronym for Computer-aided Delay or, *archaic*, Computer-aided Design.] The automation of the traditionally *manual* delays between the various stages of product development: research and development, drawing office, prototyping, testing, pre-production planning, etc. The improved delays invariably lead to better products.

CAI *n.* [Computer-aided Instruction.] The misguided attempt to replace each teacher in the Bronx with 60 on-line terminals. *Compare* CAL.

CAL *n.* **1** [Acronym for CALifornia or, *archaic*, Computer-aided Learning.] A superior West Coast (U.S.A.) version of CAI in which each teacher is replaced by 25 on-line terminals. **2** [Acronym for Computer-aided Litigation.] The automated circumvention of the law. *More at* DP ATTORNEY; PATENT; WRIT-ONLY.

⇒Our increasingly litigious citizenry, of whom the majority are now blessed with appropriate law degrees and willing to act contingently for the minority, and to whom every action entails an actionable tort, has found CAL programs to be a WRIT-ONLY blessing. Object-oriented versions of CAL have emerged to deal with class actions.

call *n.* [Origin: theater, as in the traditional request "Five minutes, darling!"] A polite but rarely heeded plea for help from one piece of troubled coding (the *caller*) to another (the *callee*). Subsequent, less polite, calls are known as *yells* and *screams*. *See also* ARGUMENT; GOSUB; WIRTH; RETURN.

⇒The vexatious taxonomy of "calls" includes "by name," "by value," "by location," "for conference papers," and, in emergencies, "by dialing 911." Further spice is added to the situation by allowing the callee to act as caller, and so on down a long dusty, nested road. Signs that say "Please leave the STACK as you found it," are regularly ignored, and some callers risk blindness by calling themselves.

callback *adj.* [From the popular lie "I'll call you back on that...."] In WINDOWS, of a user-defined function waiting indefinitely for the big EVENT.

campus *n.* [Latin *campus* "field (of battle)."] An area of scholastic and riotous endeavor offering students their first real opportunity to freak a large timesharing system. *See also* RESPONSE TIME.

CAPA [Overloaded acronym: Comité d'Action pour la Productivité dans l'Assurance; Closet Accordion Players of America.]

⇒Those who claim that no real overloading is likely between such distinctive semantic domains must be unaware of Zachary Beausoleil, FIA, FCA, FAA, the Cajun actuary, who regularly performs in both NAMESPACES.

card *n.* **1** Also **board**. A rectangular ratbag of components intended to add FUNCTIONALITY to a PC. In real life, the PC seldom has matching, or any, card SLOTS to fulfill this promise. **2** *Also called* **punch card, punched card, tab card, Hollerith card**. [Origin: from earlier, more predictable games of chance and necromantic divination.] A 7 3/8-inch × 3 1/4-inch looseleaf scratchpad system designed to fit normal shirt pockets (other sizes are available for the abnormal), but sometimes (with growing rarity) underused as an 80 × 12 analog-digital matrix. "If T. J. Watson, Sr., had played his cards right, he could have made his name in computing" (M. Thumps).

⇒The optimum size of the 80-column card is a strange accident arising from the parsimony of Dr. Herman Hollerith, who wanted a cheap filing system for his card-based census of 1890. He therefore designed his card to fit the filing trays available, which were based on the dimensions of the 1890 dollar bill. The latter, naturally, had been created with standard wallet and shirt-pocket sizes in mind. Despite the ravages of inflation, Herman's card survives. Rival formats come and go, but nothing can budge the diehard chemisier.

card, blank *n. See* BLANK CARD.

cascaded *or* **cascading** *adj.* (Of a GUI menu system) sisyphean, with the happy SIDE-EFFECT of delaying, or postponing indefinitely, the USER's access to an application.

⇒A recent ANSI Mouse standard decrees that the depth of a cascaded menu system must not exceed the maximum rated MCBF (Mean Clicks Between Failure).

case *n.* **1** A keyword in several computer languages that avoids the ignominy of multiple conditional GOTOs without reducing the dangers. *See also* DEFAULT; TRAPDOOR. **2** (Archaism) the state of a keyboard or character (upper or lower). The term is yet another survivor from earlier printing technology when capital letters were stored in cases (boxes) above the small-letter cases.

CASE *n.* [Acronym for Computer-aided Software Engineering.] *See* CA-; SOFTWARE ENGINEERING; METHODOLOGY.

⇒Thick layers between the programmer and a running application are known as UPPER CASE tools; the thinner versions as lower case. Some see Abe Lincoln as a pioneer of the latter: "As our case is new, we must think anew" (Dec. 1862).

case-insensitive *adj.* (Of terminologists and trademarkers) woefully indifferent to the horrors of interword case shifts.

⇒A random scan of the advertiser index reveals AutoSystems, CompuExpo, CoSession, EasySpooler, QualTrack, SunPro, and UniPress. But the greatest of these is NeXT.

case-insensitivity *n.* The thoughtless promulgation of unnaturally case-sensitive or typographically challenging trade names. *See also* CASE-INSENSITIVE.

⇒Thus we encounter offenders such as NeXT, dBASE, eXceed, PEXlib, aD nAuSeaM. These abominations are proudly protected by law. Perhaps abomination is too strong: imagine the infinite horror of reading "*Endlösung*™ is a trademark of H. Goering Enterprises, May 1941."

Knuth's text formatter $T_E X$ is a forgivable, outrageously special case: (i) writing it as TeX or TEX means you are not using $T_E X$ (ii) The final "X" is really a Greek upper-case *chi* and calls for a touch of Scouse-fricative expectoration. *More at* $T_E X$, TNHD.

cast *n. & v. trans.* [Origin Biblical: "...and they shall cast them into an unclean place..." (Leviticus 14:40).] *Also called* **type-cast**. **1** *n.* The conversion of a variable from its correct DATA TYPE. If the variable objects, the conversion is known as coercion. **2** *v. trans.* To circumvent the safety of data typing; thus, strongly-typed languages can be rendered weak, and weakly-typed languages given the *coup de boutoir*. *See also* OVERCAST

⇒Another text confirming the dangers of miscasting has Moses struggling with heterogeneous joins on a primitive SQL system: "And I took the two tables, and cast them out...and brake them before your eyes" (Deuteronomy 9:17).

Catastrophe *n. See* SEVEN CATASTROPHES OF COMPUTING, THE.

Cauchy-Schwarz Inequality *n.* Baron Cauchy gets the green card; Schwarz is deported.

CDC *Abbrev.* Control Data Corporation; Center for Disease Control. *Warning* Often resists contextual disambiguation.

CD-ROM *n.* *Pronounced* seedy-romm.\\ [Acronym for Compact Disk Read-Only Memory.] A 680 MB platter of "electronic papyrus" exploiting the COMPTON EFFECT.

⇒Fifteen CD-ROMs will hold Wagner's Ring cycle or an animated version of the Windows NT32 Help file. The choice, America, is *yours!*

CEU *n.* [Continuing Education Unit.] One of a sequence of random integers issued in a version of keno known as *adult education.*

⇒Players achieving certain preordained totals are required to yell "Ex-tra curr-i-cu-la!" before claiming their diplomas in such diverse fields as brain surgery, intermediate mollusk sexing, and nonmonotonic fuzzy logic for the small business user.

Participating readers who have successfully reached this page are entitled to deduct two CEU from their accumulated tally.

chad *n.* (plural **chadim**) A piece of confetto produced by a tape or card punch. *More at* TNHD.

chadless tape *n.* Paper tape prepared on a punch with blunt pins. *See also* CHAD.

Chain or **Cha'n, Daisy.** *See* DAISY CHAIN.

channeler *n.* *Also* SPIRIT GUIDE. Politically correct terms for DAEMON. *See also* PC UNIX.

chaos *n. & adj.* \Often *pronounced* tchowss\ [Indo-European *ghēu,* "yawn, gape," whence **ghau* and Greek *khaos,* "chasm, empty space."] **1** *n.* The boringly normal state of all computer projects. **2** *n.* The pandemonium in the popular science publishing houses when books on Catastrophe Theory failed to sell. **3** *adj.* (Of a theory) confirming the programmer's intuition that theoretically deterministic systems are in practice unsystematically indeterministic due to their sensitivity to initial conditions, especially the choice of methodologist, language, compiler, and mouse pad.

⇒It is reassuring to note that many respected cosmogenies see Chaos as the BASE CLASS of creation. For example, the goddess Tiamat (representing the chaos of the saltwater seas) is slain by the god Marduk who then creates the cosmos from her body parts.

Cherlin, Edward M. (1946–) Cofounder/Publisher of *APL News* (6611 Linville Drive, Weed, CA 96094). As an ordained priest of the Order of Buddhist Contemplatives, Cherlin is uniquely qualified to create and disseminate NULL SET jokes (*also called* Empty Array jokes), including elaborate taxonomies of the NOP. Following the publication of Robert Pirsig's novel (*Zen and the Art of Motorcycle Maintenance,* 1974), Cherlin issued an affidavit swearing never to write or refer to "Zen and the Art of Computer Programming." Others, it seems, have ignored this sensible attitude (e.g., Peter G. Neumann, "Psychosocial Implications of Computer Software Development and Use: Zen and the Art of Computing," SRI International, ACM Sigsoft, SEN, April 1982). *See also* ZADEH, LOTFI.

Chinese remainder theorem *n.* More strictly, a *conjecture* that there exists an $N >= 3$ such that after World War N the set of surviving Chinese will be nonempty. A corollary asserts that for $N + 1$ the set will be less nonempty. If the set is exhausted after M trials, we define World War M as the War to end all conjectures.

⇒United States and Soviet nuclear strategies were for many years so heavily based on this conjecture that diverse computer simulations to test its valididity were attempted. Behind the scenes, in fact, the Cold War was really a hectic ADA-APL benchmark. Both sets of models proved to be inconclusive and expensive, and there was mounting pressure to divert the Pentagonal and Soviet OR budgets into more reliable, practical experiments. Glasnost arrived, just in time…

Chinese total *n.* **1** Almost a billion. **2** A checksum METHODOLOGY originally devised for YODALS (Yangtse Opium Den Accounts Leceivable System), whence often referred to as a *hash total. Also called* (mainly in China) **Russian** or **Czech total.**

Chinese VMOS *n.* For full details, please consult the Yellow Pages. *See* NET-WOK; VMOS.

chording *n.* Replacing the keyboard with an eight-button MOUSE.

⇒The WIDE character sets needed for non-ASCII-disabled languages can be accommodated with Morse-like chord CLICKs supplemented by various button ARPEGGIOS.

circulation, controlled *n.* (Computer journalism) A method of magazine distribution financed by the advertisers. Subscribers qualify by responding optimistically to question 3: How many Crays do you hope to purchase this week?

CIS Overloaded initialism for Compuserve Information Services (also called **CI$** because of the cost); Confederation of Independent States (ex-Soviet Union).

⇒Cynics have claimed that the former is distinguishable by its chaotic mismanagement. Dick O'Connor, Washington Dept. of Fish and Wildlife, reports 103 CIS overloads including Canadian Iris Society, Catholic Information Society, and his own Coordinated Information System.

class *n. & adj.* [Origin: Latin *classis* via *calare,* "to call to arms."] **1** *n.* (Object-orienteeering) Data members encapsulated with a set of METHODs dying to get at them. **2** *n.* (Marxism) A subset of society encapsulated with a set of methods for exploiting and exterminating both itself and other subsets of society. **3** *n.* (Style) Someth'n' you jest plain got or don't. **4** *adj.* (Of a struggle) iterative, as in the attempted modularization of real-word activities. *See also* OO; C++; C+−; ENCAPSULATION; INSTANCE; INSTANTIATION; OBJECT.

click *v. trans.* To press a MOUSE button and then release it.

⇒This central GUI ritual is often touted as the epitome of INTUITIVITY. The mouse-pointing prelude to the click is readily mastered, of course, given that your balls are clean, the mouse-pad-cum-lunch-tray cleared for action, and both CURSOR and target HOT-POINT visible through the metaphorical mess. However, several aspects of the click-qua-click are far from obvious: choice of button(s), number of clicks, simultaneous use of Shift, ALT, and Ctrl keys, and what has been called the trigger-happiness factor. The ideal, single-button mouse has now given way to two- and three-button versions, offering considerable scope for non-intuitive left, middle, right, and even complex CHORDING variations. Even the most common left-or-right button choice can be clouded by the software option to reverse the button designations, offered by many GUIs to placate the vocal sinistrous minority. To discover if your mouse behavior has been re-conditioned, click on the Mouse icon using the left...oops...right button...*See also* DRAGGING; DRAG'N'DROP; DROP'N'DRAG.

client/server *also* **c/s** *adj.* [Often capitalized typographically but under-capitalized during the PILOT.] (Of a distributed information ARCHITECTURE) carrying the REMOTE fantasy that there are database systems somewhere on the NETWORK sufficiently servile to answer dumb client queries. *See also* PEER-PEER NETWORK; INTEROPERABILITY.

⇒The much-awaited client/server SILVER BULLET awaits both a standard SQL and success with the relatively simpler challenge of retrieving local data from a stand-alone database. "Whenne Sybase scorned my S-Q-L/Who was thenne the Oracle?" (Heterogenia Joyne, 1543).

close *adj. & v.* **1** *adj.* Relating to the nearest possible approach to project completion. *See* HARTREE CONSTANT. **2** *v. trans.* To protect (a file) until the next OPEN statement. **3** *v. intrans.* To invoke the "File not open" diagnostic.

closed adj. **1** (Of a fist) showing a complete lack of budgetary imagination, but prepared to counter accusations of parsimony with pugilistic rebuttal. **2** (Of a shop) Brit.: requiring job-unrelated qualifications. **3** (Of a loop) narcissistic; obsessed with its own parameters. *Compare* OPEN.

co- *prefix* Joint, fellow-.

⇒The current dearth of HYPHENs presents us with such eyesores as coauthor, coeducation, and cocitation. Worse: we meet potential ambiguities such as codeified, codeceased, and codetermined.

COBOL *n.* [Origin obscure: possibly from *cobble* "to botch," whence "A load of old Cobbolers," or *cobbing* "a way to punish sailors." Now assumed acronym for COmmon Business Oriented Language.] A procedurally disoriented, logorrheic language pioneered by Commander Grace Murray Hopper of the U.S. Navy. In keeping with naval tradition, a tot of rum is still forced down the throats of reluctant middy COBOL programmers before they swab their daily deck of cards. *See also* LEGACY.

⇒Serious attempts are now being made to add classes and objects to COBOL. One suggested name for this OOPified version is POSTFIX INCREMENT COBOL BY ONE.

code *v. intrans.* To resort, reluctantly, to the CODING phase of the programming cycle. *See* MURPHY'S LAW OF PROGRAMMING.

code bloat *n.* The predictable result of paying programmers by the line and using optimizing compilers with dumb linkers.

⇒The bloat rate is conveniently measured by plotting the size of "hello, world" programs since the Kernighan/Ritchie 4-line, 38-character (including WHITE SPACE) hello.c of 1978. The DLL was introduced specifically to keep the Windows hello.exe within a 2 MB limit. *See also* HELLO, WORLD.

coding *n.* The setting up of a 1-1 relationship between ENDLESS LOOPS on a FLOWCHART and endless loops in a PROGRAM.

cognition *n.* (**cognitive** *adj.*) Phatic embellishments adding interdisciplinary glamor and expense to the titles of academic journals. Thus: *Language and Cognitive Processes; Cognitive Neuropsychology; Cognition and Emotion; The European Journal of Cognitive Psychology; Cognition and Instruction; The Journal of Cognitive Psychosociolinguistics, The Journal of Cognitive Cognition; The Journal of Cognitive Hydrodynamics; The Journal of Cognitive Janitorial Methodologies.*

COIK *adj.* [Acronym for Clear Only If Known.] Relating to the growing number of complex computer topics that have no effective linear pedagogic strategy.

⇒Bostonian topology offers an analogy:

Lost Driver: "How do I get to Boston Common?"
Helpful Bystander: "Ah, you must start from some other place."

collective noun *n.* "A singularly euphonious appellation" (W. C. Fields). A revealing name applied to a class or aggregate, as: "a pride of lexicographers," "a doze of profredders." *See* the table on page 42. *See also* DATA.

combinatorial explosion *n.* The result of excessive node expansion, and the inescapable fate of all nontrivial computer systems unless the neo-Luddites get them first.

come from *n.* An instruction proposed by R. Lawrence Clark (1973) to resolve the GOTO controversy. The industry is still (1995) bristling with acute disbelief. *More* at TNHD.

common language *n.* **1** A language used only by the originator and his or her closest friends. **2** A grandiose scheme launched by Friden Inc. in the late 1950s to provide a paper-tape Esperanto linking all known data preparation and processing devices.

Table of Collective Nouns

Unit number	Collective noun(s)
Field engineer	An *absence* of engineers
User	A *bleat* of users *or*
	A *jury* of users
Manufacturer	A *dock* of manufacturers
DPM	A *panic* of DPMs
Systems analyst	An *expectation* of systems analysts
Programmer	A *detail* of programmers
Operator	An *indifference* of operators
Salesperson	A *trough* of salespersons
Consultant	A *retreat* of consultants
Deadline	A *sequence* of deadlines
Connector	A *conspiracy* of connectors
Dump	A *gloom* of dumps
String	A *vest* of strings
Crash	A *jangle* of crashes
Datum	A *loss* of data
High-level language	A *logomachy* of high-level languages *or*
	A *babol* of high-level languages
Competitor	A *rafter* of competitors
Senior COBOL programmer	A *load* of old Cobollers

⇒In spite of some initial success, the users' intense desire to be different led to a plethora of incompatible dialects, and the experiment foundered between the Scylla of three tape widths, two chadic states, five opaquacities, and a whole ferranti of coding variations, and the Charybdis of IBM's selfish allegiance to the CARD. *See also* BABOL; LOW-LEVEL LANGUAGE..

compatable adj. *Also* (in *archaic* systems literature) **compatible**. Pertaining to a supposed relationship between a given set of existing characteristics (known as the "installed set") and a mooted, nonexisting set (known as the "proposed set").

⇒Current DP usage allows a variety of colorful qualifications to the basic concept of compatability, including many adverbs of motion, e.g., upward, downward, sideways, recessively. Degrees of compatability are rated 1 to 10 on the Richter scale, but the measurement, so far, lacks solid scientific objectivity. For example, when the supplier of the proposed set is a competitor of the supplier of the installed set, the two suppliers' assessments have been known to differ by as much as nine Richter points. Many experienced upgraders, in fact, are opposed to *any* partial qualifications of the predicate, such as "almost compatable," "as good as compatable," "compatable except on a set of measure zero," and so on. The side effects of near "compatability," they claim, are infinitely more horrendous than those of total inconsistency.

compatible *adj. Chiefly archaic* spelling of COMPATABLE.

⇒Beware of the **compatible** variant, which indicates that the proposal was written by non-DP staff.

compiler *n.* [Possibly from Latin *compilatio* "pillaging," whence, contemptuously, "the act of gathering together documents" (Cicero); *related to* Latin *compilare*, "to pack up and take off."] **1** An instance of the SIGO principle (Source In Garbage Out). **2** The coder's *bouc émissaire*. **3** A program that, having successfully compiled itself, presumes to know more about its language than the programmer. *See also* YACC; INTERPRETER; PESSIMIZER.

compile-time 1 *adj.* (Of a binding) premature. **2** *n.* A useful, recurring break for meals between coding. *See also* BINDING TIME.

complex *n. & adj.* **1** *n.* Any system, subsystem, sub-subsystem, etc., which is priced as a separate item in a proposal, as: "The head office 6 × 4-1100 will be in a real-time on-line situation with each branch. The branch-office *complex* comprises 1 (one) teleprinter and modem." **2** *adj.* (Of a DP problem) resolvable into two parts: a real part that can be solved or shelved, and an imaginary part that requires a complete and immediate restructuring of the DP department.

compliance *n.* (**compliant** *adj.*) A state of compatibility claimed before the standard has been established.

⇒The adjectival form is often seen in forms generated from the TEMPLATE X-compliant. Popular values of X are "SAA," "POSIX," "IDAPI," and, of course, "X." The following advert may or may not contain a typo:

"...featuring integrated IBM's SAA-complaint SQL...(800-Software, *Computer Currents,* March 10, 1992).

compliment *v.* [Common DP usage.] Synonym for "complement," as in "The interface must compliment the system" (SIGSOFT SEN, April 1993). If taken literally, perhaps we should try `printf("Hello, pretty system");`

comprise *v. trans.*(?) *and/or intrans.*(?) (Mandatory DP usage) to consist: "The system comprises of the following items;" "the system is comprised with the following items."

⇒Beware of proposals using the archaic phrasal verb *consist of. Compare* COMPATIBLE.

Compton effect *n.* The hypocritical reaction of giant patent-rich companies to the CD-ROM patent gained by tiny Compton's New Media.

computable adj. *Chiefly archaic* spelling of **computible**. *Compare* COMPAT-ABLE; COMPRISE.

⇒The theoretical foundations of "computability" were exhausted by Turing and others in the mid/late 1930s and might have remained as a branch of pure mathematics had not Hitler challenged the military strength of Oxford, Cambridge, Harvard, and Princeton. From 1938 to 1946, the μ-recursive function was armed with sticky relays, glowing tubes, dry joints, and mercurious delay lines to implement the still undersung *Win World War II* package. Fascism, having alienated the best programmers, could not match the Allied ballistic, nuclear, logistic, and, perhaps of most value, cryptanalytic computational resources. (*See* Ronald Lewin, *Ultra Goes to War*, McGraw-Hill, New York, 1978.) Lest we forget…when you next run StarTrader, Hammurabi, or Battleship on your playful inhouse system, spare a thought for those who computed a real war, and won: Atanasoff, Bigelow, Churchhouse, J. P. Eckert, W. J. Eckert, Einstein, Fermi, Feynman, Goldstine, Mauchly, Newman, Oppenheimer, Telford, Turing, Ulam, von Neumann, Welchmann…

computer book *n. & adj.* A burgeoning market that stretches the definition of both words. *See also* COIK; LOW SELF-ESTEEM BOOKS; WORN; ZERO KNOWL-EDGE.

⇒Every computer book has a mandatory TARGET AUDIENCE prolegomenon. For example, the IBM OS/2 2.1 manual "Using the Operating System" starts with a section headed "Who Should Read This Book?" All agog, you then read: "Anyone who will be using OS/2 2.1 should read this book." "Wow, 'struth, you don't say, blow me," and similar (possibly) phatic expressions. But before you can discard the document, your eye catches the following imperious notice: "Keep this book as a reference."

computer journalist *n. Also called* **calumnist.** A programmer or systems analyst lured into the tabloid cesspool with false promises of shorter hours, better pay, and less attention to detail. The unsatisfied craving for an audience often leads to an early return to the former honest labors.

computer music *n.* **1** The sudden burst of silence when you switch off. **2** Any polyhedral, non-celestial approximation to spherical harmonics. *See also* SAWTEETH.

computer science *n.* [Origin: possibly Prof. P. B. Fellget's rhetorical question, "Is computer science?"] **1** A study akin to numerology and astrology, but lacking the precision of the former and the success of the latter. **2** The protracted value analysis of algorithms. **3** The costly enumeration of the obvious. **4** The boring art of coping with a large number of trivialities. **5** Tautology harnessed in the service of Man at the speed of light. **6** The Post-Turing decline in formal systems theory. "Science is to computer science as hydrodynamics is to plumbing" (Prof. M. Thump). *Compare* COMPUTING SCIENCE.

⇒The only universally accepted computer scientific theorem to emerge, so far, is my own rather depressing:

Theorem: *All programs are dull.*

Proof: Assume the contrary; i.e., the set of interesting programs is nonempty. Arrange them (or it) in order of interest (note that all sets can be well ordered, so do it properly). The minimal element is the *least interesting program*, the obvious dullness of which provides the contradictory denouement we so devoutly seek.

Some plagiarists have tried to reverse this argument to show that all programs are interesting, but all they actually prove is that there exists a *least dull program*. This I am willing to accept, since I wrote it in 1954—and I can assure you that it is no longer of any interest to me or anyone.

Computer Science in 1995 still reminds one of Ancient Egyptian Mensuration, coping quite well on a day-by-day, ad hoc, problem-solving basis, yet waiting for Geometry to happen. We have our Thales's and Pytheas's *go leor*, even the odd Pythagoras…but where is Euclid or Euclidea hiding?

computible *adj. Also* (in *archaic* systems literature) **computable**. (Of a function) listed, or claimed to be listed, in any extant manufacturer's catalog of available software.

computing science *n.* The Hoare-Dijkstra-Gries apostate church that sensibly ensures software reliability by delaying execution indefinitely, or until program correctness is proved off-line, whichever is sooner. The enormous effort and subsequent feeling of intellectual superiority in establishing correctness is known as the *Dijkstra invariant.* The COMPUTER SCIENCE jiffy-lubers, by contrast, converge with painful iterations to a dubious correctness at the whim of unproven chips and compilers. *See also* SOFTWARE ENGINEERING.

congress *n.* [From Latin *com* "together" + *gradatio* "climax" or Sanskrit (*Kama Sutra*) "intercourse between Indians of disparate endowments."] A wild CONVENTION.

conjecture *n.* **1** *Mathematics* A hypothesis in search of a counterexample. Once united, they marry, moved to the suburbs, raise a few boring lemmata, and are never heard of again.

⇒Some conjectures, alas, seem doomed to sail forever seeking conjugal resolution, allowed to come ashore but once a year. They anchor briefly near the Martin Gardner strands until the smooth rabble drives them out to sea.

2 *Data Processing* The firm, irrevocable, notarized pledge, sworn on the grave of one or both of the programmer's putative parents, that the job will run on time (excluding any delays caused or enhanced by war, civil commotion, or rioting, whether declared, spontaneous, reprehensible, or justified; undue pressure to perform, from whatsoever source: mal de mer, mal de pays, mal de siecle, mal de code, mal de machine, or any force majeure not pretofore invoked).

⇒Embarrassed with a daily richness of firm conjectures, the DPM is left with a pleasantly selective task known as scheduling.

connectionism *n. Also called* **The Connectionist Conspiracy.** The theory that for NEURAL network and MASSIVELY PARALLEL funding it's *whom* you know at DARPA rather than the merits of your proposals.

Connector Conspiracy, The *n.* A shadowy ECZEMA, ISO, and Illuminati plot to destroy civilization by randomly varying the size, shape, pin-assignments, and gender of all known plugs. *See also* WHEEL.

⇒ "Alas, the dazed democracies
Respond with muted DIN."

(V. Hampden)

console *n.* [From Latin *consolatio(n)* "comfort, spiritual solace."] A device for displaying or printing condolences and obituaries for the OPERATOR.

⇒ Randomly accessed my girl is delirious;
I even consoled her one night on the Sirius;
The Monitor printer did then overswing;
It took away one of my favorite things!

const *n. & adj.* [Origin: a constant source of vituperation between rival C++ gurus.] Keyword qualifying certain tokens as "constant" (read-only) or restricting the actions of functions.

⇒The delicate placement of `const` determines, inter alia, whether you have a constant object, a constant pointer to a variable object, a variable pointer to a constant object, or whatever—RTFM.

constructor *n.* (C++) The eponymous member function that creates and initializes instances of its CLASS. *See also* OBJECT.

consultant *n.* [From *con* "to fraud, dupe, swindle," or, possibly, French *con* (vulgar) "a person of little merit" + *sult* elliptical form of "insult."] A tipster disguised as an oracle, *esp.* one who has learned to decamp at high speed in spite of the large briefcase and heavy wallet.

⇒The earliest literary reference appears to be the ninth-century Arabic tale *Ali Baba and the Forty Consultants.*

convention *n.* [From Latin *convenire* "to come together."] An alibi; saturnalia; a gathering held at a safe distance from one's family; a place where normal behavioral conventions are suspended. *See also* CONGRESS; SYMPOSIUM.

conversion *n.* [From Latin *conversare* "to turn around frequently."] The regular, major recasting of one's software and databases to avoid the stigma of OBSOLESCENCE. *See also* UPGRADE.

copy right! *imperative* Unheeded warning to check whether COPY A B, MOV A,B, A=B, and so on, overwrites B or A.

copyleft *n.* [Playful antonym of COPYRIGHT coined by the Free Software Foundation.] A chain-letter urging you to copy and distribute the attached software free of charge to ten acquaintances together with a copy of the chain-letter. Breaking the chain, they warn, will lead to the downfall of the Soviet Union and victory for the howling jackals of Wall Street. *More in* TNHD at GPL; GENERAL PUBLIC VIRUS.

copyright *n.* The presumptuous and self-defeating boast that the attached work has INTELLECTUAL PROPERTIES worth stealing. *See also* COPYLEFT; TRADEMARK; PATENT.

⇒One can detect an analogy with the Decalogue, often viewed as the sinner's suggestive do-list: "Covet my neighbor's *ass*? Now you mention it…"

core technology *n.* **1** The attic of old memories. **2** The latest gadgetry without which all progress stops instanter. *See also* AUTO-ANTONYM.

correctrice *n.* [Feminine form of French *correcteur* "profredder."] A French preuf reeader with MIDDLEWARE and DYSLEXIA.

cpm *n.* [Charlatans Per Minute.] *Queuing theory* The arrival rate of salespersons, indicating the number of mailing lists to which the visitee has been exposed.

CPU *n.* [*Chiefly archaic* abbreviation for Central Processing Unit.] The calculating mill that Babbage dreamed on.

⇒The dream was eventually realized in the 1950s, but is now being replaced by a diffused continuum of minute noncomputing elements known as MICROPROCESSORS.

CR (Carriage Return) *n.* An ARCHAISM harking back to the days when printers had moving carriages. Now the ASCII code 13 indicating the end of a line. *Compare* LF (Line Feed).

⇒Many a fine manual devotes an early chapter to the confusing keytop equation, CR = Enter.

cracker *n.* A computer-intruder, *esp.* one who knows your wife's first name; a HACKER manqué. *More at* TNHD.

⇒ "If only they had used their terminals for niceness instead of evil" (Maxwell Smart).

crank *n. & v. trans.* **1** *n.* An incorrigible FLT prover, circle squarer, or angle trisector as tabulated by Woody Dudley (*Mathematical Cranks*, Underwood Dudley, Spectrum Series, The Mathematical Association of America, Washington, D.C., 1992). **2** *v. trans.* To churn out (results) mechanically without thought, as on a PENTIUM.

crash *n. & v.* **1** *n. Software* An audible warning that it's DOWNTIME time again.

⇒In excessively unstable environments the warnings combine to give the illusion of a continuous tone, e.g., middle C for Exec 8, Ab above middle C for OS/360, and so on, but cases have been reported in which the human audio range has been exceeded. Some Chronos II sites have specially trained watchdogs to alert the operator. The legendary St. Paul Breakpointer, it is claimed, not only whines suggestively *before* the system dies, but also points at the offending line of code.

2 *n. Hardware* The distinctive sound made by drums and disks when heads drop.

⇒Head crashes serve to resolve fundamental problems in maintaining dynamic equilibrium while the head is aquaplaning over the ill-defined magnetic oxide impurities that sometimes accumulate on the drum or disk surface. These rustlike layers are not intrinsically harmful—indeed, some claim that they actually protect the costly metal below—but they can acquire spurious, palimpsestuous images, known variously as tracks, sectors, or records. If the normal head burnishing action fails to correct these aberrations, a head crash is initiated, signaled by a triumphant rasp (the French call it "un pet de soulagement"). Well-designed drum/disk subsystems will demagnetize the surface before removing the fetid strata. Many variants are available: read after crash, crash before write, crash after crash, etc.

3 *v. trans.* To put down (a system or device). **4** *v. intrans.* (Of people) to lapse suddenly into a state of intense abulia, *esp.* at vital moments during a highly structured walk-through.

⇒Typical crash triggers are voices (including your own) announcing that (1) "We now need to look at the DMS sub-sub-subschema definitions;" (2) "When I took over the payroll package maintenance responsibility 12 years ago…"

creative *adj.* (Of an accounting system) devious, dishonest, sleazy, illegal. *See also* SPREADSHEET.

Creed *n.* A very early, dogmatic teleprinter.

⇒When they put the Apostles' Creed in,
It was soon replaced by Friden;
St. Peter has the system well in hand;
There's a name tape sent from Hell
In the ATR as well,
Typing letters of condolence to the Damned.

CRT *n.* [Cathode Ray Tube.] Originally an important storage device, developed by Prof. F.C. Williams, Manchester University, in 1947, but now relegated to trivial applications in the timesharing and entertainment environments. *See also* GLASS TTY.

CRUD *n.* [Acronym for Create-Read-Update-Delete.] The four basic threats to database integrity, leading to the eponymous state.

C/S *See* CLIENT/SERVER.

CS *See* COMPUTER SCIENCE; COMPUTING SCIENCE.

cult *n.* A group of devoted language supporters such as the BN (Branch Negative) Davidian Assemblers of God.

curry *v. trans. See* SCHOENFINKEL; LAMBDA CALCULUS.

cursor *n.* [Possibly Old Irish *cursagim* "to blame" or English *cursory* "rapid, superficial."] A faintly flickering symbol on a CRT screen, used to test the eyesight and reflexes of the operator, and indicating where the next keyed character will be rejected.

⇒In parts of England, frustrated terminal minders often refer to the *blinking* cursor. A cursor in the top left hand position of an otherwise blank screen serves to indicate that the system (with the exception of the cursor-generation module) is inoperative. In well-designed systems the cursor flicker rate is set to match the operator's alpha brain rhythm to provide an inescapably hypnotic point of interest until normal service is resumed.

The record for loyal patience belongs to the late M. Thumps, whose atrophied corpse was discovered slumped over a remote terminal of the British Rail TRAIN (Train Recovery And Identification Network)[3] complex two years after his particular line had been closed. The postmortem, performed by Terminal Diseases Inc., proudly revealed that the cursor was still flashing, a fact subsequently exploited in the manufacturer's gruesomely effective advertising campaign. Who will want to forget the full-page picture of the remains of Mr. Thumps's index finger, pitifully poised above the GO key? TOPE (the Terminal OPerators' Executive) has converted Signal Box 327, Camden Town, London, into a permanent museum-shrine in honor of Micky Thumps. A blue plaque outside bears the epitaph:

---

3. Initiated following the Great Train Robbery of 1895 but not fully operational until after the Great Train Robbery of 1963.

Young Mick stood by the empty screen
Whence all but he had fled;
In vain he waited for response,
Now, like the line, he's dead.

Inside, a tastefully cobwebbed replica of Thumps's putrified cadaver, erected by public subscription, can be seen seated at the silent, inexorable CRT, symbolizing the stubborn, pigheaded pride of the timesharer whom time has passed by. Inserting a coin of modest denomination into an adjacent slot, the pilgrim is rewarded with a macabre reenactment of Thumps's final attempt to log on. Bony fingertips scratch the keytops, the cursor blinks but does not move, and a crescendo of bleeps drowns poor Thumps's last modest screams of despair.

cursor address *n.* "Hello, cursor!"

curtation *n.* The enforced compression of a string in the fixed-length field environment.

⇒The problem of fitting extremely variable-length strings such as names, addresses, and item descriptions into fixed-length records is no trivial matter. Neglect of the subtle art of curtation has probably alienated more people than any other aspect of data processing. You order Mozart's *Don Giovanni* from your record club, and they invoice you $24.95 for MOZ DONG. The witless mapping of the sublime onto the ridiculous! WHY I DO turns out to be Bertrand Russell's *Why I do not believe in Christianity.* Equally puzzling is the curtation that produces the same eight characters: THE BEST, whether you order *The Best of Wagner, The Best of Schubert,* or *The Best of the Turds.* Similarly, wine lovers buying from computerized wineries twirl their glasses, check their delivery notes, and inform their friends, "A rather innocent, possibly overtruncated CAB SAUV 69 TAL." The squeezing of fruit into 10 columns has yielded such memorable obscenities as COX OR PIP.

The examples cited are real, and the curtational methodology which produced them is still with us. *Compare* TRUNCATE.

Cyc *n.* *pronounced* psyche.\ A complete OO database of commonsensical human knowledge started in 1984 at MCC (Marylebone Cricket Club?) by Lenat, Guha, Pittman, Pratt, and Shepherd with funding from several major computer companies. The BASE CLASS is called *Thing.*

⇒Cyc may be faced with the Tristram Shandy syndrome (it took TS a week to write up each day of his autobiography). As the growth of human knowledge outpaces that of the Cyc input and maintenance team, it may be necessary to restrict the database to universal *consensus* facts, which are known to decline as time goes by. When I last checked, Cyc "knew" it was unusual to offer a $100 bill for a Baskin-Robbins vanilla cone, but there was no reaction when I sang "You scream, I scream..."

D

daemon *n.* *pronounced* day-mon\ One of many puckish processes raising merrie hell in the bowels of UNIX.

⇒The OE spelling, by tradition, distinguishes the relatively benign *daemon* from the downright evil *demon*. The spooler daemon, for example, delights in sending your high priority reports to a paper-low printer, whereas the spooler demon prefers to direct all your print requests to a non-existent DIABLO at a remote site. PC UNIX considers both *daemon* and *demon* to be offensive to many religious groups and mandates the use of SPIRIT GUIDE or CHANNELER.

Dai Graff (1929–) Welsh linguist and *croesair* (crossword) composer, best known for allowing eponymous pairs of letters in a single square, namely ch, dd, ff, ng, ll, ph, rh, and th.

Daisy Chain *or* **Cha'n** (1831–1895) Legendary Bangkok prostitute-inventor who developed and gave her name to several anachronistic communications and printing devices.

⇒She left for the United States in 1879 ("breaking all my Thais," as she put it) and became Herman Hollerith's mistress-assistant at the Census Office. She died there in 1895 during an all-night card-joggling session. Her son, Markov, took his mother's surname, but did not inherit her practical, electro-mechanical skills. However, Markov soon showed signs of genius as a pure mathematician, and his pioneering work in the theory of stochastic processes probably helped Dr. Hollerith more than any of his mother's futuristic peripherals. Mystery surrounds the fate of Markov Chain. His evening walks became more and more erratic, and one night he simply failed to come home.

Dr. Hollerith tried, unsuccessfully, to incorporate Daisy's ideas into his hardware. Her line printer called for a horizontally rotating band on which were set, at regular intervals, 80 small windmill-like devices, free to spin a vertical plane, each carrying 96 printing elements, one at each tip of the windmill's vanes. Hollerith spent five years digesting the previous sentence, and a further five on the inertial and timing problems of his prototype. Although he never broke the 1 line per minute barrier, he accidentally—some 20 years before Sikorsky—built a two-ton monster that could hover six inches above floor level. Dr. Hollerith's dying words, in 1929, were "On mein Herz you vill find ze werd, *Gänseblümchenketterdrucker.*"

Dangling Else [Posthumous hypocorism for Elsie Batch (1940–1974).]

⇒A pioneer Pascal blaise-trailer who committed suicide after a particularly frustrating session with her primitive compiler. Her ghost is reputed to lurk yet around the computer room at North Staffs Polytechnic (Staffordshire, England), where her vengeful spirit is blamed for any otherwise unaccountable system crash. Her tombstone in the Shrewsbury Bone Orchard bears the following salutary epitaph:

⇒ "Poor Dangling Else!," her fellow users cried;
To cut her down and vet her source they tried.
"**IF** only she had **DOUBLE**-checked," they whooped,
"Her neck would not be unconditionally looped!
"Her once soft eyes would not be swollen
"**ELSE** had she spied the missing semicolon!
"Her timeshared lips would still be smiling;
"Alas, she now lies decompiling!"

> Dear Pascal users who pass by,
> O **PAUSE** a **WHILE**, and heed my cry.
> No **ARGUMENT** can bring me back
> And without **Wirth**, true **Worth** I lack!
> My tragic **CASE** should make **AMEND**;
> **BEGIN** a-**NEW**, avoid my **END**!

FOR careless coding in the young
Can leave a program, and a body, **HUNG**!

DARPA *See* ARPA.

data *n.* [Latin *dare* "to offer or give," whence *datum* "that which is offered or given."] The singular collective noun for a set of datums.

⇒Mandatory DP usage has data in the singular, without exception: "The data is punched and verified." The singularity of *data* is powerful enough to override preceding pluralities, as: "Ten thousand cards of data is punched and verified." Proposals or documents with such flashy affectations as, "Having been punched, the data are verified," are invariably dismissed as the work of pettifogging technical writers who wouldn't know a data if they tripped over one. Similar pitfalls exist in the spoken environment, although the rules are more flexible. The choice between *darter, dayter,* and *datter* (rarely *darrer*) will depend, in a most subtle manner, on the longitude of the speaker and the latitude of the audience. The received classical phonetic canon indicates the shortest vowel, but there are many gaps in our knowledge of Roman computing practice. When in doubt, a safe alternative pronunciation is *in-form-ay-shun,* provided that you are not addressing a convention of full-time semanticists. The latter incline to the view that *information* is that which is left *after* data has been processed, but the practical computerperson cannot afford to be so pessimistic.

A more fundamental attack on the validity of *data*, as used by the DP industry, has come recently from the eminent Scandinavian etymologist, Prof. M. Thumpersen. Thumpersen argues that computer science, being new, undisciplined, and lacking any widely accepted central authority in charge of nomenclature, has borrowed naively from other, more precise taxonomies. He claims, in particular, that the key word *data* is a grotesque misnomer, since computer data is never "given" and seldom "offered." Thumpersen urges a move to the more appropriate (*capio, capere, cepi, captum*) roots, i.e., a switch from the "giving" implied by *data* to the "taking" suggested by *capta*. To encourage the adoption of such phrases as *capta entry, capta processing, captabase,* and *Capta General Inc.,* he is prepared to accept that *capta* is treated as a singular noun. "It would be unrealistic," Thumpersen explains, "to expect too dramatic a change in CP usage."

data bank *n.* A place where DATA can be deposited with the traditional security associated with financial institutions, such as Equity Funding Corporation of America, IOS, Franklyn National, and BCCI, not to mention the many rock-solid S&Ls.

⇒Data bank interest can vary, but usually peaks at the moment of retrieval. As with coitus interruptus, there are substantial penalties for late withdrawal.

data hiding *n. See* HIDING, DATA.

data typing *n.* **1** (I/O) The dominant, depressing DP activity that has defied automation. *See also* SWEATSHOP. **2** (Computer Languages) A putative safety mechanism protecting variables from straying out of bounds.

⇒Alas, many data-typing schemes can be circumvented by internal, implicit DEMO-TIONS and PROMOTIONS, or CAST away by explicit coding.

Database Management System *n. Also* **DBMS.** [Origin: DATA + Latin *basus* "low, mean, vile, menial, degrading, counterfeit."] **1** *Marketing* Any filing system. **2** *Software* A complex set of interrelational data structures, allowing data to be lost in many convenient sequences while retaining a complete record of the logical relations between the missing items. *See also* RELATIONAL DATABASE MANAGEMENT SYSTEM.

DBMS *n. See* DATABASE MANAGEMENT SYSTEM.

deadline *n.* **1** *Communications* A NACKered line that rejects all handshakes, however friendly. **2** *Scheduling* One of a sequence of vague prophecies; a given date before which assignments must not be completed. *See also* HARTREE CONSTANT; REDUNDANCY.

DEBE *n.* [Acronym for Does Everything But Eat.] Supersoft Inc. (ca. 1980) An early example of blatant FEATURISM.

debugger *n.* (Anglo-Irish) The person responsible for errors in a program; the person who sold us our system.

debugging *n.* Removing a BUG, either by tinkering with the program or by amending the program specification so that the side effect of the bug is published as a desirable feature. *See also* KLUDGE; ONE-LINE PATCH; STEPWISE REFINEMENT.

⇒Fixing one's own errors is such a hazardous and humiliating process that programmers are well advised to observe the Kelly-Bootle Rule: "Avoid debugging! Get it right the first time!" Correcting the work of others, though, has its lighter moments, for it is difficult to suppress the occasional wry chuckle (pronounced *Yahoo!*) as your colleague's blatant howlers are methodically exposed and neatly patched. *See* YOUR PROGRAM.

DEC Overloaded *abbrev.* December; deceased; decrease; decrement; pour off (prescriptions); decrescendo (music); Digital Engineering Corporation. *Warning* Often resists contextual disambiguation.

decade counter *n.* A slow real-time clock used in automated news media offices. Every 10 years a signal is generated to initiate a spate of retrospection and prediction.

⇒The best known example, perhaps, is JANUS (JANuary Updating Service), which provides an annual subpulse. This trigger creates a hierarchical database of the previous year's nonevents and a selection of the more idle speculations on the year to come. The 10-year (or *decadent*) clock pulse invokes a complex collation of the previous files from which the presses and TV cameras can roll out the spiritual distillation of the (*n* × 10)'s.

decision table *n.* **1** A choice between the noise of the cabaret and the smell of the kitchen. **2** A noncomputable variant of tic-tac-toe.

declaration *n.* A cavalier statement made to a compiler or customs official.

decompiler *n.* **1** (Brooklyn English) the compiler. **2** The software needed to undo the wrongs of compilation, i.e., to repack object worms in a can of source.

decompiling, James Joyce's Law of "What's source for the goose is object for the gander."

deconstructor *n.* (C+–) The special member function of a class X named ~~X.

⇒Unlike the traditional C++ X : : ~X DESTRUCTOR, which destroys target objects immediately, the C+– deconstructor first engages the memory management system in a prolonged, acrimonious polemic, questioning the naive assumption that OOP "languages" can "model" the "real" world.

default *n.* [Possibly from Black English Vernacular "De fault wid dis system is you, man."] **1** The vain attempts to avoid errors by inactivity. "Nothing will come of nothing: speak again" (*King Lear*). **2 Default option.** A soft option.

⇒The default option is always worth a try when in doubt. The system tries to guess what you really want, and, even if it guesses wrong, at least the whole transaction is legal syntactically. Furthermore, you have a credible scapegoat, which, nowadays, is sure hard to find.

defuzzification *n.* The final stage when a FUZZY system is more or less forced off the fence, the rubber meets the road, and the FUZZ hits the fan.

degrade *v. trans.* **1** To add a terminal to (a timesharing system). **2** To promote (a programmer) to systems analyst.

delay *n.* **1** The elapsed time between successive deadlines. **2** A period of frustrating inactivity so fatal in all its consequences that no member of the DP community can relax until every single manifestation has been tracked down, identified, and stored in the pending file. *Compare* PAUSE. *See also* CAD.

delay-line storage *n.* (ca. 1948) An ecologically sound memory system using recycled pulses. The Cambridge EDSAC I, for example, employed acoustic pulses circulating in long tanks of mercury.

⇒The term "delay-line," of course, was a marketing fiasco. As a general rule, computer products should avoid names that hint, however remotely, that instant gratification is not a key FUNCTIONALITY. Repackaging under the name Green Mercurial Memory and miniaturizing with discarded clinical thermometers might yet bring back this wonderful device.

demotion *n.* **1** The announcement that an ousted CEO is being retained as a consultant at a higher salary. This is a strong indication that the toppled executive could not think of any "personal interests" worth "pursuing." **2** CASTing an **int** to a **char**. *Compare* PROMOTION.

denier *n.* [Origin: possibly French *dénier* "to refuse to recognize."] A proposed unit of coarseness which has yet to gain ISO/ASCII approval.

⇒The measure assigns *zero* to the NULL STRING, *one* to the benign strings (such as "God bless you," "Sláinte," etc.), and *infinity* to any string containing******.

depilation *n.* [Latin *de* "away" + *pilus* "hair."] The painful process whereby programs are made less HAIRY.

⇒A DP trickopathist writes: "One of life's most enduring and remunerative paradoxes is that, for every patient I have complaining of a superfluity in the trichoid environment, I can cite and bill another with the contrary affliction. Hair, or the lack of it, it seems, always looks greener on the other side. Some programmers worry unduly when their programs become *more* hairy in spite of long sessions aimed at simplification. We in the trade call this the "the third-shift shadow" problem. I advise such patients, regardless of sex, to relax, step aside from the job, retire to bed with a cheap novel, and sip my guaranteed medication. There are some horripilations, of course, beyond the grasp of trickopathy, and for those in a seriously deep trichoma we can do little more than find a scapegoat and a change of scenery.

"Hair deficiency, on the other hand or chest, can always be remedied, either by natural methods (usually by a fresh, more realistic assessment of the problem to be programmed) or by artificial complexifications. The latter techniques range from the grafting of hair to hide any thin patches of triviality, to the fitting of a global program toupee able to give to the most mundane package unimpeachable profundity and daunting opaqueness. A full refund is made if anyone spots the join!"

dereference *v.* To trace, with increasing horror, the ultimate object (*also called* the POINTEE) being pointed at by a chain of linked POINTERS. *See also* INDIRECTION; REFERENCE.

⇒In C++, the simple rule is: reference by adding an **&** and dereference by removing an *****. (Ask Bruce Eckel for the rest of the story.)

desktop *adj.* (Of a metaphor) relating to the inane, GRAND GUIGNOL mapping of a windowed computer screen to the untesselatable 3-D chaos of your real desktop.

⇒Current usage indicates that "simile" is a more accurate term for the GUI desktop. However, it seems that metaphoric paradigms are more marketable than mere similitudes (look what happened to Simile 67). Disk directories and files are certainly "like" filing cabinet drawers and folders, and some thereby justify the subsequent predominant iconography. The problem now, though, is explaining to the class of '95 exactly what a filing cabinet *is* (not to mention, Where On Earth Is Manila?). After you have described the metal boxes, sliding compartments, access to paper by indexed tags, and the rest, the kids of today say, "Oh, you mean like a hard disk with directories and files?"

Virtual Reality purists point out that a screen truly reflecting your desktop would surely display the most prominent object thereon, namely your desktop computer with its screen truly reflecting your desktop...

destructor *n.* (C++) The lonely serial killer lurking among the member functions of each class. "Whatsoever Bjarne giveth, Bjarne taketh away" (St. Bernard d'Eiffel). "Out of scope, out of heap" (Sean Bootstrap, Irish Business Machines).

⇒DP usage dithers between "X::~X destroys" and "X::~X destructs." However, the Oxford American Dictionary warns that "Careful writers use the verb *destroy* and the noun *destruction* except when referring to rockets and military devices." *See also* TEMPORARY; DECONSTRUCTOR.

Diablo *n.* A devilish slow serial printer. *See also* DAEMON.

diagnostic *n.* A person who doubts the existence of two gods.

dialog box *n.* (GUI) An inquisitive window that, if MODAL, demands an answer. Modeless dialog boxes can be ignored but you might as well click OK to keep them happy.

⇒Yet another unproductive element in the GUI canon. What started as a simple input prompt has tsunamied into a time-wasting conflict between data-entry fingers and mousing hands. One is tempted to blame the many Windows interface building packages that encourage the programmer to add just one more effortless control button to the dialog box.

digital recording *n.* My dramatic reading of π to 3,000 decimal places (PYE Records, Cambridge, England).

⇒The adventurous may prefer the hard-to-find Lithuanian Pi-recital (200 wax cylinders on the LithPhon label).

Dijkstra, E. W. Versatile computing scientist and baseball star. *See also* COMPUTING SCIENCE.

⇒To confuse the taxman, he spells his name Dykstra when playing center field for the Phillies.

Dinosaurs *n.* A CD-ROM package from Microsoft containing DOS 4.0 and Windows 1.0.

disability *n.* (PC) A hidden or euphemised deficiency.

⇒Thus 8080 SEGMENTED memory is "address-challenged." Similarly, an employer can no longer ask job-seekers if they are addicted to alcohol, absenteeism, or BASIC.

disambiguation *n.* That which contains ambiguities.

⇒Inspiration for this wordplay comes from a real anti-virus program that proclaims: "This package contains viruses."

disclaimer *n.* A message of dubious legality attached to a SHRINK-WRAPped software package confirming the user's fears that the contents are unsuited to the implied, or any, purpose. *Compare* **disowner** as in "Valid except where invalid." *See also* AS IS.

⇒Thus a box labeled Eezi-Akkounting carries the warning: "Notwithstanding the product name and the contents of the manual, it must not be construed that accounting procedures are easy, or indeed possible, by executing the enclosed programs on your past, present or future hardware configurations."

dismal *adj.* [Origin: malapropistic transformation of *decimal* "pertaining to or founded on the number 10."] **1** *Currency* Boring; lacking the traditional, sterling, and natural basal variety of a mixed duodecimal and vicenary monetary system. **2** *Adders* Not quite reliable: "In fact, we dubbed it the "dismal" adder because of its proximity to the edge of workability" (Herman Lukoff, *From Dits to Bits,* Robotics Press, 1979).

disquotational *adj.* (Of Tarski's concept of "truth" in formalized languages) true. *See also* QUOTES.

⇒More precisely, "Tarski is right" if and only if Tarski is right. And I happen to know that Tarski *is* right. You can quote me on that. Niema za co! Less formally, the Bourne and other UNIX shells daily face the disquotational challenge. A host of METACHAR-ACTERS impact the shell in diverse ways *unless* they are *quoted* or *escaped*, i.e., made to behave *literally*. Thus, **cat** is a command but "cat" is a feline string. SPACE PRE-CLUDES a full exegesis…

documentation *n.* [Latin *docomentum* "warning."] **1** The promised litera-ture that fails to arrive with the supporting hardware. **2** A single, illegible, photocopied page of proprietary caveats and suggested infractions. **3** The detailed, unindexed description of a superseded package. *See also* DOXOLOGY; RTEM.

⇒"Documentation is like the weather—everyone talks about it but nobody does any-thing about it" (Michael Marcotty).

dope *n.* The Philosopher's Stone of electronic alchemy.

⇒Cynics have noted the cussedness of 20th-century alchemy, in which a deliberate impurity (or fix) transmutes pure silicon into base transistors.

doryphore *n.* [Greek *doru* "lance" + *pherein* "to carry." Whence "spear car-rier," whence suborder of Coleoptera, whence "nit-picker."] One who takes excessive delight in spotting small errors. *See also* LINT.

DOS *n.* A series of fatal PC VIRUSes distributed by MICROSOFT. *Also called* MS-DOS.

⇒Warning: most PCs now arrive pre-infected.

DOS-2evsky *n.* An early Russian version of DOS generally believed to have been a leading factor in the Evil Empire's downfall.

DOS for Dummies *See* LOW-SELF-ESTEEM BOOKS.

DOSKEY *n.* *pronounced* Доский \ Pirated version of DOS 4.0 available on the Arbat for 100 roubles (2 sold since 1990).

double-sided drum *n.* [© Irish Business Machines.] A discontinued device aimed at storing data on both surfaces of a hollow cylinder. The increase in storage capacity was vitiated by the disastrous reduction in angular momen-tum. *Compare* FASTRAND.

down *n.* [From Old Norse *dunn* "the soft plumage of a seabird's tits," whence, a feather bed."] Moving from an upright, operational, busy, and bor-ing posture to one of horizontal relaxation. *Compare* UP.

downsize *v. intrans.& v. trans. See* RIGHTSIZE.

downtime *n.* The period during which a system is error-free and immune from user input. *Compare* UPTIME. *See also* CRASH.

doxology *n.* (*Rare*) a hymn of praise for the technical writer.

DP attorney *n.* An attorney whose own law firm has not yet computerized, and who is therefore able to exude a proper and expensive objectivity when faced with the tiresome loops of litigation between user and manufacturer.

⇒Until juries are selected by technical rather than common-sense qualifications, a heavy burden rests on the attorneys involved in complex DP actions. There is little point in the aspiring Perry Mason yelling at the jury: "This so-called programmer, cowering in the dock behind a patently false beard, would have you believe that, on the night of the 25th, when all the operators were in the rest rooms and he alone was at the console, that my client's widely respected operating system suddenly and without premeditation killed Job 148, a harmless FORTRAN background batch routine that had been idly ticking over for 18 hours at least. Need I remind you, sweet members, that Job 148 has run regularly each week for 25 years, taking, typically, 19.6 hours with no observable degradation of the timesharing service? Exhibits 23 through 7856, showing the relevant operator log sheets since September 1965, can leave you in no doubt about this. The plaintiff's absurd counter that the log for December 24, 1990, is missing is a despicable red herring underlining the poverty of his submission. Why, then, I pray, would Job 148 on this fateful night be aborted by the system? You have no doubt studied Exhibits 1 through 5, the basic documentation of my client's OS. In any of the nine hundred pages, I ask, is there the remotest sign of instability, the merest suspicion of nonresolvable conflict between batch and timesharing resource allocation? Who had the most to gain from the untimely demise of Job 148? I direct your attention, members of the jury, to exhibits 7857 through 12,345, the actual, unarguable hexdump printouts that the plaintiff tried to shred on the morning of the 26th. The shredder would not swallow such infamy, and neither will this court! Observe the 29765A34F in column 5 of p. 3451. The most innumerate of plaintiffs could not deny the damning significance of this. It is, I submit, the smoking revolver, the flagrant delicto, the reason the accused is now attempting to escape via the window behind the dock. Yes, *he* killed Job 148! *He* wanted to load the 960K SNOBOL compiler. Our case rests, Your Honor. Forgive me if I feel and appear a little Godlike; a touch of the Ellery Queens. I must go now and bill."

DP dictionary *n. Also called* **DP glossary.** An attempt to freeze the volatile vocabulary of an illiterate industry. This work is the first such to succeed.

DP fraud *n.* **1** The supplier's 300 percent markup. **2** The user's refusal to pay because of petty contractual quibbles, such as nondelivery, nonperformance, force mineure, and bankruptcy. **3** (*Rare*) An individual's failure to report the unexpected bank credits or undercalculated invoices.

DP litigation *n.* Formerly the IBM-Justice Department antitrust action but now *chiefly* the LOOK'N'FEEL closed-loop marathon devoted to the artistic comparison of TRASH CAN icons.

⇒The few DP ATTORNEYs who were not engaged in the IBM monopoly affair usually acted on behalf of one or more of IBM's bickering rivals (known then as the Seven Dwarves). Minimum punitive damages of $1 billion were regularly claimed from IBM (but never received) on the grounds that IBM's successful and profitable policy of keeping most of their customers happy constituted unfair competition and restraint of trade. This line of argument evaporated in the mid 1980s.

Other areas of DP litigation that arise from time to time include the vexing problem of copyright. One defendant, accused of copying a general ledger package, received the following solomonic judgment: "The jury has, quite correctly in my view, found you guilty, and my first reaction was to grant you the maximum sentence permitted under the 1980 Protection of Packages (Whether Operational or Not) Act, namely 10 years confined to your present terminal with no upgrade options. On further, more merciful reflection, it being but your sixth offence this year, it occurred to both the plaintiff and this judgeship that your unique ability to duplicate diskettes using COPFLOP level 3.4 and FLOPCOP level 4.3 on the plaintiff's system arouses such a heady mix of curiosity, admiration, and disbelief that the more appropriate punishment, subject to your approval, ultra vires and nolo contendere, would be an immediate and indefinite promotion to DPM at the plaintiff's site, full costs in this matter, and an irrevocable undertaking on your part to devote your undoubted talents to the greed of the plaintiff rather than to your own.

The court be now upstanding until the Friday forenoon following the next St. Presper's Day."

The 1980 act (op. cit.) was carefully drafted to prevent countersuits from those who illegally copied inefficient or bug-ridden software. The notorious sequence of English cases (*Bloggs v. Lloyds*; *Bloggs v. Rex*, and *Bloggs v. Regina*) stretching from 1940 to 1972 clearly influenced the law remakers. As is now widely known, an admitted safe cracker, Lord "Pete Blower" Bloggs, damaged his heavily insured fingertips while attempting to test the security of a Lloyds Bank deposit box outside the normal business hours of the Park Lane branch, London, England, as 1939 was staggering to an indifferent conclusion. Bloggs's counsel argued persuasively that while the normally expected combinatorial defenses were perfectly "valeat quantum valere potest," the bona fide "furunculus armariolorum" (innocent tester of small safes) should not also have to cope with dangerously burred edges on the coded knobs. Lloyds had clearly violated the Office Appliance Safety Ordinances of 1896 and the many amendments thereto (1901–1948). Further, the plaintiff had failed to secure any financial compensation from his "actus non facit reum, nisi mens est rea." The plaintiff's injury and wrongful incarceration had deprived the plaintiff and the plaintiff's backers of proven recidivist income. "While the plaintiff is unable to engage in his trade," urged counsel, "employing skills to which we all have contributed, Society itself is in the dock." Counsel then joined the jury in a spirited rendition of:

The banks are made of marble
With a guard at every door;
And the vaults are stuffed with silver
That Lord Bloggs sweated for!

(Lee Rice, "The Banks of Marble")[4]

Less dramatic but equally relevant actions have followed. Burglars, slipping as they benchmarked suburban hallways in full pursuit of their vocational expectations, have successfully sued not only the hallway owner, but also the Shiny Wax Corporation. Correcting these anomalies, the 1980 Package Protection Act can be summed up as "Caveat Fur" (let the thief beware!), or, to paraphrase Iago, "Who pirates my file, steals trash" (*Othello*).

DPM *n.* [Diplomatic Psychiatric Mediator *or* Demented Programmer Minder. *Rare* Data Processing Manager.]

⇒In a typical medium-sized commercial installation, the DPM ensures that the payroll runs on time, that the month-to-date errors are cleared each month, and that the quarter-to-date errors are cleared each quarter. Typically, the DPM becomes a free agent before the year-to-date discrepancies ruin the office Christmas party.

DP VOGUE *n.* A daily glossy magazine devoted to the transitory topics of computer science. Originally modeled on the eponymous sartorial monthly, it soon required a higher publicational frequency. DP Daily now copes (barely) with the swings and arrows of fashionable computing.

drag'n'drop *v.* To throw away your mouse after the first attempt to copy a file leads to its deletion. *See also* TRASH CAN.

dragging *n.* The canonical GUI method of moving a WIDGET to a point on the screen determined by the unencumbered areas of your MOUSE PAD. *See also* CLICK; MOUSE; DRAG'N'DROP.

drag queen *n.* A move in GUI chess.

drop'n'drag *v.* A basic Polish GUI gambit. *Compare* shoot'n'point. *See also* ETHNOLOGY.

dryadic *adj.* (Of a function) taking two wood-nymph arguments.

⇒Do not confuse with GONADIC.

DTP [Desktop Publishing.] *n.* An advanced word-processing application that warns you after each page that you have used only 15 of the available 60 fonts.

dump *n. & v. intrans.* [Origin: English *dump* "a dull, gloomy state of mind, low spirits; a thick, ill-shaped lump or hunk of anything; to deposit something

---

in a heap or unshaped mass, as from a cart."] *Rather archaic* **1** *n. also called* **postmortem dump** and **core dump.** The bewildered, numerical mapping of each molecule of a corpse in order to establish the cause of death. The excessive volume of evidence is self-defeating, insofar as putrefaction outpaces analysis. **2** *v. intrans.* To test the "0" and "1" printer or display elements at random intervals. More advanced dumps may also exercise the "2" through "7" printer capabilities, while state-of-the-art dumps provide tests for some of the alphabetic characters.

⇒Dumps *are* rather depressing, but looking on the bright side, they provide an excellent check on the paper-low warning device.

DWIM *pronounced* dwim.\ [Acronym for Do What I Mean.] The frustrated cry of the programmer lost in the chasm between syntax and semantics. *See also* INTELLISENSE.

dyadic *adj.* (Of a function) exposed to two arguments. *See also* DRYADIC.

dynamic *adj.* **1** (Of a RAM) in need of constant refreshment. **2** (Of a dump) unexpected, unwelcome. **3** (Of a young executive) despised, short-lived. **4** (Of an IBM system/370 model 155, 165 Address Translator) expensive. **5** (Of a salesperson) early bounding. **6** (Of a variable) late BINDING. *Compare* STATIC.

⇒The mathematical equations for chaotic systems contain two classes of variables: static and dynamic. DP chaos mirrors this with compile-time-bound and run-time-unbounded variables. A third category is meal-time-binding, the result of programmers' bad eating habits.

dynamic halt *n.* The name given, retrospectively, to an endless loop discovered in MY PROGRAM.

dyslexia *n.* [Greek *dys-* "with difficulty, abnormal" + *lexia* "reading."] A disease pandemic among cheap input peripherals, wealthy illiterates, and prrofredders. *Compare* ADD.

dyxlesia *n.* The self-diagnosis of a dyslectic. *See* DYSLEXIA.

⇒Whence the famous graffito: "Dyxlesia Rules, KO?"

E

E *n.* Yet another SINGLE-CHAR LANGUAGE, devised by Richardson, Carey, and Schuh (University of Wisconsin). E can be interpreted as either (C++)++ or, considering the high-mortality rate of even the best academic languages, short for Ephemeral. E increments C++ with the power of creating PERSISTENT objects, and one hopes that this power extends to the language itself.

E13B *n.* A font designed for Madison Avenue and check sorters at the expense of human legibility.

EBCDIC *n.* \Pronounced *ebb-see-dick*\ [Acronym for Extended Binary-Coded Decimal Interchange Code.] An 8-bit code devised for the IBM System/360 and based on the earlier 12-bit IBM card code. *Compare* ASCII.

⇒Initial objections from the Jacquard Weaving Syndicate (JAWS) were quickly silenced by the allocation of codes for CC (Change Color), EW (End Woof), TWE (Time Warp Escape), SLCSM (Switch to Low-Cost String Manipulation), and FB (Fairisle Begin).

editor *n.* **1** (Software) A product capable of generating copies of a text with random variations. *See also* TEXT EDITOR; TEXTUAL HARASSMENT; UNDO.

⇒These variations usually arise from spurious mutations triggered by the editor itself, but sometimes the user is allowed to collate his or her own random strings, known as *changes*. If the *edited* copy is usefully near to the original, it is called a VERSION; otherwise, it is referred to as a BACKUP.

2 (Primate, possibly human) A much maligned scapegoat, paid by the SQUIGGLE. Payment is determined by weighing the target manuscript before and after assault, whence the terms "heavy" and "light" editing. The rare absence of squiggles is known as a "copy edit."

⇒Unlike Ambrose Bierce, whose entry at "editor" is one of the longest and most sarcastic in *The Devil's Dictionary,* this chicken lexicographer is unwilling to provoke editorial revenge. Nevertheless, diverse editors (non-MIT Press, of course) have contrived to improve submitted texts in unexpected ways: the "3-M cartridge" (as manufactured in Minnesota) emerged as a "3 MB cartridge," and my witty "easier done than **sed**" in an essay on **vi**, came out as "easier said than done."

electron *n.* [Origin: eponymous heroine of the Greek novel *Forever Amber.*] The smallest and most mobile of the charged elementary particles.

⇒Luckily for the industry named after her, the electron is also the most enduring, in spite of her driving habits. She consistently ignores the road signs on circuit diagrams and drives on the right against the arrows, from output to input, flagrantly violating the clearly marked potential gradients. *See also* LOGICAL DIAGRAM.

Else, Dangling *See* DANGLING ELSE.

e-mail, email *n.* *pronounced* ee-mail\ *Abbrev.* electronic mail. A picaresque novella (also known as the header) listing the sequence of gateways, nodes, mailers, and protocols responsible for garbling the appended one-line message.

⇒The OED has a semi-prophetic citation: *emailed* (1480) "…arranged in net or open work." *More at* TNHD.

e-mail humor *n.* A measure of risibility inversely proportional to the number of grinning glyphs embedded in the text. Such glyphs, known as EMOTICONS or SMILEYS, are the printed equivalent of the bar-room bore's nudge-nudge or the sitcom's unrelenting laugh track. *More at* TNHD.

⇒There are now over 650 variations on Scott Fahlman's original sideways "have-a-nice-day" :-). *See* David Sanderson, *Smileys* (Sebastopol, Calif.: O'Reilly & Associates, 1993). Peter Kirwin has mooted an email-aware extension of C known as C:=). He also reports that "The emoticon appears to have been anticipated by that great combinatorialist and controversialist, Vladimir Nabokov. I quote from a 1969 interview reprinted in *Strong Opinions*:

'Q: How do you rank yourself among writers (living) and of the immediate past?

A: I often think there should exist a special typographical sign for a smile—some sort of concave mark, a supine round bracket, which I would now like to trace in reply to your question.'"

EMI (Overloaded Acronym) **1** English Musical Industries. **2** Experiments in Musical Intelligence. **3** Electromagnetic Interference.

⇒Whence "EMI's EMI caused EMI" provides yet another daft challenge for automated contextual disambiguation.

emoticon *n. Also called* SMILEY. *See* E-MAIL HUMOR.

empowerment *n.* The Clinton-Gore plan to provide the homeless with high-speed, waterproof modems. *See also* SUPER DIGITAL HIGHWAY.

emulation *n.* [Latin *emulgere* "to drain out, exhaust."] A pack of hardware and software tricks dealt by the manufacturer, allowing the user to acquire a more expensive replacement system without the attendant miseries, or improvements, of an UPGRADE. *See also* LIBERATION; SIDEGRADE.

⇒The main commercial advantage of the generality of the general-purpose computer is that machine *A* can be so programmed and interfaced that the user encounters patterns of error and delay normally associated with machine *B*. Indeed, if the emulation is extended to repainting the cabinets and falsifying the invoice letterhead, the user may well remain unaware of the switch. Emulating slow, sequential processors on fast, parallel systems (while retaining all the idiosyncrasies of card-based batchness and parlaying years of RPG effort) has proved so successful that one wonders why, for example, there are still IBM 1400 installations not yet sidegraded to the 360/370 elysium. Current, and more challenging, research centers on the problem of emulating large-scale efficient mainframe systems on hordes of tiny, inefficient MICROPROCESSORS.

encapsulation *n. Also* **incapsulation** (rare). *Preferred usage*: "Incapsulation ensures that..." but "Encapsulation insures that..." **1** Hiding the details *esp.* from those who need to know. **2** Two of the seven pillars of OBJECT ORIENTEERING. The other five are INHERITANCE, POLYMORPHISM, and BRADY GOOCH. *See also* CLASS; HIDING, DATA.

⇒Incapsulation ensures that data members are incarcerated with the very methods bent on sodomy. Data members evading such attacks (failing to get the message) inevitably succumb to FRIENDly fire.

endless loop *n. See* LOOP, ENDLESS.

⇒In YOUR PROGRAM, an endless loop is known as an *elementary blunder*, whereas in MY PROGRAM it is called a DYNAMIC HALT. See the accompanying illustration.

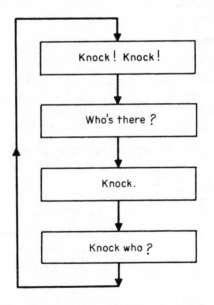

end user *n.* [Origin: from *end* "the point in time at which something ceases, termination of existence, death, fragment, remnant," + USER. **1** Plankton in the DP food chain. **2** A user forced to accept the fact that the blissful days awaiting delivery will never return. *See also* REALITY.

English *n.* [® [sic] Microdata Corporation.] **1** The least unnatural of the natural languages, likely to spread from Bawston to other parts of the United States. **2** A programming language supported by the Logical Machine Corporation's ADAM, and the Microdata Corporation REALITY systems. "Do not adjust your terminal, there is a fault with Reality."

⇒The Reality programmer's guide includes the complete *Oxford English Dictionary*, ample proof of their claim that it offers the most exhausting documentation. Since English® is, perforce, absent any formal metaspeak on the upperdeck of the Clapham omnibus, specified in English, it seems to meet Wirth's challenge that any decent language compiler should be written in its own language.

English++ *n.* An object-oriented extension of ENGLISH.

⇒Initially mooted in a well-worn CompuServe CLFORUM thread by, *inter alia*, Larry O'Brien, Jim Kyle, John Dlugosz, Ben Sano, Brian Hall, Rudyard Merriam, and SK-B, English++ seeks to regulate the many ambiguities of "standard" English. Thus the polymorphic "overloading" and late bindings of virtual verbs and prepositions help resolve zeugma ("Kill the boys and the luggage" [Shakespeare]) and syllepsis ("He left with misgivings and Doris" [SK-B]). Similarly, "The family is ready to eat" and "The duck is ready to eat," can be safely combined in English++ to allow "The family and the duck are ready to eat."

enterprisewidth *n.* Corporate measure determining the potential for right-sizing.

⇒The only applications worthy of attention at the moment seem to be user-centered, prompt-to-market, mission-critical, open, scalable, seamlessly interoperable, and enterprise-wide. The self-employed will be delighted to note that such applications are provably attainable iff enterprisewidth = 1. *See also* RIGHTSIZE.

environment *n.* One of many phatic circumlocutions originating in the DP environment and now spreading to other environments.

Table of Environments*

In the office	In an office environment**
On the moon	In a lunar environment
In vacuo	In an empty environment
At home	In an in-house environment
Under UNIX	In a UNIX environment
Crashed	In a nonfunctioning environment
Chaotic	In an unstructured environment

*Since weight and weightiness are highly regarded in DP documentation, the right hand column variations should be used on all occasions.
**Note the common shift from the definite to the indefinite article.

Note: From the San Francisco *Examiner/Chronicle,* Sunday, November 9, 1980:

During the sentencing, judge Stanley Frosh said Melton needed a more structured environment, such as a pre-release camp. It was then that Melton reached into his pocket and swallowed the poison, calmly washing it down with a glass of water, witnesses said. His wife, after fondly patting her husband, swallowed the white powder before a deputy could stop her.

Moral: The phrase "structured environment" should be avoided.

EOF *n.* Possibly overloaded *abbrev.*: End Of File; Extremely Old Fart.

⇒TNHD defines OF (Old Fart) as "Tribal elder. A title self-assumed with remarkable frequency by (esp.) USENETters who have been programming for more than about 25 years … This is a term of insult in the second or third person but one of pride in first person."

I suppose that we EDSAC I-ers from the 1950s might consider 25 years as the *young* fart boundary, mere upstarts, *pieds tendres*, and *cornichons*; but to maintain the OF jargon, let us introduce and bask in the designation EOF:

> "Keep right on to the end of the file,
> "(Smile you bastards, smile)
> "Keep right on to the end;
> "Though the strings be long,
> "And your **getchar()** wrong,
> "Keep right on round the bend!
> "Though you're tired and weary
> "Still journey on,
> "'Til you come to your happy abode;
> "Where all you love
> "And you're dreaming of…
> (Never dull, the final NULL)
> "Will be there…
> "At the end of the file."

EPSS *n. See* EXPERIMENTAL PACKAGE SWITCHING SYSTEM.

ER Overloaded *abbrevs.*: Entity Relationship; Elizabeth Regina.

⇒Both Rule, OK?

eristic *n. & adj.* [From Greek *eris* "strife."] The dominant mode of disputation that, having victory as its goal, is willing to bypass reason, truth, and other flimsy obstacles.

⇒Euclid of Megara (not to be confused with the Alexandrian geometer) became a full-time eristic, and his ghost can be heard daily in the Senate.

A mild eristic manifestation is "proof by assertion," often accompanied by the waving of hands or, clinch-clinch, the banging of tables. Deities from day one have reveled in more forceful argument-winning variants: smite is right! The Greek goddess Eris (known as Discordia to the Romans) owns the copyright, but the whirlwind eristic prize goes to Yahweh, thundering at Job:

"Who is this that darkeneth counsel by words without knowledge?...Where wast thou when I laid the foundations of the earth?...Hast thou commanded the morning since thy day; and caused the dayspring to know his place?" (Job 38:2–12)

Weak echoes of this form of reasoning can be still be heard as old farts browbeat their upstart critics: "Where were *you* when the EDSAC I initial orders were written?"

ESP Overloaded *abbrev.*: Embedded Systems Programming; Extra Sensory Perception. *Warning* Often resists contextual disambiguation.

⇒No connection?

Ethelred OS *n.* An operating system aimed at the ongoing nonuser environment. *See* SUPERCOMPUTER.

⇒Non-ICL users, as opposed to ICL nonusers, will need reminding that when the British company International Computers Limited launched its 1900 series in 1959, it was faced with two minor embarrassments. First, there were predictable sniggers, fostered by the competition, that 1900 was the design vintage. These jokes, in fact, backfired, since the average English prospect reckoned that 1900 was *a very good year,* suggesting systems of imperious, Victorian stability, in contrast to the ghastly frog-plagued times evoked by a Univac 1108, or the futuristic uncertainties of a CDC 6400. Second, ICL had embarked on a sequence of reignwise-refined operating systems called George I, George II,...while a breathless, indifferent, historically confused market checked the diverse merits of the Hanoverian succession. Would George III madly relinquish the American market? The Ethelred OS was introduced at this point to initiate a new, more honest, regal software genealogy.

ethnology *n.* "The science that treats of the various tribes of Man, as robbers, thieves, swindlers, dunces, lunatics, idiots and ethnologists" (Ambrose Bierce, ca. 1881).

⇒Alas, our tribes continue to cultivate mutual disdain, and ethnic jokes countenance ethnic cleansing. The chilling fact is that the most decent and tolerant of our species can chuckle over tales that enforce cruel and unjust group and racial stereotypes (see, for example, Alan Dundes, *Cracking Jokes—Studies of Sick Humor Cycles and Stereotypes* (Berkeley, Calif.: Ten Speed Press, 1987). As an Anglo-Irish-French-Polish family unit with Jewish, Basque, Welsh, and Scottish overtones, we present a broad target for ethnic slurs but retaliate only against the Frisians. Perhaps "tribal" maturity is reached when the "jokes" no longer offend.

Although I count Łukasiewicz, Kuratowski, Chwistek, Ulam, Mazur, Banach, Tarski, and Sierpiński among my heldenest heroes (my preferred Polish stereotype being the brilliant logician-mathematician), I can still smile at the Polish Shoot'n'Point Camera, the Polish doctor who treats hemophiliacs with acupuncture, and the outrageous catechism: Q. What has an IQ of 300? A. Poland. Yet I wince at the story of the Pole who learned English so that he could read Joseph Conrad in the original (ibid. p. 136). Polish/Ukrainian-born, trilingual Conrad wrote *all* his masterpieces in English, which is a sound enough reason for anyone to master that language. A more complex version of this joke would have a Frenchman learning English so that he could read Samuel Beckett in the original. *Waiting for Godot,* of course, to name but one, was composed first in French (*En attendant Godot*), while Beckett's later works were written in English or no language at all. I decided to unlearn all my languages so that I could read Beckett's *Breath* in the original. *See also* HUNGARIAN ALGORITHM; IRISH SEARCH; POLISH NOTATION.

Euskera Batua *n.* All your Basques in one exit.

⇒Is there a UNIX angle to the long struggle by Euskaltzaindia (the Basque Language Academy) formed in 1918 to establish a unified written version, Euskera Batua, from the five major dialects (bizkaiera, gipuzkoera, lapurdiera, benafarrera, and zuberoera/xiberoera)? Bai, halaxe da (yes, that is so)! It is summed up in Gabriel Aresti's well-known plea: "Euskara bizi dadin, euskarak hiltzeko dira" (In order for Basque to survive, the dialects must die) (Gorka Aulestia, *Basque-English Dictionary* [Reno and Las Vegas, University of Nevada Press, 1993]). Note that even the Basque for Basque-the-language has regional variants: *Euskera* and *Euskara*, and you still find the unified language described as both *Euskera Batua* and *Euskara Batua*. An analogy might be calling a unified UNIX both *Common UNIX* and *Common XENIX.*

event-driven *adj.* [From *event,* "whatever happens" + *driven,* "compelled to succeed."] (Of a disastrous programming paradigm) forced to anticipate the unpredictable with an evergrowing switch-case statement.

⇒In happier, unwindowed days, USERs, enjoying a finite choice of rational, sequentially menued options, knew and loved their subservient place. GUI madness, however, spurred by the makers of RAM, has encouraged user-centric, asynchronous anarchy. The event-driven programmer's *angst de minuit* is "What if the dextrous bugger double-left-clicks while holding down Ctrl-Shift-F12?"

EWOM *n.* [Acronym for Erasable Write-Only Memory. © Irish Business Machines.] A refinement of the WOM (Write-Only Memory) allowing the chip to be erased by (1) a fresh write sequence, (2) exposure to infrared light, (3) in-depth frying for two hours with a portion of rock salmon, (4) a stick of gelignite.

exception reporting *n.* A system with intermittent printer problems.

exit *v. intrans.* To attempt to leave the current program by typing a sequence of ignored farewells. *See also* HALTING PROBLEM.

⇒Many interactive systems shyly resist invocation, but once invoked, stubbornly refuse to step down at the user's request. If the mandatory signing-off slogan is not immediately available or effective, try a harmless prime number sieve, and await the machine's natural rejection. *See* MTBF; INTELLISENSE.

There is, as yet, no standard string for use in the discontinuant or cessational environments. Contenders under urgent review include BYE, PISS OFF, END, ADIEU, BREAK, PARTING IS SUCH SWEET SORROW, and the ANSI 14-pound hammer aimed at the screen (or two such hammers for the Ctrl+C interrupt option). LISP addicts will need to surround their Abschied or Hammerschaft with a reasonable number of parentheses.

More recent annoyances are guilt-inducing regimes such as WINDOWS that seek your confirmation: "Are you *really* sure you want to exit? Click away, you lousy cop out!"

expansion *adj.* (Of a sports franchise or PC board) Freshly inserted among the scornful status quo and doomed to struggle for five seasons.

Experimental Package Switching System *n. Also called* **EPSS.** An on-going, potentially never-ending project dedicated to ensuring the consistent misdirection of long messages in large communications networks. *See also* SDH.

⇒The misrouting of stringent strings, e.g., telegraphic platitudes of five words or less, even under the primitive protocols of Chappe, Edelcrantz, Morse, Baudot and Don Ameche, can be achieved with the minimum of effort, and is subject to the Shannon-Heisenberg uncertainty principle, "If the *content* of a message is 'fixed,' there is an unavoidable error in determining its *destination,* and vice-versa." This delicate balance between message mutilation and misdirection seems to break down with strings of higher DENIER and increased signaling rates. Attempts to introduce new conceptual invariants, such as the *charm* of the longer message, were vitiated by recent ALLC experiments in which the entire text of *Gone with the Wind* was injected into the ARPA network. The message emerged, with less than the predicted number of stylistic aber-rations, on the TRS-80 cassette library of X. P. Qume in Ottumwa, Iowa. It appears that the extra momentum of heavy, fast-moving messages overcomes the intended switch-ing strategy at certain nodes, rather as a runaway locomotive jumps the points.

expert *n.* One of an opinionated group (*esp.* Economics Nobel laureates) holding views that are mutually incompatible with the views of all others in the group. *See also* NIH.

⇒When the Great Day comes, we'll have but one expert per topic. The Dublin horol-ogist, Tim O'Day, was asked why each of his sixty clocks registered a different time. "Bejays," says he, "if they all showed the same, I'd only need the one."

expert system *n.* The sad reduction of AI's nobler aims to a sequence of "IF Nelly claims THEN...ELSE..."

⇒Nelly from Liverpool is the archetypical expert. "Sitting next to Nelly" remains the primary pedagogic strategy in diverse industrial disciplines, ranging from gutting fish to stuffing black puddings. If the trainee asks why she graded the apple as 3, Nelly will say "Well, it's better than a 4, but never a 2, you daft sod."

Extended BASIC *n.* [From *extended* "fully stretched, prolonged" + BASIC.] **1** "Shit with icing" (P. B. Fellget). **2** Any BASIC compiler or interpreter enhanced with features stolen from COBOL and C and meeting any two of the following conditions: (1) the cost exceeds $39.95, (2) line numbers can be incremented automatically or omitted, (3) labels can be alpha-numeric, (4) tape cassettes are not supported, (5) A$ is an object.

F

FAQ *n.* Frequently Asked Question. What's a FAQ? How is FAQ pronounced? *See* TNHD and *UNIX Review,* July 1994.

FASTRAND *n.* [© Sperry Rand Corporation.] A nonfloppy rotating cylindrical device used for storing angular momentum.

⇒In the event of power failure, the FASTRAND can be coupled to a standby generator for several days. Note that the total angular momentum available is slightly reduced if the data-storage option is fitted, owing to the braking effect of the read-write heads on the magnetized drum surface. Three or more FASTRANDs should not be switched on simultaneously at the same site without consulting Sperry's in-house geophysicist. The latter will also advise on the correct latitude-dependent orientation of the drum axis to avoid data loss due to coriolis forces.

fault-tolerant *adj.* **1** (Of a Quality Assurance Department) tolerant to a fault; willing to overlook defects in the noble pursuit of timely deliveries. **2** (Of a system) earthquake-proofed to survive the BIG ONE.

featurism *n.* *Usual usage* **blatant featurism.** Term of abuse applied to the more richly endowed products of your competitors.

FHF [Free Hardware Foundation.] A mooted extension to the FSF (Free Software Foundation).

FIFO *adj.* [Acronym for First In, First Out.] (Of a STACK) Able to "deal from the bottom," using legersdestack. *Compare* LIFO; LINO.

finite-state *adj.* **1** (Of a sales tax) ranging from 0 to 100 percent, depending on the state. **2** (Of a machine) having a limited repertoire.

⇒It can be proved that if a finite-state machine is left to run long enough—for 24 hours prior to a payroll deadline, say—at least one machine state will recur. This is known as the *error state. See also* TURING MACHINE; UTM.

firewall *n.* **1** A desperate but inevitably flammable barrier between the CRACKER and the cracked. **2** An inscrutable modem and protocol manual. *More at* TNHD.

⇒The honest CRACKER is not only determined to test your defenses, but having broken in, is resolved to check the rest of your vulnerable system. Your firewall, therefore, should be constructed more as an appraisal than as a moat: Whom do you trust to debug your kernel and test the relational integrity of your databases?

firmware *n.* A neutral, noware zone between hardware and software, free to deflect blame in either direction, and enabling problems to be solved by three sets of modifications rather than one.

first-time *adj.* (Of a user) virginal and secretly panting for the salesperson's sacrificial knife.

⇒A few first-time users somehow survive the bloody initiation.

> "I didn't like it the first time.
> But, Oh! how it grew on me."
>
> (Julie Lee, "The Spinach Song")

fix *n. & v. trans.* [Latin *figere* "to attack with reproaches, to render immovable."] **1** *n.* A palliative shot in the system's arm, becoming less effective with each application. **2** *v. trans.* To remove (a BUG) by redefining the program specification in order to take advantage of an unexpected feature. *See also* DEBUGGING.

fleep *n.* *Also called* **feep, bleep, beep.** [From JARGON FILE.] The soft bell sound emitted by a display terminal.

⇒The softness of the fleep varies according to the VDU and the calamity signaled. The fleep of the VT-52 has been compared to the sound of a '52 Chevy stripping its gears.

flip-flop *n.* **1** A primitive and noisy bistable device.

⇒ Flip; flip-flop;
The circuit keeps a squeggin'
And it won't stop;
Flip; flip-flop;
I guess I'll have to change it
To a good Kipp;
What is it, it does to me?
What mad kind of thrill do I find?
Switchin' on the HT, the LT;
Don't know it's alive but
It's driving me out of my…
Flip; flip-flop;
The circuit keeps a squeggin'
And it just won't stop…flip-flop!

2. A double-sided FLOPPETTE.

⇒As in the pop record industry, the interesting tracks are usually stored on the *flip* side.

floating-point *adj.* *Also* **FP.** (Of a number) able to keep its head above water during the most crunching of computations. *See also* NUMBER CRUNCHER.

floppette *n.* *Also called* **floppy, floppy disk, diskette.** [Diminutive of *flop* "failure."] Any of various non-hard memory devices with non-soft error propensities. *See also* FLIP-FLOP; FLOPPY DRUM.

⇒Floppy disks must be handed with great care. Keep away from tobacco smoke, grease, nuclear reactors, gravitational fields, ballpoint pens, fingers, meteorites, untreated sewage, and floppy drives. Always store away from strong moonlight at 0 kelvin in a neutrino-free environment. Before discarding used, that is, encoded, floppies, read Irish Business Machines' racy leaflet *1001 Things to Do with Old Floppettes*. Table mats, coasters, flower-pot drainers, and models of the Taj Mahal are among the many bright gift ideas.

Note that the use of "le floppy" in Francophone domains is punishable by death. The Académie-ordained term is *le disque souple*.

floppy drum *n.* [© Irish Business Machines.] An early low-cost mass memory device, now superseded by the FLOPPETTE.

⇒Conversion from floppy drum to disk is not difficult, and can be undertaken by any user of average intelligence using everyday household tools. Simply cut along the dotted line and reshape as required. (See the accompanying illustration.) IBM provide free 5- and 8-inch templates: send the crate tops from three 370/168 systems plus $1.98 for postage, packing, and insurance.

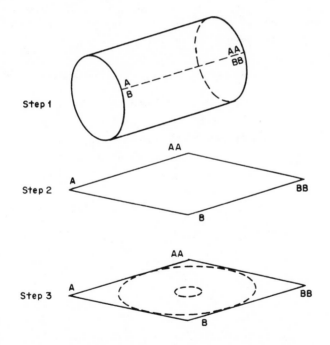

FLOPS *n.* [Rare: Acronym for Floating Point Operations Per Second.] Now replaced with KFLOPS (kilo), MFLOPS (mega), GFLOPS (giga), and, next week, TFLOPS (tera). *Compare* MIPS.

⇒Note that the final "S" does not indicate a plural, so correct usage is 1 FLOPS, 2 FLOPS, etc. The solecism "1 FLOP" is as rare as a coprocessor chip with such dismal performance, but "1 MFLOP" is often encountered.

flowchart *n. & v.* [From *flow* "to ripple down in rich profusion, as hair" + *chart* "a cryptic hidden-treasure map designed to mislead the uninitiated."] **1** *n.* The solution, if any, to a class of Mascheroni construction problems in which given algorithms require geometrical representation using only the 35 basic ideograms of the ANSI template. **2** *n.* Neronic doodling while the system burns. **3** *n.* A low-cost substitute for wallpaper. **4** *n.* The innumerate leading the illiterate. "A thousand pictures is worth ten lines of code" (Mao Tse T'umps, *The Programmer's Little Red Vade Mecum,* Subversive Software Publications, 1968). **5** *n.* A set of systems analysts' Rausch tests, revealing their innermost, twisted procedural fantasies. (See the accompanying illustration.) **6** *v. intrans.* To produce flowcharts with no particular object in mind. **7** *v. trans.* To obfuscate (a problem) with esoteric cartoons.

⇒The flowchart fell into disrepute during the 1980s as higher-level languages emerged of which the source code proved to be more legible than endless reams of linked, annotated boxes. The arrival of VISUAL programming in the 1990s has, alas, put the clock back with a vengeance.

Algorithm for maximizing human happiness

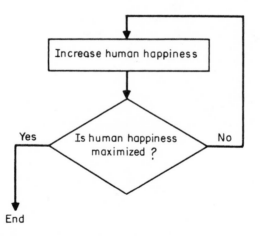

foolproof *adj.* (Of a system) inaccessible by the USER. *Compare* INTUITIVITY.

footprint *n.* Desktop indentations revealing the size and weight of your devotion to personal productivity. *See also* PLATFORM.

foot worm *n. Also called* **ring worm.** A graduate INCH WORM who, forsaking marigolds, mensurates on the branches of labeled trees.

forecasting *n.* An activity to be avoided, especially in relation to future events (*attrib.* Oscar Wilde).

⇒DP prophets, a burgeoning subset of industry watchers and analysts, face a tricky balancing act. Their clients are impressed by "spurious accuracy," whereby a firm predicted annual PowerPC growth rate of 9.61 percent carries considerable weight and billability. Post factum factoring, however, favors less precise prognostications of "about 10 percent," qualified with phrases such as "other things being equal," or "depending on what the buggers at Intel do."

The literature reveals some prime examples of rash prophecy:

- In 1989 John C. Dvorak claimed that NEURAL Networks would be able to predict the scores of NFL games "to within a point" during 1990.
- "The market for LISP machines should exceed $1.2 billion in 1990." (*ComputerWorld*, 16 April 1986).
- "Three EDSAC machines will satisfy the computing needs of all UK universities for the foreseeable future."

Forth *n. Often caps* **FORTH.** A unique, stack-oriented programming cult invented by Charles H. (Chuck) Moore ca. 1970. *See also* SINGLE-CHAR LANGUAGE.

⇒Astrophysicist-cowboy Moore originally brought forth FOURTH (as in next generation) but was forced to drop the "U" in order to meet the five-character naming limitation of the then available operating system (*compare* FORTRA and FORTRAN). Although Forth never became a major, mainstream success like C, it has, like APL, nurtured a pleasantly fanatic set of groupies. Forth's famed resource-wise parsimony has proved especially attractive in embedded systems applications. Folklore has it that Jean Sammet excluded Forth from HOPL-I (ACM's first History of Programming Languages conference) on the grounds that a computer language, by definition, must have a syntax. This omission was happily corrected for HOPL-II (*See ACM SIGPLAN Notices* 28, no. 3 [March 1993], ed. Richard L. Wexelblat).

FORTRA *n.* An early FORTRAN implemented on the IBM/704 that limited identifiers to the first six (upper case) letters (Henry G. Baker).

FORTRAN *n.* [Acronym for FORmula TRANslating system.] One of the earliest languages of any real height, level-wise, developed out of Speedcoding by Backus and Ziller for the IBM/704 in the mid-1950s in order to boost the sales of 80-column cards to engineers.

⇒In spite of regular improvements (including a recent option called STRUCTURE), it remains popular among engineers but despised elsewhere. Many rivals, with the benefit of hindsight, have crossed swords with the old workhorse! Yet FORTRAN gallops on, warts and all, fired by a bottomless pit of proven libraries. Lacking the compact power of APL, the intellectually satisfying elegance of ALGOL 68, the didactic incision of Pascal, the spurned universality of PL/1, the military might of Ada, and the exciting dangers of C, FORTRAN survives, nay, flourishes, thanks to a superior investmental inertia.

forward *adj.* (Of a reasoning chain) presumptuous; jumping to conclusions, as in

```
IF BALANCE<0 THEN PRINT "You are overdrawn"
```

See also BACKWARD.

FPU Floating Point Unit. Formerly a separate math coprocessor chip but now added to the main microprocessor together with a heatsink and a fan.

free loader *n.* The despised linker that comes with your compiler (Henry G. Baker).

freelance *adj.* [Origin: either *free* "expensive" (as, "the best things in life are free") + *lance* a large lancelet, a not-so-diminutive fishlike animal," or from 15th-century weapons sales jingle: "Buy three lances, get one free!"] Immune from litigation.

freeware *n.* **1** A program that is not worth pirating. **2** The main vehicle for the dissemination of VIRUSes. "Who steals my code, steals trash" (Immanuel Agogo). *See also* SHAREWARE; FSF; PIRACY.

friend *n.* (C++ keyword) A non-member, granted membership privileges. If class *X* says you are a friend, you can access *X*'s private and protected parts with no risk of costly litigation. As in real life, friendship is not necessarily transitive. (*X* is a friend of *Y*) and (*Y* is a friend of *Z*) does not imply that (*X* is a friend of *Z*), but where I live, *X* and *Z* have already shacked up and dropped *Y*.

FS *n.* [Future Series. © IBM.] *Also called* Freundliches Schwert (Friendly Sword). [© Richard Wagner.] A sword of Damocles for the non-IBM minority. *See also* VAPORWARE; NT.

⇒IBM's next product announcement, or possibly the one after the next. Who knows if the FS if really hanging over the marketplace? IBM's announcement that "FS is suspended" is ambiguous, to say the least. Cynics say that FS will be a 1401 for $20 (printer ribbons and software not included); others say it will be level 3 of ACF/NCP/VS or a 7090 emulator for the 4331. Myth has it that a Heldenprogrammer will one day descend on the misty Poughkeepsie Nibelheim singing "I'm busy doing Notung"; he will reforge the mighty FS, rescue Grace Brünhopper from a burning Blübell mountaintop, and restore IBM's rightful 100 percent share of the market. For was it not written:

Da hast du die Stücken,	(Well, there are the bits,
schändlicher Stümper	You blundering botcher!
. . . .	. . . .
Warst du entzwei	You were unstable
ich zwang dich zu ganz;	But I have made you whole;
kein Schlag soll nun dich mehr	You are now completely user-
zerschlagen	proof)
	(Richard Wagner, *Siegfried*, act 1, tr. SK-B)

FSF [Free Software Foundation.] Richard Stallman's brave but doomed attempt to bankrupt the "free market" software industry. *See also* FHF; GNU; COPYLEFT.

FUBAR [Acronym for F***ed Up Beyond All Recognition.] British Army slang now gentrified to "foobar," a popular metasyntactic variable. *More at* TNHD.

function *n.* **1** (Math. and CS) a mechanism for mapping a domain of dubious ARGUMENTs into (*rare* onto) a range of unreliable results. **2** (General) the stated action or purpose of something, later denied in a small-print fitness-for-use footnote.

functionality *n.* Preferred usage: **added** or **improved functionality.** Marketese inflation of FUNCTION (2). *See also* CARD.

fuzz *n.* [Backformed from *adj.* FUZZY.] **1** That which prevents U.S. research projects from being funded and papers on topology from being published. **2** That which makes Japanese trains and dishwashers run on time. *Compare* HAIR.

fuzzy *adj.* [Origin: possible corruption of Farsi.] **1** (Of a logic) one in which *modus ponens* is replaced with *modus vivendi.* **2** (Of a set) *a* Colonialist poet Kipling's wuzzy warriors. *b* "Slightly-too-naive" for Halmos. *See also* FUZZ; ZADEH, LOTFI.

⇒Although it means "clever" to Japanese Fifth *et seq.* Generations, for Western ears "fuzzy" can never quite escape the overtones of fluff and imprecision. Thus, when Canon proudly introduced a "fuzzy lens," the news was greeted differently in Tokyo and Leipzig. However, as with CHAOS, the formal definitions of "fuzzy" are firmly planted in a non-fluffy determinism of Calvinistic proportions. Whether "big," "tall," and "big'n'tall" are points or ranges, sooner or later membership is determined by a flag in the CCR (Condition Control Register) following a boring sequence of BLEs (Branch Less than or Equal).

Fuzzy-alone is no longer a marketable predicate, so one must batten down for a deluge of neural-fuzzy-object-based thingies.

G

G \giga\ The SI (Système International) prefix multiplying by either 10^9 or 2^{30} depending on whether you are buying or selling.

⇒Once considered exotic, the Gbyte (often called a "gig") is now commonplace; indeed it is fast becoming laughably inadequate for both disk and RAM if decent OS/2 or Windows NT performance is required. To end the boring debate over pronunciation, be it forthwith mandated that both "g"s are *hard*. This avoids the real possibility of confusion with "jigger" (Scouse [Liverpool] dialect for a "back entry dividing a row of terraced houses"), "jidger" (the didgeridoo-player's embouchure), and "gijah" (a short truce during a Moslem holy war). One is reminded of Genene, the former CEO of ITT, who is reputed to have told a confused underling that "The 'g' is soft as in Jesus, not hard as in God."

gainsay *v.* To deny.

⇒"There's no gain saying that the (CIS) CompuServe Information Service can be, at times, monumental in size and scope" (Editorial in *CompuServe Magazine,* October 1992).

The difference between "no gain saying" and "no gainsaying" is quite subtle. In "gainsay," *sans* space, we have a transitive verb derived from Middle English *gayn*, "against" and *sayen*, "to say." To "gainsay" is to speak against, to contradict, to deny. But in "gain saying" we have a different "gain," from ME *gayne*, with the familiar notion of "increase" or "profit." As luck would have it, the quoted passage makes sense in both contexts. With the space removed (as intended, I'm sure), the editor is saying "There's no denying that..." As printed, it says "Why bother saying that..." Of course, the "at times" is rather inappropriate, implying that the size and scope of CIS can, on occasions, oscillate between "monumental" and "non-monumental" states.

gangpunch *v. trans.* To ensure that a sequence of cards is mispunched consistently.

garbage *n. & adj.* *pronounced* gar-bidge but often pseudo-refined to garbarge. *cf.* garage, barrage, cleavage.\ **1** *n.* Rubbish, trash; the defining by-products of an effluent society. **2** *n.* User-perpetrated input. **3** *n.* (RAM) Essential, well-tried data unjustly denigrated by programs unable to gain access. **4** *adj.* (Of a collection) relating to frantic, futile, low-level attempts to avoid insufficient-memory errors by incurring insufficient-time errors. *See also* GIGO.

gate *n.* One of the nine Apollinarian "portes" to algorasmic bliss.

Gates, William (member FDIC, *aka* **Bellevue Billy**) Founder/CEO of Microsoft Corporation, and youthfully, richly immune to jealous satire. As the second wealthiest U.S. billionaire, he tries harder. *See also* MAW; UNDOCU-MENTED; WINDOWS.

⇒Bill sensibly disputes the *Forbes*'s annual wealth tables. A minor fluctuation in Microsoft share values can increase or decrease his net worth by untold millions. We, *los decamisados,* must count our blessings.

gee whiz *adj.* Relating to some superficially flashy aspect of technology intended to amuse and distract the layperson.

GBH [Putative origin: *Brit. abbrev.* Grievous Bodily Harm.] The aggravatingly red nano-mouse located at the centroid of the "G," "B," and "H" keys of an IBM notebook.

gender *n.* The earthling nexus of connector conspiracies.

⇒On other planets, enjoying more exotic coupling methodologies, added *angsts du jour* are the number and size of the pins:

"Whip Jamboree, Whip Jamboree,
"Momentum equals ΣMV,
"Them three-legged gals are the ones for me,
"Keep her on the orbit, son."
  (Stan Kelly, "Space Shanty," *Liverpool Lullabies* London: Heathside/SING,
1964)

genetic *adj.* (Of an algorithm) Evolving instantly to the worst case after billions of divergent mutations. *See also* GRANDFATHER-FATHER-SON.

⇒"The drosophilia's fleeting moment in the sun is now but a floating point in the SUN" (Sol Stein, "Darwin Deconstructed").

general-purpose graphs *n.* [© Irish Business Machines.] A set of graphical visual aids designed to reduce your overhead overheads. See the illustration on pp. 80–81.

Gershwin's law It ain't necessarily so.

GFE (The Pick Operating System) Originally, *abbrev.* General Format Error, now interpreted as Gone For Ever. *See also* SARCONYM.

⇒The Pick OS has a brilliant but volatile file structure much loved by the purveyors of the UPS (Uninterrupted Power Supply).

GIGO *n.* Acronym for Gospel In, GARBAGE Out.

gilding the lily *n.* The fruitless attempt to improve an already perfect system, e.g., by replacing a data cassette with a floppy disk, or by upgrading from Solaris 2.1 to 2.2.

glass tty *n.* *pronounced* glass titty.\\ A CRT terminal so lacking in features that it behaves like a TTY. *More at* TNHD.

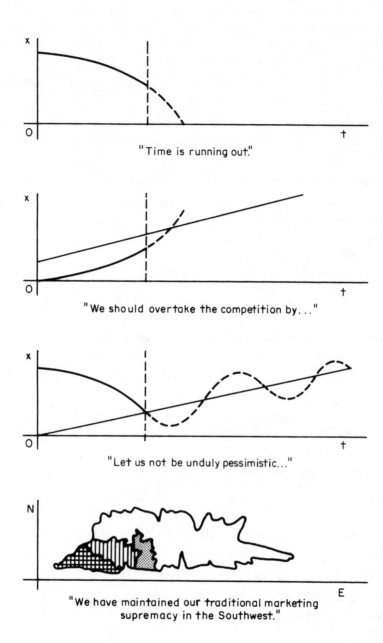

"Time is running out."

"We should overtake the competition by..."

"Let us not be unduly pessimistic..."

"We have maintained our traditional marketing
supremacy in the Southwest."

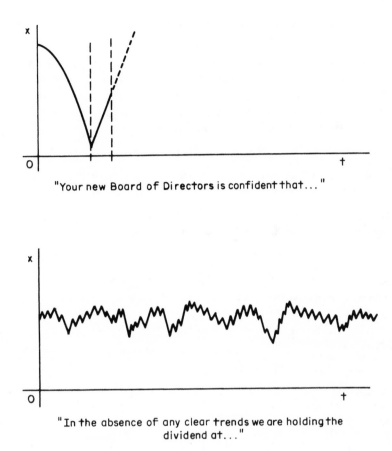

"Your new Board of Directors is confident that..."

"In the absence of any clear trends we are holding the dividend at..."

glitch *n. & v. trans.* [Origin: possibly blend of *glitter* + *hitch* or Yiddish *glitsh-'n* "skip, skid."] **1** *n.* Any unexpected and transient fluctuation in the power supply or, by extension, any sudden change for the worse in the status quo. **2** *v. trans.* To upset (a component or system) by the, usually unintentional, addition of a glitch. **3** *v. trans.* (local usage, Stanford University, California.) To engage in SCROLLING (on a display screen). *See also* GRITCH. *More at* TNHD.

global *adj.* [Latin *globus* "a ball."] **1** (Of a variable) able to bounce around the system, transferring arbitrary values to and from unconnected programs. **2** (Of an error) ideal; detectable; correctable; minor. *Compare* LOCAL.

⇒All unavoidable errors should be made global. Local errors can lurk around unnoticed for months, gathering malignant momentum, suppurating behind the scenes until the system suddenly collapses from the sheer mass of smegmous accretion. *See* SOFT-WARE ROT.

GNU *n.* [Recursive acronym: GNU is Not UNIX.] *pronounced* G-noo\ Richard M. Stallman's noble attempt to restore UNIX to its primordial, off-licensed anarchy. *Malgré cela*, a host of entrepreneurs are waxing fat by installing, debugging, maintaining, and trans-licensing GNU software. *See* FHF; FSF; COPYLEFT; RMS. *More at* TNHD; *Compare* INCA.

GOD *n.* Acronym for General Oracle Dispenser. *See* SUPERCOMPUTER.

Godot *n.* A sarcastic name applied generally to any project or device which fails to materialize after the *n*th deadline. *See also* ETHELRED OS.

golf ball *n.* A spherical printing device, so called from its early propensity to fly off in random directions to unpredictable places.

⇒An Olivetti model (serial #098-43245) holds the world record for distance: 546 yards at St. Andrews University, Scotland, on January 3, 1969, using a specially dimpled character set. M. Thumps holds the record for the most golf balls lost during a single round of on-line editing. In a 12-hour session at the IBM Selectric Rail TRAIN system terminal (*see* CURSOR), Thumps lost 89 golf balls (comprising 16 distinct typefaces). During this period, incidentally, he also lost five trains, three friends, a $500 productivity bonus, and his job.

A hole in one has been claimed by Ann Arbor University, Michigan, but the details are too disgusting to merit objective reportage.

gonadic *adj. See* DYADIC.

gosub *n.* [From verb "go" and Latin *sub* "under."] A CALL made on some nonexistent or noncooperative routine, resulting in instant downage.

goto *n. & v. & adj.* **1** *n.* A GOTO ORDER. **2** *v. trans.* to transfer control (to a distant line or label). **3** *v. intrans.* To transfer control to nowhere in particular. **4** *adj.* (Of an order or instruction) hazardous, irresponsible, fatal, inviting contempt. **5** *n.* A minor flaw in the C language. *See also* CASE.

goto order *n.* [Origin: possibly biblical: "Go to, let us go down and confound their language."—Jehovah at Babel (*Genesis* 11:7); or possible metathesis of "order *to go*, (U.S.) term used in the cafeteria system.] A delightful but dangerous feature of many primitive (unstructured) mid-level languages, whereby a programmer can pass control to some remote, unwritten part of a program and break for coffee. *Compare* COME FROM.

⇒The powerful academic lobby promoting GOTOless programming [e.g., al-Khāsī (1449), Dijkstra (1968), Wirth (1970), and Knuth (1970)] received support from an unexpected direction when Anthony Newley's recording of *Where Shall I Goto?* made the charts in 1976.

Grand GUIgnol *n.* [French: *Un spectacle d'une horreur sanglante et mélodramatique.*] *See* DESKTOP; GUI.

grandfather-father-son *adj.* Being or pertaining to three files believed to have some genealogical relationship. Owing to the hazards of updating and GENETIC mutation (*see also* SOFTWARE ROT), the grandfather, if still alive, carries more authority.

⇒Those who seek some neo-Darwinian interpretation of the evolution of programs and data files are thwarted by the complexities of ONE-LINE PATCHES, the conflicting definitions of fitness and survival, the apparent death wish of DPMs, and the morphogenetic instability of the editing process. "For the sins of Mk I shall visit Ye, yea unto the *N*th generation" (St. Presper's *Stridor Dentium*, Incisor IV, molar iii).

graphical *adj.* (Of a system) capable of, and mainly engaged in, the display or printing of continuous-line Snoopy renditions. *See also* GUI.

great moments in computing history *n.* A collection of boring anecdotes: as,

"Paging Mr. Samas, paging Mr. Samas…There's a Mr. Powers on the line…"

"Professor Wilkes, the man's here with the mercury…"

"T.J., I think we should call it virtual memory…"

"Yes, I know it's small, but we can still use the big cabinets…"

"But, Grace, darling, that will allow *anyone* to program…"

"Bill Gates is offering $20,000 for our non-reentrant DOS?"

green adj. (Of a PC) PC.

gritch *n. & v.* [Origin: possibly exclamation "Grrr" + "hitch" or corruption of GLITCH.] **1** *n.* A complaint or expression of frustration (usually following a glitch). **2** *v. intrans.* To complain.

Grosch's law [Formulated by Herbert R. J. Grosch in the late 1940s.] "Computing power is proportional to the square of system cost."

⇒K.E. Knight has shown that up to 1976, in spite of diverse changes in technology, leasing policies, and inflation, Grosch's law had been religiously observed by the costing and marketing departments of the major DP manufacturers. "And so it was done that the Grosch prophet be maintained" (St. Presper's *Admonishments to the Parasites,* Level III, release iv). To some, the mini- and micro-revolutions have obscured the validity of Grosch's law, but it remains honored in the canon of mainframe orthodoxy. Indeed, cynics in the latter camp point out that the equation

$$P = kC^2$$

where P = computing power, C = cost, and k is the Grosch constant of proportionality, is vacuously true for mini- and microcomputers, with $P = k = 0$ for all values of C. The nonabashed mainframer still dreams of exploiting Grosch's law by buying bigger and costlier systems, and sections of the industry will forever try to oblige. *See* GROSCH'S LAW, COROLLARY TO; SUPERCOMPUTER.

Grosch's law, corollary to "Development cost is proportional to the cube of the target performance." *See also* GROSCH'S LAW; SUPERCOMPUTER.

grunge *n.* [Origin obscure; possibly onomatopoeic blend of *grunt* and *cringe.*] The patina that eventually enhances all hardware and software exposed to the human environment.

⇒A janitorian writes: "A really healthy grunge takes time and should not be rushed. Smegmologists worth their salt can sniff out an artificially accelerated layer of grunge with instant disdain. Genuine grunge is not only an object of sublime beauty, a palimpsest of DP endeavor, but also a threatened source of information to the industrial microarcheologist. Many installations, despite regular upgrades, retain some vestigial reminders of earlier, happier days—a bypassed accounting machine, a 90-column sorter, perhaps, a sales analysis written in RPG-1, or a real-time TurboProlog-controlled trephine—either for sentimental reasons or from sheer necessity. Patient probing of the grungial strata residing on these bygones can reveal unexpected facts about earlier DP cultures. Our present knowledge, however scanty, of the Collator People, for example, stems entirely from nanodigs made in the 1970s at MIT, a site still rated highly by grunge sifters and DP historians. The janitorial fellowship is united in its effort to avoid the mindless removal of vital evidence from computer equipment. As Dr. Thumpton, the doyen of DP microarcheology, once explained, "Each console fingermark, each keyboard coffee stain, each half-removed adhesive label is a priceless, sacred token of our heritage.""

GUI *pronounced* gooey, rhyming with phooey\\ [Graphical User Interface.] A massive and successful conspiracy to sell MIPS and RAM to the illiterate. *See also* ICON; TUI; TRASH CAN.

guru *n.* [Origin: Hinduism, "spiritual guide."] (UNIX) The local Shiva who, being one *Vedic* man page ahead of the site, can create and destroy as the whim dictates. *See also* METHODOLOGY; SYSADMIN.

H

h file *n.* [Originally from "header file" but now often referred to as "headache file."] *Also called* **include file.** **1** A C file with the extension **.h** used to increase the size of files with the extension **.exe.** **2** A device for OVERLOADING your NAMESPACE (Henry G. Baker). *See also* CODE BLOAT.

HA *adj.* [Origin: exclamation of doubt, surprise, and/or amusement but now presumed *prefix* for Human-assisted.] (Of computing) as seen by a tolerant computer. *See also* BA; CA.

hacker *n.* One who hacks real good. *Much more at* TNHD.

hair *n.* The subsumed substance that makes problems, programs, and devices HAIRY. *See also* HIRSUTE; FUZZ.

⇒The Scouse dialect, as spoke in Liverpool and contagious suburbs, has a similar adjective-to-noun transformation. Anything that is "tatty" owes its "tattiness" to the presence of "tats" (Frank Shaw, Fritz Spiegl, and Stan Kelly-Bootle, *Lern Yerself Scouse: How to Talk Proper in Liverpool* [Liverpool, England: Scouse Press, 1966]).

hairy *adj.* **1** (Of a program or system) unduly complex, overly convoluted, beyond fathomage, trichomatic. **2** (Of a person) weak-chinned, complexifying, able to add or substract HAIR according to demand. "For I am an hairy man, but Alan was an smooth man" (St. Presper, *De Arte Publica Statuque Artis [Concerning the Art of the State and the State of the Art]*). *See also* DEPILATION.

Halting problem *n.* **1** *DP* The problem of stopping a computation between crashes.

⇒A halting engineer writes: "Users sometimes want to interrupt a job without waiting for the system to abort. If the machine has no stop or suspend facility (or if these functions fail to work), we recommend the use of the power-off switch rather than removing the power plug. The latter action occasionally invokes a standby UPS (if fitted), and your unwanted job or endless loop will continue. Even the power-off switch will not always guarantee termination because of what we engineers call the *running-on problem.* As with the analogous automotive problem, the cure is to clean all the contacts, check the timing, and try a higher-octane power supply."

2 *Computer science* The abstract problem, solved negatively by Alan M. Turing, which, essentially, seeks a general method for deciding whether an arbitrary program will terminate or not in the crashless environment.

⇒Turing's formal proof of the nonexistence of the programmer's much-needed touchstone is closely related to Gödel's work on undecidable propositions. The curious laity should read Douglas R. Hofstadter, *Gödel, Escher, Bach: An Eternal Golden Braid* (New York: Basic Books, 1979). The undercurious are referred to the accompanying illustration, which, according to DP folklore, was jotted on the back of an envelope by Turing during a London-Cambridge train journey with Strachey.

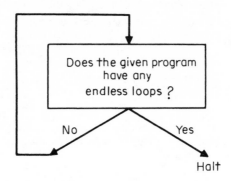

handle *n.* **1** An alias allowing remote, guilt-free mutilation. **2** A POINTER to a pointer or "passing-the-buck-squared." *See also* INDIRECTION; POINTEE; HIDING, DATA.

⇒Borrowed from the phrase "getting a handle on things," the DP handle is a homely, reassuring concept hiding, *inter alia*, several layers of complexity. The handle-as-pointer can remain fixed while the target structure is casually relocated by the memory mismanagement system. *Warning:* the purists who hate pointers and loathe all forms of hiding are made doubly mad by any reference to this term. In particular, avoid making declarations such as `Handle messiah;`.

hangup, hang up, hang-up *n. & v.* **1** *n.* The condonable murder of an intrusive communicator and the brief period of guilt following the deed. **2** *n.* (Archaism) a command in the discontinuant environment harking back to the time when telephones were vertical.

hard sector *n.* An area of a disk resisting access.

hardware *n.* The easy part of the system. *Compare* FIRMWARE; MIDDLEWARE; SOFTWARE; VAPORWARE.

⇒The callosity of a *ware* is best judged by considering the difficulties faced by the goods inward clerk as incoming items are checked against the supplier's advice note. Receipts such as:

4-off Frames, boards, mother, holding, S-100, 6″ bolts, retaining, hexagonal, tapping, self, aluminum. Part #360/168-PDQ-362516526/A

present fewer problems than, say:

1-off Disk, floppy, teeny-weeny Pascal, level 56.127, contains all fixes in appendices 12–68 of attached release dated 12/10/90.

or:

1-MB add-on virtual memory.

Hartree constant *n. Also called* **Hartree's constant.** [After Douglas Raynor Hartree (1897–1958), English physicist and computer pioneer.] The fixed time interval H between now t and the time T_a when any given DP project is completed.

⇒If T_i is the time when a promise is made to complete a project at time T_p then

$$T_a > t >= T_p >= T_i$$

and

$$T_a - t = H$$

It follows that

$$\lim_{t \to \infty} T_a = \infty$$

i.e., DP projects are never completed.

hello, world *n.* [Often confused with the verbose "hello, world!"] The prototypical nerdstring displayed by compiling and executing **hello.c**, the *Urquelle* (primary source) code from p. 6 of K&R (Brian W. Kernighan and Dennis M. Ritchie, *The C Programming Language* [Prentice-Hall, 1978]). *See* C (as the blues rider say).

⇒The "world" responded to this greeting with instant devotion, probably, hint the cynics, because the full syntax of **printf()** was not revealed until p. 145 (IBID BEN PASSIM). Progress in language, compiler, and GUI design since K&R has been warily correlated, often inversely, with the increasing size of "hello, world" executables. Not content with the original, one-line, legible, monospaced ASCII text, as God intended, current implementors are tempted into resizable, in-your-face, spiraling fonts, exploding dialog boxes, and background video clips from Haydn's *Creation*.

help *n.* A torrent of irrelevant information invoked by the F1 key.

⇒The tree-saving crusade to replace hard-copy documentation with on-line HYPERTEXT is vitiated by the fact that most users harbor a deep-rooted distrust of volatile screen displays.

Henny Thumpman *See* KING OF THE ONE-LINE PATCHERS.

heuristics *n.* **1** The art of looking busy when seated at a terminal. **2** An upmarket problem-solving METHODOLOGY still seeking a worthy class of problems. **3** A formal approach to idle speculation.

⇒"Giving strong technical advice for writing a good informal strategy is hard, due to its informal nature. We think therefore that better ways of discovering objects, classes and operations have to be found." (C. J. and A. Strohmeier, "An experience in teaching OOD for Ada software," *SEN,* October 1990, ACM Press).

hexadecimal *adj. Also called* **hexadismal.** [Greek *hexe* "witch," whence "evil spell" + Latin *decem* "ten."] Relating to a much-cursed method of alphanumerological counting, whereby two spiders can be dissected for the hellbroth cauldron. Cordon Bleu hags intone 0 through 9 as they toss in the first ten tarantulid tarsi; the remaining six stumps carry the mnemonical incantation A through F: "Azazel, Beelzebub, Cacodemon, Diablo, Eblis, Fiend."

⇒Current DP usage retains the demonic, hexadecimal notation 0 to 9, A to F for the bit patterns 0000 to 1111, but William Barden, Jr. (*TRS-80 Assembly Language Programming,* Radio Shack, 1979) has updated the mnemonic to: Actinium, Barium, Curium, Dysprosium, Erbium, Fermium."

hiding, data *n.* [From *hiding* "a severe thrashing" + "data."] The inevitable fate of your datums, however cunningly concealed. *See also* ENCAPSULATION

high-level language *n.* **1** Any of a set of acronyms devised by the manufacturer's marketing division. **2** A natural language purged of ambiguity *and* semantics, but with compensatory punctuational and diacritical extensions aimed at increasing the complexity of the syntactical structure. **3** A method of slowing down the system to allow the innumerate to cope.

hirsute *adj.* Humorously endowed with a pleonasm of plethoric profundity, i.e., HAIR.

hole *n.* **1** The space in a medium formerly occupied by a CHAD. **2** The resulting region of a Babbage wooden memory board when a knot-hole is reset. *See also* NOT-; PUNCH.

hole, black, computing *n. See* SUPERCOMPUTER.

HOPL [Acronym for History Of Programming Languages.] A conference organized by the ACM so that rival language designers can feign a three-day friendship every ten years.

hot *adj.* (Of a chip) **1** Successful. **2** Unsuccessful. *See* PENTIUM.

⇒By a Voltairean quirk of fate, the design of hot chips has kept pace with the design of tiny fans and large sinks.

hot-point *n.* **1** The pixel-group just beyond the reach of your MOUSE. **2** The

Comdex booth featuring LaToya Jackson's "A Survey of ANSI C++ Exception-Handling Methodologies." *See also* CLICK.

however *conj. Also called* **the big BUT.** A disjunctive used to separate the assertion of a proposition and the immediate assertion of its negation: "We plan to market tomorrow; however, the FDIV subroutine still leaves much to be desired." "We accept your quotation and performance estimates; however, we await the results of the benchmark promised last June."

howler *n.* A solecism too gross and commonplace to excite the true DORYPHORE.

⇒Let us not treat a misplaced diaeresis as a daughter lost:

"Howl, howl, howl, howl! O, you are men of stones:
"Had I your tongues and eyes, I'ld use them so
"That heaven's vault should crack…"

(*King Lear,* act 5, scene 3)

Hungarian algorithm *n.* "First, pirate a copy of Borland C++…" *See also* ETHNOLOGY.

Hungarian notation *n.* The naming of variables using mnemonically data-typifying prefixial agglutination.

⇒Thus, **hMessiah** is a HANDLE, **dwFooFoo** is a double-word, **szTring** (pronounced "string") is a null- (zero-) terminated sequence of characters, and **sTring** (pronounced "shtring") is probably Pascalian. The incomparable status of Thomas Stephen Szasz (1920–) is not affected.

hype *n.* Any document headed "For immediate release."

hyper- *prefix* [Greek *hyper,* "over and above."] A modifier, once certain to hyperventilate the most Laconian Spartan, but now diluted by mindless application. *See also* HYPERTEXT; M; VLSI.

⇒"If 'super' be 'superfluous,' then 'hyper' be 'hyperfluous'" (John Philoponus).

hypertext *n.* A game played with a possibly empty set of text files each of which (if any) contains zero or more characters and zero or more randomly embedded pointers, some or all of which may be null. Each non-null pointer (if any) points to a character (if any) in a text file (if any) or to another pointer (if any). Players are given no prior information as to the structure or cyclicity or absence thereof of the graphs established by the possibly void pointer chains. The object (if any) of the game is to traverse and ingest the entire textset from pointer to pointer without losing your f***ing mind (if any).

⇒Hypertext emerges as an unwitting vindication of both Derrida's deconstructionist (compare with null-pointer dereferencing) *hors-texte* ("there is nothing outside the text") and Barthes's post-structuralism ("writable [*scriptible*] text has no determinate meaning...but is a seamless weave of codes and fragments of codes, through which the critic may cut his [sic] own errant path. There are no beginnings and no ends, no sequences which cannot be reversed, no hierarchy of textual 'levels' to tell you what is more or less significant.")[5] *See also* BROWSE.

hyphen *n.* The ultimate curse of typography, inappropriately dropped by editorial whim or added (by your friendly syllable processor) to cope with finite column widths.

⇒"Nature abhors the vacuum, and TIME (magazine) abhors the hyphen..." (Anon). Thus we endure the ugly "multiaccess" and the ambiguous "recreation" (as in "recreate" a file: come on file, time for walkies...). The AFL/CIO call to "unionize," as noted by Renata Holland, can appear as the chemist's "un-ionize." Is your "prescience" prescientific? Did you "codecease" spousally, as required by the Pru, or did your program abort? "Codetermination" is no help here. The usage needs "codification," not to be confused, as if, with "codeification."

Spurious hyphens are also dangerous. Computer magazines with narrow column formats are especially vulnerable, often inserting hyphens in command lines, program identifiers, and e-mail addresses that can drive the innocent reader insane.

The wiser Welsh-language hyphenators formally distinguish the *cyslltnod* (connecting mark) and the *cyplysnod* (coupling mark), which helps both phonetically, as stress indicators, and etymologically. Thus, "slaughterhouse," *lladd-dy* avoids the ugly, ambiguous cluster *ddd* and reveals the origins (*lladd* "kill" and *t[d]y* "house"). Welsh hyphens also play a semantic role: *bendigedig* means "blessed, wonderful," but writing it as *ben-di-ged-ig* adds the superlative touch, "O My God, how blessed can you get?" (Robert A. Fowkes, "Teithi'r Iaith," *Ninnau* 19, no 2 [December 1993]).

Consider the appalling "cocitation," without which no book on Bibliometrics can survive. This naughty eye (*et le bon!*), despite Miltonic side-effects, sees some possibly illegal hanky-panky. But the Welsh "co-" prefix *cyd* insists on a hyphen: *cyd-ddyn* for "fellow man." *En passant*, "hanky-panky" and similar "jingle-jangle" collocations, carry hyphens in both Welsh and English. For example, "helter-skelter" is marvelously rendered as *strim-stram-strellach*. *See also* LEXICAL SCOPE.

---

5. Terry Eagleton, *Literary Theory, An Introduction* (Minneapolis: University of Minnesota Press, 1983).

I

Ibid Ben Passim (?35–?100 B.C.E.) The oft-quoted Eastern scholar.

IBM [pre-1981.] *n.* [International Business Machines Corporation.] *Also called* **Itty Bitty Machines, Snow White, The VS Pioneer, The Lawyer's Friend.** The dominant force in computer marketing, having, worldwide, supplied some 75 percent of all known hardware and 10 percent of all known software. To protect itself from the litigious envy of less successful organizations, such as the U.S. government, IBM employs 68 percent of all known ex-attorneys general.

⇒An IBM watcher writes: "I am often asked to explain IBM's leading position in data processing. My reply, in a word, *infallibility.* No cheap tricks or gimmicks. No loss-making innovations. Just honest-to-goodness, expensive *infallibility.* If IBM's rivals—formerly called the Seven Dwarfs, with Univac as Doc and Telex as Grumpy, but now more accurately referred to as the Seven Hundred Midgets—would only eschew their fruitless, vindictive crusades against the one, true, everlasting orthodoxy and attend to their own blatant fallibilities, we would see fewer fatalities in the DP marketplace." *See also* ABM; FS; THINK SIGN.

IBM [1981–1993.] A sad victim of its own successful open PC architecture. A DP Historian (limited to one sentence) writes: "The masters of the unclonable mainframe with proprietary operating systems failed to predict that Intel and Microsoft would quickly convert the noddy 6MHz, segmented-address 8088 running DietPlan under CP/M into a screaming-hot 66MHz, large linear-memory PENTIUM multi-database server running under Windows NT."

⇒"...how are the mighty fallen! Tell it not in Armonk; publish it not in the streets of Poughkeepsie; lest the daughters of the Gates rejoice..." (2 Samuel 1:20, New MS Translation).

See also OS/2; MICROSOFT.

IBM [post-1993.] No longer the old monopolistic dreadnought, but a rejuvenated, optimistic fleet of slim cruisers each able independently to dodge the minefields at the risk of occasional inter-squadron collisions. A DP Seer predicts: "Having admitted 'OEM' into its vocabulary and forged allegiances with former enemies to fight the real foe, IBM's survival seems assured. Whether the decision to offer OS/2 for Windows at $49.95 (with a $39.95 screen-saver thrown in for free), turns out to promote OS/2 sales or depress the Windows market, remains to be seen..."

ICARUS *n.* [Acronym for Infallible, Comprehensive, And Running User Software.] A software house that aimed too high and was mortally singed. *See also* VAPORWARE.

⇒The staff made redundant by the ICARUS dive have both forsaken the cruel world of computing and are now working for DEC.

ICL [International Computers Ltd.] *pronounced* "I see hell"\ *See also* ETHELRED.

icon *n.* [Origin: either Greek *eikon* "an image, *esp.* one held to be sacred," or possibly from the song "Anything you can do, Icons do better..."] **1** (Computer books) The front-cover picture of John C. Dvorak or Peter Norton. **2** (GUI) An illiterate PROMPT; a SEMIOTIC retrogression. *See also* TRASH CAN.

⇒Iconoclasts decry the outrageous, GRAND GUIGNOL attempt to replace a crisp, unambiguous, text-based command-line syntax with a quilt of grunting caveman pictograms. Overnight, they assert, we have undone the hard-gained evolution in linguistic sophistication from primitive glyphs, via Linears A, B, C, P, and L, to the majesty of phonetic syllabaries and alphabets. Further, if GUIcon designers persist in litigating to keep their little pixel-clumps private and proprietary, then the claimed semantic universality and immediacy of icons flies out the Window. Incidentally, there may be a lesson in the fact that the Mayan glyphs, which were originally open, widely understood but non-phonetic symbols, proved more difficult to decipher than the secret, priestly Egyptian hieroglyphs that had acquired a phonetic structure. The emerging generation of computer users is more likely to be familiar with disk files than with manila folders and filing cabinets, so an icon-metaphor that explains the former in terms of the latter proves to be a quaint anachronism. Why not have antimacassar icons to signify the presence of a diskette write-protection tab?

Ideal Business Machine *n.* A sublime, cost-no-object VTMI (Very Total Management Information) system being developed for the 1999 Meanman-Narkus personal computer catalog.

⇒The architecture is the joint responsibility of von Neumann and Turing assisted by Wilkes, Eckert, Mauchly, Hartree, Cray, Amdahl, Babbage, Williams, Leibnitz, and Pascal, based on Carver Mead components supplied by English Eclectic. Analog options are by Mike Godfrey. The systems and applications software team includes Gill, Knuth, Strachey, Hopper, Stroustrup, Ritchie, Thompson, Kernighan, Wirth, McCarthy, Dijkstra, Newell, Simon, Minsky, Wheeler, Arbib, Popplestone, Winograd, van Wijngaarden, Backus, Naur, Kleene, Łukasiewicz, Iverson, Landin, Hoare, Floyd, Chomsky, Scott, Park, Peterson, Michaelson, Michie, Steele, Tarski, me, and Shannon.

Project Director is Lord Flowers, helped by Oppenheimer, Hartley, Teffler, Goldstine, and Wotan. Russell, Whitehead, Wittgenstein, and Dylan Thomas are handling the documentation (a much-needed blend of wit, fantasy, and precision).

Bill Gates, T. J. Watson, Sr., Billy Graham, and Steve Jobs are running the marketing division, while N. Bonaparte heads up field service. Site preparation is in the experienced hands of G. Khan, P. Kahn, Capability Brown, and A. Le Nôtre.

Fully comprehensive, bundled, and infallible packages have been ordained in a newly resurrected ALGOL++ by our shit-hot package kings, Buddha, Shiva,

Mahomet, and Christ (proprietary rights fully protected). The other two major high-level languages, EV-LISP and EVQ-LISP are also supported.

Initial master file data will be keyed in by K. Marx and verified by F. Engels. A real Meanman-Narkus coup has been the signing of A. Einstein and H. Poincaré to oversee the file-maintenance group (any three of the nine muses, according to availability). The day-to-day data-entry team has been recruited from the Dallas Cowboy Cheerleaders, trained by Minerva, and supervised by Pope John Paul II and the Ayatollah Ruhollah Khomeini.

An all-Greek squad of factory-trained operators will be provided, comprising of (sic) Plato, Socrates, Aristotle, *more,* under the watchful eye of GUI whiz-kid Zeus. On-line prognostics are guaranteed by the Delphic Service Center.

The total up-and-running ballpark end-user price has not yet been announced, but is likely to be high. But when was the *best* ever cheap? Also, some slippage timewise has been mooted. But when were such experts ever able to agree? The lengthy stand-off between Zeus and Shiva over character sets has been particularly annoying to the lets-ship-next-quarter crowd. But when was the *best* not worth waiting for, indefinitely if need be?

identifier *n.* A string devised to obscure the program's semantics. "Today we have the 'Naming of the VARs'" (Army Programming Lecture).

⇒J. B. Priestly once observed that from the moment "Enter Ophelia" is written, the playwright is in the hands of a blonde who is sleeping with the producer. Likewise, a programmer declaring `Net_Income` as `double` immediately saddles a chunk of memory with extraneous semantic baggage well beyond its machine-specific floating-point representation. Subsequent code, for all we know, might dictate that

```
Net_Income = Gross_Income + Deductions;
```

leading some to view "identifiable identifiers" as a mixed blessing. Parnassian fields, named (by me) for D. L. Parnas ("On the Criteria to Be Used in Decomposing Systems into Modules," *Communications of the ACM* 5, no. 12 [December 1972]) are deliberately non-mnemonic. Parnas would prefer the arbitrary A1, X3, etc., as forced on us by early BASICs. Maintainabilty, he claims, which depends on understanding what the code actually does, should never rely on the "natural language" interpretation of `Net_Income` as someone's net income.

An onomaticonian writes: "Close to the theme of maintaining legacies are the interesting shifts in identifier-naming fashions. Over the code-forsaken years, I've been compiling lists of bizarre variable and function names encountered in programs, both mine and others'. In the Modula-2 FileSystem module, for example, there's a SET OF Flag data type called FlagSet, and I could never resist declaring

```
VAR Kirsten: FlagSet;
```

Even when upper-case and *maxLenVarString* restrictions eased for many language/OS combinations (the jump from 2 to 6 was particularly memorable with wild dancing in the streets of Dartmouth), the old miserly habits often persisted, leading to some risible overloading. The table on pp. 94–95 lists some of the polysemous substrings that can perplex the maintainer.

Table of Substrings

Substring	Meanings and Examples
alt	alternative (AltVar); altitude (VarAlt); alteration
blt	built; blit; bacon-lettuce-tomato
cap	capital-capitalization (CapDef); ceiling (CapCap); upper-case (LowToCap)
cat	catalog; category; (con)catenate (Unix); feline
check	test; mark[6]
const	constant; constructor
corr	correction (CorrCorr); correlation (CorrCorr)
cur	current (GetCurCur); cursor (GetCurCur); canine
db	database; decibel
dec	decrement; decimal; Digital Equipment Corp.
def	define (defunc); defunct; deficit; default (DefFunc); definite (DefInt[egral])
diag	diagnosis; diagonal
firm	agreed/settled (FirmQuote); company (FirmName)
han	handle; handler[7]
ind	index (IndTab); indent (IndTab)
int	integer (IntRef); integrity (RefInt); integral-calculus (DefInt); interval (DefIntInt)
inv	invoice (InvTot); invalid (InvTot); invert (InvMat); inverse (InvLog)
lf	linefeed; logical font (Windows)
ln	natural log; link; line
log	log-file (ErrorLog); log (LogOn); logarithm (logX); logical (LogError); "loss of generality"[8]
man	manual-method (ManIP); manual-book (ProgMan); manager (progman); male
mat	matrix (TransMat); material (TransMat)
mess	message (ClearMess); mess/garbage (ClearMess)
min	minute (time); minimum
ord	order/billing; order/ordinal
org	origin/cartesian; original[9]; orgasm (GetBrushOrg); organisation; organism

6. As in `CheckMenuItem()`, a toggle that also "unchecks."
7. A sequence that puzzles at first glance is the Borland OWL function, `eventhan()`, which one reads as "even than" but which turns out to be an event handler.
8. As in "wlog, we can assume that...," meaning "without loss of generality...." Often, though, the following assumption demands a huge gain in particularity, leading cynics to take the "w" as "with." Compare "wa" = with average.
9. Thus `OrgOrg` means the original coordinate origin. To add to the confusion, `org` sometimes means "previous."

post	temporal (PostProcess); transactional (PostMessage); mail (PostIt).
ps	pointer-to-string; postscript; process-status (Unix)
ref	reference (IntRef); referential (RefInt)
rep	repeat; representative; repository
res	resource; result; resolution; reserve; restore
sec	second (time); secant
set	collection (FlagSet); assignment (SetFlag)
str	string; strict; struct; street; strip
sub	subtract; subscription; subsidiary; subscript-font
sz	size (StringSz); zero-terminated string (HUNGARIAN NOTATION: szString)
tab	table (IndTab); tabulate/indent (IndTab)
tm	textmetric (Windows); trademark; transcendental meditation
trans	transpose; transport
val	value; valid (ValValChk);
var	variable; variance; value-added reseller
win	window (FailWin); victory (WinWin) cf. Nelson's WinMain().

if *conj.* **1** (Poetic) Kiplingian milestones on the road to mandelayhood and gambler's ruin. **2** (CS) One of many conditional control-flow obstacles faced by a process linearly anxious to complete the next instruction without tiresome, trivial, testing diversions.

⇒Some programmers see if as the soul of machine intelligence. Thus,

```
if (CurBankBal <= 0) errmsg("Spendthrift scoundrel!");
    else exit(0);
```

forms the core of many a smart, ethical money manager. The home-exit loving, non-judgmental process, however, reluctantly forced to test transient bits of registers, is tempted to rule in favor of else. Baudelaire predicts these nuances in *Les Hiboux*: "Sous les ifs noirs qui les abritent...." In some computer languages, a nested if is terminated with endif or the more attractive, Shakespearean mirror-image, fi. The ifs in procedural computer languages are followed by BOOLEan expressions that reduce at runtime to TRUE or FALSE. Logical implication is replaced by material implication: TRUE implies that the then clause (possibly empty) is obeyed, while FALSE triggers the else clause (also possibly empty). Note that we lose the asymmetry of logical implication (true implies true, but false implies anything), and you are free to interchange FALSE and TRUE: they are essentially arbitrary attributes with no semantic significance. You are equally free to switch your then and else clauses.

C is rather different. The interesting quirk with C, in the absence of a dedicated Boolean type, is that zero is Boolean FALSE, while nonzero is TRUE. An expression such as (1 != 1), which most would regard as patently false, does indeed evaluate to zero; (2 == 2) evaluates to the integer 1, which is abundantly nonzero and eminently true.

The interesting point is that FALSE is single-valued (I exclude the metaphysics of null pointers, huge, near, and far) while TRUE is legion. There may be a Zarathustrian strand here: the diabolical equivalence of all dark lies contrasting with a billion points of light? However, when you want a function to return TRUE for success and FALSE for failure, a perfectly natural, dare I say, intuitive ploy, you hit a snag. Success is a one-of-a-kind blessing, failure comes in whole battalions. To have the function return an instructive error code, it is necessary to rephrase the question pessimistically: Did the function fail? Yes, TRUE! Why did it fail? Test the nonzero return value:

```
if ( e = f() ) {    // did f() fail?
            switch (e) {       // why?
            case 1: // one reason for failure
               . . .
            case 2:// and another
               . . .
            case n:// no end?
               . . .
            break;
      }
   }
   // success
```

Some see life itself as a *huge* case statement. *See also* EVENT-DRIVEN.

iff 1 [*abbrev.* "if and only if."] "*A* iff *B*" means not only that "*A* if *B*" (*B* implies *A*, so *B* is a sufficient condition for *A*) but also that "*A* only if *B*" (*A* implies *B*, so *B* is necessary condition for *A*). The prevalent confusion between the statements "*A* if *B*, "*B* if *A*," and "*A* iff *B*," is, echoing Maxwell Smart's Control/Chaos crises, the major threat to civilization as we know it. Thus, if *A* = "it is sweet" and *B* = "it is sugar," then "*A* if *B*." So, sugarity is a sufficient condition for sweetness. However, sugarity is not a necessary condition for sweetness, since there are many non-sugar substances that are (nutra)-sweet. From *B* we can impute *A*, but from *A* we cannot indict *B*. In everyday domestic discourse, the threat "I'll kill you if you say that again," should be countered by a calm request to clarify the spelling of "if."

⇒A non-tenured logician writes "My salary is necessary but not sufficient." David Gries[10] tells the following story:

"The notation *iff* is used for 'if and only if.' A few years ago, while lecturing in Denmark, I used *fif* instead, reasoning that since 'if and only if' was a symmetric concept its notation should be symmetric also. Without knowing it, I had punned in Danish and the audience laughed, for *fif* in Danish means 'a little trick.' I resolved thereafter to use *fif* so I could tell my little joke, but my colleagues talked me out of it."

10. David Gries, *The Science of Programming* (Berlin: Springer-Verlag, 1981).

2 [*abbrev.* Identification Friend or Foe.] A key aim of the UK radar systems deployed during World War II.

⇒It is worth noting that in addition to the hush-hush Turing-Newman Enigma code-breaking exploits at Bletchley Park, the computer age owes much to the digital-processing radar techniques developed in the 1940s. [Maurice Wilkes, *Memoirs of a Computer Pioneer* (Cambridge, Mass.: The MIT Press, 1985.)

IMP *n.* [Acronym for Integrated Morticians Package © ICARUS.] A comprehensive, heart-warming package which has literally buried the competition after prolonged, in-depth trials at the Lombard Happy-Landing Chapel of Sweet Repose, Gardena, California.

⇒The IMP package is a real eye-opener, and a lesson to less lively vertical markets in the proper exploitation of such modern DP techniques as postmortem dumps, drag'n'-drop, and decompilation. We quote from the ICARUS brochure *Stretching Your Bereavement Processing Dollar* (1994 edition):

"The cult-independent IMP package is written in racy, portable, uncontroversial MIDTRAN: ('For He shall choose between the QUIKTRAN and the DEAD-TRAN.' [St. Presper, *Epistolary Update to the Algolites,* level IX, release viii])."

IMP's truly revelationary documentation will take you painlessly, step by joyous step, through the once-irksome keening cycle.

Say *goodbye* to digging holes and punching cards!

Shout *farewell* to unsightly chadim on your vestments!

Scream *adieu* to clay on your boots!

Yell *no-more* to unjustified memorial epigraphy!

IMP offers the LOT! IMP prepares the LOT! IMP consecrates the LOT! Check out the advantages!

Only IMP gives you:

Full pre- and post-need casket accounting

On-line floral tributation

Next-of-kin mailing shots

Obituarial word processing

Probate litigation (normal or noncontingency)

Retrospective Living Trusts

Will-call validation

Realtime corpse count

Interment logistics and plot plotting

Armband inventory control

Reusable coffins via nondestructive crematorial temperature gradients

Automatic tombstone engraving (choice of 15 Gothic fonts)

Jazz bands (New Orleans branch only—"When the Saints": $50 surcharge)

Internet séances (subject to domain accessibility)

Firecrackers (optional)

Hertz Rent-a-Hearse network

Pre-need enrollment and training

Cosmetics (departed *and* departee)

Cryogenics or mummification to persistencize your dear ones

Cross-religion hymn selection menus

Cross-deity placations

Creative condolences (with optional personalization)

Computer-aided design (mausolea, caskets, cuisine, etc.)

FREE repeat business voucher (valid for 3 days)

All listings/invites/invoices in tasteful HAMLET-black

PLUS PLUS PLUS...the real killer:

The Merry Survivor option!!!

A discreet, no-questions-asked COMPU-DATE™ service offering confidential, computer-matched social introductions for the semi-inconsolable!

IMP carefully vets all post-funereal dates!

NO boring fortune hunters!

NO overrated gigolos!

NO dumb gold diggers (unless box 47 checked)

NO racial, religious, or sexual prejudice (unless box 89 checked)

The Merry Survivor option keeps YOU, the mortician, in an ongoing, profitable situation with otherwise transitory clients.

impersonal computing *n.* Routine, run-of-the-mill commercial data processing, in which the scrawled schedules Scotch-taped to the console have not been changed for three years. *Compare* PERSONAL COMPUTING.

implementation *n.* The fruitless struggle by the talented and underpaid to fulfill promises made by the rich and ignorant.

implementation-dependent *adj.* (Of a STANDARD requirement) non-standard; worse than unpredictable; much loved by implementors.

⇒Cobbler, heal thyself! There seems to be no standard set of terms in the standards lexicon. The ANSI C standard uses *implementation-defined* for non-portable features or actions left to the "whim of whomever." However, *conforming* implementations *shall* publicly document such quirks. Standards use *shall*, by the way, with Levitical regularity. Note that a *strictly conforming* implementation *shall* eschew *implementation-defined* features. Or ELSE!

INCA [It's Not Called APL] An APL derivative from Manugistics introducing such avant-garde horrors as objects, hierarchical name spaces, right-to-left parsing, C-type primitives, and, the ultimate heresy, structured flow-control mechanisms. *See also* RECURSIVE ACRONYM; GNU.

inch worm *n.* One engaged in spurious quantification on a small scale.

⇒ Inch worm, inch worm, measuring your marigolds,
You and your arithmetic will probably go far;
Inch worm, inch worm, measuring your marigolds,
Seems to me you should stop and see
How beautiful they are.[11]

Compare FOOT WORM; NUMEROLATRY.

incompleteness theorem *n.* **1** *Formal systems theory* A theorem establishing the incompleteness of a certain set of axioms, as: "The second-order predicate calculus is incomplete (K. Gödel [1931]). **2** *Informal systems theory* The empirically unimpeachable fact that at least one vital element in the system will not be delivered, as: "Where's the ****ing power lead?" (M. Thumps [1976]).

indirection *n.* The leap of faith from address to contents, from POINTER to POINTEE. *See also* DEREFERENCE; HANDLE.

inferencing *adj.* (Of an engine) inferring with a 22.22 percent overhead. *See also* IF; MARGIE. *Compare* METHODOLOGY.

⇒Yet another example of M'AS-TU-VU syllable-bloat. From the verbal forms "infer, inferred, inferring" comes the noun "inference" (the act of inferring), whence a sequence of IF-THEN statements dressed-to-sell as an "inferencing engine." Such devices have done little to resolve the bitter-long arguments as to whether "infer" means "hint, suggest, surmise" or "derive by sound reasoning." To update an old aphorism: "Inferencings are made, implicationings are discovered."

infinity *n.* More than enough, as in 640 KB (1980) or 4 GB (1990).

⇒ "Is not thy wickedness great? and thine iniquities infinite?" (Job 22:5 KJV).

inheritance *n.* **1** Two of the seven pillars of OBJECT ORIENTEERING. The other five are ENCAPSULATION, POLYMORPHISM, and BRADY GOOCH. **2** (For OOPstarters) a mechanism for deriving sports cars from baser modes of transportation.

---

11. "The Inch Worm" from *Hans Christian Andersen* by Frank Loesser. © 1951, 1952 Frank Music Corp. © Renewed 1979, 1980 Frank Music Corp. International Copyright secured. All Rights Reserved. Used by permission.

⇒There are now more OOP books than objects, and most of them confuse taxonomic ("is a") and meronymic ("part of") inheritances. Does the derived class "specialize" by adding and overriding base members, or does it "refine" the base by removing impurities? St Paul's answer: "...neither doth corruption inherit incorruption" (1 Corinthians 15:50 KJV).

Neo-Freudian standup comic: "Why is the class hierarchy a barren concept? Because the private members are not inherited!"

in-house *adj.* [Origin: "Is there a doctor in-house?"—traditional appeal to a theater audience.] Relating to any job that the user's staff can screw up without outside help. *Compare* OUTSOURCED.

insinnuendo *n.* [Origin: Malapudlianism (Scouse dialect, Liverpool, for malapropistic portmanteau) from *insinuate* + *innuendo.*] The oblique implication that a certain feature or device is available as a result of its being named in a specification, proposal, or quotation.

install *v.* [Etym. obscure: possibly from prefix *in* and *stall,* either "evasive, deceitful delay," or "a cattle-shed reeking of stale, piss-ridden straw."] The first command required of the neophyte USER and, by SOD'S LAW, the one most likely to freeze the system. *See also* UNINSTALL.

⇒The more creative install programs not only crash after the sixteenth floppy has been inserted, but also re-write essential ini files in order to inhibit rebootage.

Polite versions have been known to advise the user to "Grab a coffee or two," or even "This is a good time to watch a movie or two; Fritz Lang's *Nibelungen* trilogy is highly recommended."

instance *n. See* INSTANTIATION.

instantiation *n.* **1** *Object-orienteering* The birth of a CLASS instance, that is, an OBJECT saddled with the diverse data members ordained for that class, and the methods trained to corrupt them. **2** *Beverages* The reduction of various plants to their time-saving, inorganic substitutes.

⇒In the vast OOP tutorial literature, instantiations invariably betray egotistical declarations. Thus, the profusion of subjective objects:

```
MyWindow     TWindow;
MyWay        TWay;
MonDieu      TDieu;
MeinKampf    TKampf;
```

Alas, before the parent classes and FRIENDS can light their cigars, destructive caducity strikes: out of scope, out of luck.

integral *adj.* (Of a solution) accurate to the nearest whole number, as: "The PENTIUM has an integral FPU."

intellectual property *n. Law* An expensive, on-going, possibly oxymoronic, attempt to solve the mind-matter problem. "Who would have thought that 'NBC' and 'intellectual property' would ever occur in the same sentence?" (D. Letterman disputing the ownership of the phrase "The Tonight Show").

⇒Distinguishing between creative cerebral activity and its recordable, copyable, and protectable manifestations remains an intractable legal and technological challenge. Be warned, though, that I have archived my brain-wave graphs, both sleep and wake, and preserved all my shopping lists since birth. Any infringement in whole or part, conscious or otherwise, on these declared embodiments constitutes a grave *Casus Melvin Belli. See also* PATENT.

IntelliSense™ "It's built-in technology that senses what you want to do and produces the desired result." (MICROSOFT advert). (Submitted by a puzzled Mitchell McConnell.)

⇒Those who believe in Chairman Bill's total prescience (hyphen optional) are puzzled by the need for explicit *sensing*. Our unfolding requirements are surely *preknown* and can be satisfied autoexecutably each time we power up. IntelliSense also has important consequences in the discontinuant and cessational environments. Prior knowledge of your impending Ctrl+C or Break provides the application with diverse salvific strategies. *See* GATES, WILLIAM.

interface *n. & v. trans.* [Origin: Possible contraction of "In your face."] Mandatory usage: **seamless interface. 1** *n.* An arbitrary line of demarcation set up in order to apportion the blame for malfunctions. **2** *v. trans.* To redesign (two working subsystems) so that they can go wrong symbiotically. *See also* GUI.

Internet *n.* The anarchic mother of all networked networks, dedicated to the memory and upholding the aims of the Catalan and Basque insurgents in the Spanish Civil War (1936–1939).

⇒"Mother" is to be taken here in the Black-American elliptical sense. Apart from a few O'Reilly & Associates authors, nobody really understands or needs to know how Internet works (stretching the word "works" beyond its usual semantic web). Individual users are content to acquire access via a chain of generous nodal gateways, each of which may or may not form part of the user's Internet "address." The Catch-22 is that inter-communication is rarely possible until either party has successfully reached the other. A typical Internet message, therefore, consists of a two-page header listing each store-and-forward gateway routing (with many disconcerting "Apparently-to" strings), followed by a plaintive one-liner: "Let me know if you don't receive this."

Reaching out to touch someone electronically is further complicated by the coexistence of Internet and UUCPNET (uunet) addressing protocols. The former has the pattern name@site.domain while the latter uses the so-called BANG notation:

uunet!site.domain!name. The site and domain fields may be extended to reflect the chain of intermediate gateways. Suffice it to note that your importance in the e-mail food-chain is, in general, inversely proportional to the total length of your accessible address. Thus, as the UNIX Review Avocado Diaboli, I am beast!stan, Bjarne Stroustrup is bs@research, the Trinity is god!god!god and Mahomet is m@islam.mil. *More at* TNHD under "Internet address."

interoperability *n.* An octosyllabic drain on Press Release productivity.

interpreter *n.* **1** (Human) "One who enables two persons of different languages to understand each other by repeating to each what it would have been to the interpreter's advantage for the other to have said" (Ambrose Bierce). **2** (Computer) One that is quick to chide but slow to run. *See also* COMPILER.

introspect *n.* A VIRTUAL prospect added to forecasts in order to placate sales management and remove the finiteness restriction from the TRAVELING SALES-PERSON PROBLEM.

intuitivity *n.* (Preferred DP form for *intuition* and *intuitiveness*) Innate user knowledge prior to reading the manuals. *See also* RTFM.

⇒Thus, in TAPCIS, Shift-F7 and "!" both give "print with form-feed" while "*" gives "print with no form-feed."

IO *n.* [Origin obscure: from Greek *io!* "a shout of joy following the successful mounting of a cow," or, possibly, abbreviation for Input/Output.] The Alpha and Omega of computing, and the only two aspects thereof that the layperson understands and desires. Unfortunately, the DP professional intervenes with Beta through Psi. If Omega should be reached, the cry "IO" is raised, initiating a prolonged bacchanal.

IOU *n.* *pronounced* I owe you\\ [Input/Output Unit.] A promissory instrument that is rarely honored. *See also* IO.

Irish search *n. See* BEST-LAST SEARCH; ETHNOLOGY.

IRQ *pronounced* irk.\\ Interrupt Request—ill-timed and invariably disdained.

irregular verbs In addition to the irregular conjugations found in Standard English (e.g., *I am, you are, he is*), DP English has generated local deviant conjugations of interest to the sociolinguist.

Table of Irregular Verbs

I construct algorithms
You program
He/she uses Visual BASIC

I consult
You freelance
He/she moonlights

I chart
You code
He/she runs

I was with IBM
You were with UNIVAC
He/she was with NCR
They were with Ashton-Tate

I refine
You debug
He/she patches
They kludge

I assemble
You compile
He/she/it interprets

I market
You sell
He/she peddles

I manufacture
You sell
He/she suffers

I heurist
You try and err
He/she flounders

I interact
You timeshare
He/she hogs

I extrapolate
You conjecture
He/she guesses

I was Turing
You were Turing
He/she Tured

I verify
You punch
He/she joggles

I curtate
You truncate
He/she shortens

IRS *n.* [Internal Revision Service.]

⇒Each year the IRS meets with AUGRATIN (Amalgamated Union of General Rewriters, Amenders, Tinkerers, and INterpolators) to determine which changes in the withholding algorithms will cause the maximum dislocation to existing PAYROLL packages. Experience has shown that it is the small, apparently insignificant variations in the taxiomatic schema that create more havoc and consultancy fees than any major recasting of the income-truncation METHODOLOGY. Mooted changes are tested on the joint IRS/AUGRATIN Cray Mk.II, which holds models of over 7000 payroll implementations, and refined to maximize conversion cost.

ISAM file *n.* [Acronym for Intrinsically Slow Access Method *or* (rare) Indexed Sequential Access Method.] One of the most successful data-security systems so far devised. Information is protected from all but the most persistent, patient, and devious.

ISDN *See* SARCONYM.

ISO *n.* [Origin: possibly Greek *iso* "equal" but now presumed acronym for International Standards Organization.] A meta-standards organization set up in 1947 in order to establish standards for the setting up of standard organizations. *See also* ANSI; ASCII; STANDARD.

⇒Having failed in this exordial assignment, and in order to regain some credibility among the growing number of national standards bodies (for each emerging nation, it seems, considers itself not fully emerged until it has an airline, ethnic strife, and a standards association), ISO directed its taxonomic skills to the creation of a standard for toilet seats, to which end a widely spaced sample of assholes was recruited and exposed to the mensurational rigors of statistical humiliation. This ongoing (in both senses of the word) project is likely to be vitiated by the arrival on earth of extraterrestrial globs with nonstandard excretive methodologies.

J

J *n.* Ken Iverson's more elegant, more powerful, more ASCII, less scrutable son-of-APL.

⇒Some see the language J (unrelated to *The Book of J)* as Mao-tse-Ken's Cultural Revolution, but one played out on an uninhabited, off-shore Taiwanese island. *See* Murray Eisenberg and Howard A. Peelie, "Confessions of Two APL Educators Learning J," *APL'93 Conference Proceedings, APL Quote Quad.* 24, no. 1 (August 1993). *See also* APL; MISFILED BOOKS.

JANUS *n.* [Acronym for JANuary Updating Service.] *See* DECADE COUNTER.

JARGON file *n.* An on-line hackers' glossary-thesaurus originated and maintained at SAIL (Stanford AI Laboratory) and MIT (Massachusetts Institute of Technology) by Mark Crispin, Raphael Finkel, Guy L. Steele Jr., and Donald Woods, with assistance from the MIT and Stanford AI communities and Worcester Polytechnic Institute. This definitive repository of programming wit and folklore was published on real paper to great acclaim in 1983 as THD (*The Hacker's Dictionary* [The MIT Press]). Reflecting changes in the ever-volatile DP culture and lexicon, TNHD (*The New Hacker's Dictionary),* also from MIT Press, appeared in 1990, compiled by Eric S. Raymond, with a foreword and zany, Crunchly, ad-hackery cartoons by Guy L. Steele Jr. A second edition, TNHD-2, quickly followed (1993) with over 250 new entries. Matching the fame of K&R, TNHD is also known as R&S.

⇒Entries from the original Jargon file are reproduced with the permission of the above-mentioned compilers. Legends such as *See also* TNHD mandate inspection of the indicated urtext.

JCL *n.* [Job Control Language.] A deliberately abstruse software barrier between the USER and the OPERATING SYSTEM, set up to prevent ordinary programmers from running their own programs.

⇒As the name partly implies, JCL was devised to create jobs for otherwise displaced intellectuals, and to thwart the gloomy predictions of computer-induced unemployment made in the 1950s.

job trickle *n., also (archaic)* **job stream**. The system's attempt to match the rate of execution to the programmer's coding rate.

Jobs' Comforters [from Steve Jobs, cofounder of Apple Corporation and founder/loser of NeXT Inc.] **1** Canon Corporation. **2** Sun Microsystems Inc. *See also* NEXT.

⇒Currently, NeXT Inc. has cleverly eschewed loss-certain hardware in favor of loss-possible software.

John Birch machine *n.* [From M. A. Arbib, 1969.] A finite-state machine in which the tape moves to the right after each computation.

Jolt Award *n.* [From Jolt™, an explosively caffeinated "soft" drink much favored by all-night programmers.] The software-developers' Oscar, launched in 1991 by Larry O'Brien (editor, Miller-Freeman's Computer Language Magazine, now called Software Development).

⇒As on Hollywood's academe, the Jolt categories are yearly becoming increasingly bizarre, combining particularity and universality to ensure that everyone wins. Thus, to mirror "Best French Movie Not Starring Any Depardieux," we have "Least Offensive GUI Builder Running In Under 8 MB."

K

K *prefix* [Kilo-.] **1** *Science* 10^3-fold, as: "40K brothers/Could not, with all their quantity of love,/Make up my sum" (*Hamlet*). **2** *Finance* 2^{10}-fold, providing a hidden 2.4 percent hedge against impoverishment. *Compare* M.

⇒Computer sales proposals operate in both environments and tend to fluctuate between the two K modes without proper warning. When in doubt, you should assume the worst case, e.g., "Each additional 8K of memory will cost $1K," means you get 8000 *bits* for $1024, whereas "We offer to buy back each surplus 8K memory board for $1K" should be taken as an offer of $1000 for 8192 *longwords*.

K&R *n.* *Also* **K&&R.** A reverential reference to Brian W. Kernighan and Dennis M. Ritchie, *The C Programming Language* (Prentice-Hall, 1978). *See also* C; R&S; HELLO, WORLD.

⇒In the ASCII encodement, 'K' = 1001011 and 'R' = 1010010, so some literally bitwise idiots take K & R to be 1000010, which, alas, is the ASCII value for 'B'. The more logical approach is K && R which evaluates to TRUE.

KBMT *n.* (Knowledge-based Machine Translation) The long-overdue attempt to improve MT by supplying some appropriate facts about the source and target languages. *See also* NLP.

⇒In spite of copious multilingual databases, the SYSTRAN KBMT service offered by the EEC (European Economic Community) continues to confuse and divide its members: "Les agriculteurs vis à vis de la politique agricole commune..." reached the English bureaucrats as "farmers live to screw the common agricultural policy..." A clear case of *In MT veritas*. "Nous avions" came out as "we airplanes."

kernel *n.* [Etym. OE *cyrnel*, a little corn.] *Preferred DP spelling* **kernal**, as in Kernal Data Systems, Pleasanton, Calif. The OS seedling lurking inside the SHELL.

⇒Old-soldiering UNIX farts are fond of the World War I song: "If you want to hack the kernel, I know where it is, I know where it is..."

keyword *n.* *Also called* **reserved word.** An identifier with prescribed syntax and semantics, so don't argue.

⇒Whether NL has any keywords is an open question.

kibitzer *n.* [Yiddish *kibits'r* "onlooker, meddler."] The maddening stranger who leans over your shoulder and whispers "Your Queen is *en prise*" or "You missed a 'p' in 'append.'"

⇒With the GUI invasion, a new breed of kibitzer has appeared who dares to fondle your mouse while you are typing.

king of the one-line patchers. Byname for Henny Thumpman (1906–), stand-up programmer and court jester for Jewish Business Machines, and enumerator of such overexposed catch strings as: "I *love* this environment"; "Take my system!"; "*That* you call a callback?" "The 586, but for *you,* 585.99927"; "Compatible, schcompatible, so you wanna hold up progress?"; "My wife's so dumb, she wants that syntax should increase by 10 percent!"

kludge *n. & v. trans., also called* **kluge** [Possibly from Yiddish *klug* "smart," or Polish *kluczka,* a trick or hook.] \preferred pronunciation klooj.\ **1** *n.* The programmers' vaseline. **2** *n.* A retrograde step in a STEPWISE REFINEMENT. **3** *n.* [From JARGON FILE.] Something that works for the wrong reasons. **4** *v. trans.* To fix (a problem) quickly and dirtily by applying a kludge. *See also* BUG; ONE-LINE PATCH; PTF. *More at* TNHD.

⇒There is no dispute concerning the meaning and usefulness of kludge/kluge in the electronics and computer trades, although many lay dictionaries sadly mislead. However, even within the DP laxicon, its spelling, pronunciation, etymology and citationography are still delightfully controversial.[12] A Yiddish, rather than Teutonic, *klug* is the preferred origin in order to explain the obvious irony: "That you call smart?"

The sound of the final "g," of course, can readily fricate your velum at diverse points beyond IPA encoding, from a simple "k" (Gielgud's "Leave not a rack behind") via a romantic, Hispanic "j" (as in *mujer*), to the depths of a fatal, Xhosa, heavy-smoker's phlegm-throwing *graillon* (as in the Scouse *f**k off*). Generally speaking, though, the word is rhymed with "refuge" rather than with "fudge." In spite of this, the preferred spelling must remain "kludge." As Terry Lambert explains:[13] "...this allows easy distinction between people who know what they are talking about and people pretending to know what they are talking about." *Compare* SQL.

---

12. John A. Barry, *Technobabble* (Cambridge, Mass.: The MIT Press, 1991), pp 145–149, provides an excellent summary.

13. Devil's Advocate, *UNIX Review,* March 1991. Further kludging can be found in ibid November 1990 and January 1991; Doug Parr of Cubix Corporation, Carson City, Nevada, has sent me the earliest written kluge citation so far: a story published in 1961 in the *Life Treasury of American Folklore* (New York: Time Inc.). It tells of Murgatroyd, a newly-enlisted sailor who gives his civilian occupation as "kluge maker." None of Murgatroyd's superiors is willing to appear ignorant by asking what a kluge is. Our hero enjoys a quiet service life until eventually a captain insists that a kluge be made for the admiral's inspection. Murgatroyd employs delaying tactics by ordering a long list of tools and material. Finally the kluge, the "damnedst-looking thing you ever saw—wires and springs sticking out in every direction," is presented to the admiral. The admiral, too, cannot appear ignorant, so he says "It looks like a perfect kluge . . . let's see it work." A nervous, on-the-spot Murgatroyd drops the object overboard as the admiral, captain and crew watch in suspense. As it sinks into the ocean, it goes "kkluuge."

Well, now, how far does this citation help us pin down the origin of the computer kluge/kludge? In the Murgatroyd story, almost any onomatopoetic term would work. Indeed, the Life editors report similar tales: Davy Crockett's blacksmith who made a "skow" and Abraham Lincoln's story of the "fizzle." Joseph M. Perret of La Crescenta, Calif., has been exploring the

knerd *n.* A NERD with a Stanford degree.

knowledge-based *adj. Rare* (Of a program) gnostically generated as opposed to the bulk of software that is based entirely on hearsay, anecdote, and superstition. *See also* KBMT; ZERO-KNOWLEDGE.

Knuth, Don Rockne (1928–) Legendary sports coach turned computer scientist.

⇒From a recent interview in *Sports WEB Annotated*:

SWA: Are you pleased with progress so far?

DRK: Well Stan, we have some real coding talent on the team; if we can stay healthy, I think we'll do what we have to do…we're still just taking it one line at a time…

KSAM file *n.* [Acronym for Key Sequential Access Method.] A place where only *key* items get lost. *Compare* ISAM.

Kuhn Blue Book [Named for Thomas Samuel Kuhn (1922–), American philosopher and historian of science.] The definitive guide for those buying, selling and trading PARADIGMS.

⇒However, don't expect much of a trade-in on your old paradigm: "I hope you won't take offense, Sir, but, really…O dear me…we haven't seen one of *those* in years…Have you tried the Smithsonian?"

kummerbund, Irish *n.* The two-inch band of Jockey shorts that shows above your trouser belt. *See also* ETHNOLOGY.

---

oral traditions, and sends me a fascinating letter from his uncle, Joseph A. Perret who worked on the Univac I in the early 50s. Joseph A. writes: "Kluge as it was spelled then, was a familiar term to me; and I can date it back to the mid 50s…the term in those days, however, was not used in the context of software, but was always used in connection with hardware." He then gives some examples. A typical "kluge" was a single-purpose box designed "to interface two incompatible computer systems." In particular, when First National Bank of Boston needed to exchange data between a Honeywell 3" wide metal tape (sic!) and a 1/2" IBM mylar tape, "Ben Taunton, their computer specialist told me that they were thinking of 'kluging it'…."

The search continues. Note that words do not demand an apodictic etymology. They can arise through playfulness, both drunk and sober. Recall Shakespeare's deflation of the scholar seeking the origin of "Hey nonny": Bill the Quill effectively says, "'Tis a device to call fools into the Ring."

L

label *n. & v. trans.* **1** *n. Programming* An arbitrary but often mnemonic string assigned to a line in a program to which subsequent GOTO or preceding COME FROM instructions can be referenced. Labels are mainly used to distinguish the various ENDLESS LOOPS in a program. **2** *n. Magnetic media* A physical identification up front, showing author, date, content, author's bio and previous convictions, number of undetected errors, proprietary caveats, waivers re consequential damage, and the address of the nearest attorney. Cautious users have the foregoing both dymo'd *and* digitally encoded on the leader of the medium. **3** *v. trans.* To invoke the message "duplicate label" until a unique label has been assigned (to a program line or statement).

⇒Current lawyer-aware marketing brings forth the idiot-proof, catch-all warning label. Thus, a formerly harmless keyboard must carry the caveats: "Do not type nonstop with extended wrists for more than 48 hours (see diagram 3, p. 48). Further, on no account must you prise off the Escape keytop and insert it in your ear, nose, mouth or rectum, or the ear, nose, mouth or rectum of your friends, enemies or pets without their express written consent (see diagram 8, p. 69)..." Warnings about the contents of food and drinks have reached a Zen nadir: the Hakutsuru Saké bottle declares "Contains sulfites not detected," the software equivalent of "QA has not yet found the bugs, but we're sure they're lurking about somewhere."

labor-hour *n. See* PERSON-HOUR.

lambda calculus *n.* **1** Lamed calculus for the goyim. **2** The one true model Church of Computability (Alonzo Church: "The calculi of lambda-conversion," *Annals of Math. Studies* 6, Princeton). *See also* SCHOENFINKEL.

lambada calculus *n.* [Inspired by Matthew Rabuzzi, 1992] A set of algorithms to determine the maximum number of dancing angels per pinhead.

⇒"Discussions about programming languages often resemble medieval debates about the number of angels that can dance on the head of a pin instead of exciting contests between fundamentally differing concepts" (J. Backus, ACM Turing Lecture, 1977).

lambdacism *n.* *pronouced* rambdacism.\ Excessive use of the LAMBDA CALCULUS.

laptop *adj. Also called* **lappable.** *Marketing* (Of a computer) weighing less than 80 lbs.

⇒In fact, recent lappability STUDIES have shown that most users can survive four hours with a 100-lb computer on their knees before terminal thrombo-phlebitis sets in. Laptop manufacturers are cooperating by ensuring that battery life is limited to three hours.

Last Action Hero *n.* The QA manager who stamped "Ready to ship" on Microsoft WINDOWS 1.0.

⇒Popular variants indict Sun's Solaris 2.0 and the Titanic.

latch-lifter *n.* [Scouse (Liverpool) argot] **1** The price of admission, leading to the possibility of free rounds. **2** The HACKER effort expended to gain initial access to a site.

⇒The Stoic ethics of Merseyside pub crawling demands that you pay for your first bevvy (drink), figuratively "lifting the latch" and gaining a valued place at the bar as a bona-fide customer. Thereafter, endless ploys are available to sponge from friend and stranger. Thus, you may challenge all upstanding (if any) to name the last man to box Gentleman Jim (the undertaker); seek the dead center of town (Anfield Cemetery); or ask who played for both Liverpool and Everton at the same derby soccer match (the Royal Marines Band). Additionally, there are many bets you can place on factual (name the referee and linesmen at the 1913 FA Cup Final) or Smullyan-type (is A telling the truth about what B is saying about Pascal?) trivia.

latest version *n.* See VERSION, LATEST.

law *n.* **1** (usually capitalized as **The Law**) Antonym for both "justice" and "mercy." **2** Any statement in the aphoristic environment, coined to amuse and distract regardless of apodictic truth or empirical verifiability.

⇒Some meta-laws escape the latter qualifications, e.g.,

Kelly's pith-poor law: "Terseness is not enough."

G.B. Shaw's golden rule: "There are no golden rules."

Following a spate of undisciplined lawmaking, ANSI established the Solon Committee in 1978 to devise guidelines for the formulation of laws and their preferred typography in two major categories:

The standard ANSI 1.75-inch diameter lapel button.

The standard ANSI 11.25-inch car bumper sticker.

The rival Hammurapi Committee, set up by ISO in 1979, has accepted the latter standard, subject to some minor revisions, but utterly rejects the antiquated ANSI button size as an unjustified curb on creativity. The ISO 5.139-cm-diameter button will probably prevail, in spite of the earnest 1.845-inch compromise proposal from the United Kingdom representative.

SEE FOLLOWING ENTRIES*

Decompiling, James Joyce's law of

Gershwin's law

Grosch's law

Grosch's law, corollary to

Murphy's law of programming

Voltaire-Candide, law of

Welfare, Burns' law of

---

*A database of tarnished truisms initiated by Conrad Scheiker is being maintained at the Computer Center, University of Arizona, Tucson, Arizona, 85721 by Gregg Townsend.

laxicon *n.* THIS dictionary.

layering n. The creation of impassable FIREWALLs between arbitrary levels of a PROTOCOL.

leader *n.* **1** (Of a project) the person at the front, followed blindly until the break occurs. **2** (Of a magnetic or paper tape) the piece at the front, followed blindly until the break occurs. **3** (Of a punched-card deck) the veteran, battle-hardened card placed at the front of the pack to soften the defensive jaws of the opposing card reader. *Compare* TRAILER.

⇒ As me an' me marrer was reading' a tyape,
The tyape gave a shriek mark an' tried tae escyape;
It skipped ower the gyate tae the end of the field,
An' jigged oot the room wi' a spool an' a reel!
Follow the leader, Johnny me laddie,
Follow it through, me canny lad O;
Follow the transport, Johny me laddie,
Away, lad, lie away, canny lad O!

(Industrial Ballad, Durham, N.E. England)

leading *n.* *pronounced* ledding.\\ *Archaism* A line-space unit formerly allocated intuitively by inserting strips of real, metallic lead between lines of real, metallic font. The DTP (Desktop Publishing) equivalent, taking Word Perfect for Windows 5.2 as an example, will drive you insane. The Reference Manual index points to "Leading, adjustment—page 574," "Leading, initial setting—page 636," and "Leading *see* Whitespace—page 283." Pages 574 and 283 do not contain the string "leading," while page 636 says "Line Height (Leading) Adjustment between Lines = 0 inches; between Paragraphs = 0 inches." If you have survived this run-around, you may decide to consult the twenty-one index entries under "Line Height." One of them refers to page 574 (déjà vu); here the para headed "Line Height Adjustment" ends with the helpful, "For further information, see *Line Height Adjustment* in *Reference*."

leading-edge *adj.* **1** (Of a technology) a few microns blunter than STATE-OF-THE-ART. **2** (Of a tab-card feeding option) two of the eight possibilities.

Whenever practical, tab cards should be submitted to the card reader so that the least significant columns are chewed up first.

learning curve *n.* The plotting of *K,* knowledge-gained (y-axis), against *t,* time-expended (x-axis).

⇒The possibly fractal results indicate how you might master or forget a subject as time goes by. In spite of well-established graphing conventions for *dK/dt,* the rate of knowledge acquisition, the DP literature often bemoans, rather than celebrates, a "steep learning curve." A happier trend is emerging whereby the learning curve is characterized as "easy," "gentle," "short," or "difficult" without explicitly specifying the gradient. However, a new confusion has appeared: "Without a proven solution, you risk absorbing startup costs in your first project. To avoid such problems, you need to travel the learning curve quickly" (Alsys real-time Ada development brochure). Here we seem to be violating all the known (so far) laws of physics by trying to dash along the learning curve in better than real time. In fact, there is no absolute learning curve that each of us must navigate. For any given target system and individual exposed thereto, there is no shortage of soft scientists who will plot, plot, plot to produce learning curves for various didactic methodologies (they get paid by the syllabus and by the syllable). Whether such curves are relevant to other learners is extremely moot. Adjust the curve if you can, but the x-axis represents Ol' Man riverrun Time, who jest keep rollin' along. A fruitful extension is to consider the learning curve as hysteresial: from *t* = 0, our *K* builds up with monotonously malleable monotonicity. Soon *dK/dt* tails off to zero as we ask "Who needs all this? Will it butter my parsnips?" and *K* peaks with boredom and/or saturation. At the drop of a cusp, *K* suddenly starts declining as we find better ways to spend our x-axis. The curve, alas, does not return to zero: retentivity ensures that we'll remember unto death some stupid, irrelevant subset of *K* (typically that Shift+F7 stores and prints the current message).

lebensRAM *n.* The GUI conspiracy presaged in Adolf Hitler's *Mein Kampf:* "4 MB is my *final* demand."

legacy *adj.* **1** (Of software) mature, reliable, unfashionable. **2** (Of hardware) soldiering on; desperately seeking spare parts. *See also* MAINFRAME; PASTEMIC.

⇒I first encountered the *adjective* "legacy," in a KnowledgeWare leaflet describing the mind-reeling, reel-winding mounds of ancient, unportable, pastemic code that survive throughout our fair planet in installations large and small. I pictured the unveiling of the old Coboller's Last Will & Testament. The lawyer reads to the acquisitive and mutually jealous next-of-kin. They grow edgy during the long preamble: "Little did I envisage when I wrote my first divide subroutine...and how we longed for Knuth's next volume...." Who'll get the collectible collator? She always promised me the embalmed bug. O Lord, the bugger's left me the payroll suite on 30,000 soggy cards!

The lucky, but rare, legatees are those who have not changed their differential equations or bookkeeping methods since the first Univacs or 1401s were painfully programmed thirty years or more ago. "We ain't *never* goin' through all that again," they swore as the years rolled by with ever-increasing bpb (bangs per buck) vitiated by ever-loftier, less efficient languages. IPS (instructions per second) moved up via KIPS to and beyond MIPS as they switched to 1401-emulating 360s, 360-emulating Honeywells, and, for all I know, Honeywell-emulating SparcStations. But the good old reliable legacy code hangs in there, or rather, refuses to hang!

LEGOL *n.* A high-level billable language embodying the wisdom and precision accrued over 300,000 lawyer-years of patient litigation during March 1994 in California. *More at* legalese, TNHD.

⇒Let a simple example suffice: the C statement

```
int i = 1;
```

translates to LEGOL as

Be It Understood And Acknowledged By These Presents That

the newly created object is herewith to be named and referred to as "i" within the scope determined by the preferred embodiment of the previously submitted namespace patent hereby incorporated by reference and further that "i" being of the type declared known and widely recognized as integer it shall straightway without let or hindrance be assigned and allotted ne quid nimis the value 1 (ONE) and shall retain that value sub tegmine fagi until such time or times if any that some other value within the jurisdiction of the Type Safety (Promotions) Act may be assigned and alloted thereto. Notwithstanding the aforementioned assignment the said value of "i" shall be subject to male parta male dilabuntur and all liability due to mal de chip or mal de code is expressly excluded.

LEGOL also allows a variant of the `#include` directive:

```
#including_but_not_limited_to
```

lemma three *n.* More strictly, a conjecture; even more strictly, a possible conjecture, insofar as Pierre de Fermat's dying marginalia in 1665 read: "Ah, pauv'cons, you zink zat my penultimate conjecteure was incroyable...*mais*, et c'est un grand *mais*...it is but un cas spécial of my jolie troisième lemmère, qu'on voit danser le long des golfes clairs...Mon dieu, I have a precise upper bound for the Selmer group in the semistable case of the symmetric square representation associated to a modular form...Mi par di veder un gran lume...Gaston, de l'encre et encore une autre marge!...arrgh!" The search continues.

⇒ CHORUS   Lemma three, very pretty, and the converse pretty too;
But only God and Fermat know which of them is true.

VERSE 1   When I studied number theory, I was happy in me prime,
And all them wild conjectures, I knocked them two at a time, but...

CHORUS

VERSE 2   Last week, at supervision, Ken Ribet said to me:
           "Did you discover the deliberate mistake in lemma number three?"

CHORUS

VERSE 3   Lemma three it has puzzled mathematicians by the score,
           But Max Newman has engulfed it, and it won't be seen no more.

CHORUS

VERSE 4   Well, the axiom of choice, it is very clear to me:
           If you wanna choose a lemma, boys, then don't choose lemma three,
           for...

CHORUS

VERSE 5   And it's black and white together, we shall not be moved,
           But the four-color theorem, it hasn't yet been proved,[14] (last time
           now...)

CHORUS   Lemma three, very pretty, and the converse pretty too;
           But only God and Andrew know which of them is true.

(Words by SK-B, based with deep respect on "The Lemon Tree," Will Holt, Dolfi
Music Inc., Chappell Music Company, New York.)

less than *pronounced* <.\ A symbol of inequality and victimization having
precedence over all other symbols of disparity.

⇒The less than symbol is located betwen such pairs of variables as: {C, C++};
{YourDoxy, MyDoxy}, {YOURGOL, MYGOL}, and {MyPay, MyWorth}.

lexical scope *n.* One of natural language's many risible barriers to disambiguation. *See also* HYPHEN.

⇒Thus, the Small Computer Book Club promises to "Hone your small computer
skills," to which we say, "With insults like this, the Club is likely to remain small." In
other parts of the literature, we read of "hard disk problems" and "Real-Time
Marketing Managers." In the absence of scoping indications, we could have "Real-
Time (Marketing Managers)" or "(Real-Time Marketing) Managers." We are left to
ponder whether they solve "quickly enough" each marketing problem as it comes
along, or whether they tackle real-time-marketing problems in their own time. We need
to be told.

---

14. If you have read, understood, and LINTed Appel & Haken's program, you can skip this pre-
1976 verse.

along, or whether they tackle real-time-marketing problems in their own time. We need to be told.

Paul A. Wax reports a paper called "Eating Disordered Women in the Workplace," by Susan Gale Hanchey, Ph.D., and notes that "Dr Hanchey never takes a position for or against this practice, I'm sorry to say."

LF *n.* **1** (1929) Handout. **2** (1970) ASCII Line Feed. *See also* CR.

⇒ "I do love my boss, he's a great pal of mine;
"And that's why I'm standing in this here bread line;
"Hallelujah, I'm a bum, hallelujah, bum again;
"Hallelujah, give us a handout to revive us again."

(Anon. Wobbly Hymn)

liberation *n.* [Latin *Liber* "a deity associated with the Greek Bacchus."] A specialized, heady form of emulation, allowing the user to switch rapidly from one manufacturer (usually IBM) to another (usually Honeywell) during an orgiastic "half-price-but-hurry" period known as the "happy hour."

LIFO *adj.* [Acronym for Last In, First Out.] **1** (Of a STACK) being analogous to the central deck of cards in gin rummy, where (*pace* card sharping) cards are taken from or placed on the top position only. As with gin rummy, the top item in the stack has usually been discarded by someone else and is not the item you are seeking. *Compare* FIFO; LINO. **2** (Of industrial relations) related to a commonly observed situation where the most recently employed are the first to strike.

linear *adj.* Evenly proportioned; scalable; soluble; predictable; unrealistic. *Compare* SEGMENTED.

linear programming *n.* *Also called* **LP.** A tidy method of programming in which the horizontal strings of source code are kept strictly parallel and right-hand justified, while all indentions are set to offer a pleasing trompe l'oeil vertical aspect. Borrowing the traditional engineering design axiom, some say "If the program *looks* good, it's probably correct."

⇒Early, random tests by DPM proctors, aimed at eradicating insobriety and nonlinearity among programmers, included such odious practices as FORTRAN smear tests, SNOBOL uroscopies, and extended BASIC breathalyzers. The request to "blow into this bag" was often unsuccessfully countered by the rejoinder, "Why? Are your chips too hot?" The IUP (International Union of Programmers) has now negotiated a more humane regimen, whereby the proctor must have reasonable doubts regarding the state of the suspect programmer before demanding two simple, physical tasks: first, the programmer must circumnavigate a prescribed flowchart or class hierarchy without throwing up; second, the programmer must thrice intone, without undue sibilation, "The LISP parenthesis doth perennially pisseth us off."

LINO Last In Never Out. A stack uncertain whether Pascal or C argument conventions prevail.

lint *n. & v. More correctly* **de-lint** [Cotton trade: *lint* "nasty bits of waste yarn causing 'trouble at'*MILL*.'"] (*Chiefly* UNIX and C) **1** *n.* A doryphoric (nit-combing) filter program claiming to report those inevitable syntactic, semantic, and stylistic errors that are presumably undetectable by any compiler/linker. **2** *v.* To subject or expose (source code) to the lint program. *See also* DORYPHORE. *Compare* HAIR. *More at* TNHD.

⇒The lint.c source itself, of course, should be linted relintlessly. The homely Liverpudlian analog is a nested (i.e., infested) array of biddy-combs, each capable of cleaning its successor, nay, unto the root.

Liquid Paper® The Gillette Company, Stationery Products Division. Supplied with all Frisian word processors for on-screen corrections. *See also* ETHNOLOGY.

LISP *n.* Preferred plural, at least for Francophones: **LISPen.** **1** LISt Processing language, J. McCarthy (MIT, late 1950s), but often mistaken as acronym for Lots of Irritating Spurious (or Superfluous) Parentheses.[15] *More at* TNHD. *See also* LOGOMACHY.

2 Laser Impulse Space Propulsion, Los Alamos National Laboratory, 1993.

⇒Which of the two LISPen will survive this millennium remains to be seen. The rocket system may turn out to be *in loco parens*, destined to discover some distant, advanced galaxy where dedicated LISP-the-language machines are built and sold profitably.

list *n.* The sinking feeling induced by excessive documentation.

local *adj.* [Spanish *loco* "foolish, mad, irresponsible."] **1** (Of a site, terminal, node, branch, user, agent, object) being, rightly, kept in ignorance of the policies, strategies, and protocols devised, and daily refined, by some centralized pool of superior intelligence. **2** (Of a variable) confined; stunted; unable to spread its erroneous wings, and doomed to flap forever in some obscure, somber, scope-ridden block. **3** (Of an error) latent; malignant; lurkful; ticking away. **4** (Of a pub) the nearest and dearest, providing minimal LATCH LIFTERS, a tabula rasable credit slate, and an armory of personalized "arrers" (darts). *Compare* GLOBAL.

locale *n.* An ANSI-approved ethnic stereotype.

---

15. For the definitive, picaresque tale see Guy L. Steele Jr. and Richard P. Gabriel, "The Evolution of LISP," *ACM SIGPLAN, HOPL-II Conference Proceedings* 28, no. 3.

logical diagram *n.* The graphical idealization of a circuit, indicating by means of lines, arrows, and symbols the various conflicting choices facing any electron rash enough to venture therein.

logomachy *n.* **1** *1960s* The good-humored altercations between supporters of EV-LISP and of EVQ-LISP. **2** *1980s* The good-humored altercations between members of the Common LISP committee. See note 15.

⇒As John McCarthy once said, "It doesn't really matter which language you choose; they're both very good."

look'n'feel *n.* [Look and feel] The ill-defined, superficial but legally protectable property of a user interface, *esp.* where the underlying application has been stolen from others.

loop *n. & v. intrans.* [From Middle English *loupe* "a noose, a circle of rope used in applied knot theory to enforce suspended judgments; a device similar to the one recommended by Polonius for garroting one's friends."] **1** *n.* *Programming* The frantic rehearsal of a certain sequence of program steps until the system "gets it right," failing which the loop is branded *endless*; the repetition of a certain sequence of program steps WHILE, and only while, a set of unforeseen circumstances prevails; an algorithmic recycling; a piece of code in search of a LOOPHOLE. **2** *n.* *Control theory Also called* **feed-back loop.** The amplification and regurgitation of error signals in order to achieve any desired degree of instability. **3** *v. intrans.* *Programming* To relinquish command for an unspecified period, as: "D'you mind taking over the console, I'm looping for a while." *See also* DYNAMIC HALT; ENDLESS LOOP.

loop, endless *n. See* ENDLESS LOOP.

loophole *n.* **1** The escape route sought by a LOOP. **2** *Metacomputer science* The conceptual gap left when a loop migrates to another part of the metasystem. Any fresh loop nearby will be attracted into the hole, and so on. **3** *Marketing* A deficiency in the jurisprudential environment that allows overselling on the grounds of diminished responsibility, knowledge, and honesty.

Lord High Fixer *n.* For any given installation, the oldest living member of the original programming team. *See also* GURU.

⇒Unfortunately, the Lord High Fixer, when needed, will be found to have moved to a distant, competitive site or to have set up as an independent consultant.

Lotus *n.* A sleep-inducing corporation claiming ownership of the sequence 1-2-3, and hence, via Peano's axioms, threatening dominion over Z+ the set of natural numbers. *See also* PATENT.

⇒The Lotus 1-2-3 trademark may clash with my prior claim over all subsets in the decimal expansion of π. Are the courts number-theoretically ready to try such cases?

Borland, paradoxically, has the upper hand, since they now control (figuratively) the zero spreadsheet. Lotus may well rue the day they did not follow the C option-base convention: Lotus 0-1-2.

low-level language *n.* **1** A primitive programming language in which each line of code needs, but never gets, 20 lines of comment. **2** *Also called* **common language.** Imprecatory, often scatological strings aimed at an ailing system.

⇒If delivered with sufficiently high DENIER, genuinely anthropomorphic venom, and heavy, reed-bending keyboard ostinato, such inputs have been known to shame the operating system into a belated response. The system's own obscure introspections will be suspended briefly while a conciliatory message is flashed to the user. *Compare* HIGH-LEVEL LANGUAGE.

low memory *adj.* (Of a GUI system) having 4 MB RAM. Systems with less than 4 MB are now called "no memory systems."

low-self-esteem books *n. Also called* **books for the baffled.** Any book riding on the huge success of *DOS for Dummies* (Dan Gookin, IDG Books, San Mateo, Calif.).

⇒My contest for rival titles (*UNIX Review,* October 1993) invoked: Visual BASIC for the Blind; MIDI for the Deaf; Pacsal for the Dyxlesic; REXX for Ex-Monarchs; C++ for the Nonplussed; dBASE for the Debased; Quicken for the Dead; 1-2-3 for the Innumerate; CLU for the Clueless; and LISP for the Listless. In spite of this ridicule, the genre has grown to include *The Complete Idiot's Guide to Brain Surgery.*

LP *n.* [Gramophonic *abbrev.*: Long Playing—sometimes confused, under-standably, with the abbreviation for LINEAR PROGRAMMING.] The recording of Paul Erdös's recitation of *e* to 80,000 places, available in Hungarian, German, Russian, Hebrew, and English. The rare, collectible 1972 edition has a small error in the 34,034th digit. *See also* DIGITAL RECORDING; OVERLOADING.

⇒In the audio-reproductive vinyllic environment, we have progressed leisurely from 78 rpm via 45 rpm (misnamed EP for Extended Play in view of the reduced diameter) to 33 1/3 rpm (LP) formats with severe but correctable discontinuities in locational central-hole-size methodologies. Terminologists were presumably ready with ELP (Extended Long Play) or perhaps SP (Super Play) if the 16 2/3 rpm record had appeared, but the digital magic of the CD (Compact Disc) arrived to upturn-tables on the analog-scratch of groove-grinding needles. Offsetting the claimed loss of ambience and the joys of hand-sharpening bamboo styli, one must acknowledge that Solti's CD Decca Ring cycle now occupies 85 percent less shelf space ($5.75'' \times 6'' \times 5''$ CD versus $7'' \times 13'' \times 13''$ LP).

Luddite *n.* [Origin: from "King" Ned Ludd, legendary victim of enforced automation during the Industrial Revolution, Yorkshire, England (ca. 1780).] One who, Canute-like, attempts to stem the tide of computerization. Having failed by stapling checks, folding tabcards, defacing OCR documents, demagnetizing credit cards, and part-paying utility and telephone accounts, the diehard Luddite resolves to continue the struggle from within by becoming an undercover programmer.

⇒Ironically, most Luddite programmers quickly achieve DPM status, which denies them both the inclination and the opportunity to sabotage:

> The Luddite class can kiss my ass,
> I've got the foreman's job at last.[16]

The DP counter-counterrevolution, though, must not become complacent. Three-shift vigilance should be the battle cry. Spotting the traitor coder in your midst is not easy— only the most naive Luddite will punch the giveaway *X* in column 5—since, nowadays, *all* programmers have the shifty, rebellious aspect of a communard freshly scraped off a disputed barricade, or the truculent sneer of one who has marched ten thousand miles with Mao to get to work. Similarly, the abnormality of program error distribution precludes any positive discrimination between *deliberate* and *standard* coding blunders.

Some overzealous vigilante groups still string up a suspect programmer at the drop of a semicolon, and although several studies show this to be a cost-effective method of improving program quality (e.g., *Bonus Payments or Lynching?: A Comparative Study*—Judge Thumphreys, *Journal of the Institute for Software Productivity and Discipline* 9, no. 3 [1979]), too many bright Luddites evade justice. Emerging as the least fallible indicator of the non-wasp in your system's bosom is the "punctuality test." Programmers consistently arriving on-site at the preordained time are doubly suspect. Why are they so anxious to "get at" the system? And how did they avoid the general state of abulia and debility induced in all genuine programmers by the previous session? Is there a time bomb ticking away in your cherished database? Your punctual, hard-working, over-reliable apostates, they know, they know! Do not hang or fire them! Promote them quickly, the higher, the better!

---

16. Compare with Leon Rosselson's anti-Labour Party parody, "We'll sing the Red Flag once a year."

M

M *prefix* [Mega-] Either 1000^2 or 2^{20} depending upon the financial implications. *Compare* K. *More at* TNHD at quantifiers.

⇒Sadly, in natural discourse, *mega* has become a vapid, ho-hum amplifier lurking fuzzily within the shifting showbiz range of *superdooper* to *hyperdyper*. Once you have tagged your best-selling trend as *mega*, your rivals will scoff "If that's all there is, then let's keep dancing...." From the "merely mega," they'll trot out the whole SI (Système International) sequence: *giga, tera, peta, exa,...*

"Some said *exa*, I said 'More Yet';
"Some said *zetta*, and it's 'More Yet';
"Some said *yotta*, I said 'More Yet';
"The name of this song is 'More Yet.'"

(adapted from Leadbelly, "More Yet")

Mac, MAC *n.* [Gaelic: son of, whence patronymic prefixes, *Mac* and *Mc*; the young of any animal; a term of endearment; anonymous person, what's-yer-name (cf. French *machin*).]

⇒Relating these simple origins to the current MacOverload is a tempting but fruitless (and possibly actionable) exercise. The litigious claims over this ancient prefix in the audio, computer, and hamburger environments have apparently led to the withdrawal of the Scottish Play (Shakespeare's *Macbeth)* from the theatrical repertoire.

1 [*Abbrev.* via the McDonald's fast-food chain to its eponymous products] The universal, uniformly distributed, triadic meal, variously relished. Its remarkable impact on the world's cuisinary sensibilities extends to "les arrondissements les plus chic de Paris," where "le Big Mac" has revived a million jaded palates.

2 [*Abbrev.* Apple Macintosh; *also called* (derog.) **Macintoy, Macintrash.**] A popular GUI PC invented at Xerox Park, built in Malaysia, and reputedly marketed from Cupertino.

⇒One of the profoundest mysteries of the PC jungle is why the freedom-loving, people-empowering Apple Macintosh acquired a fiercely protected, over-priced, closed architecture, while IBM, the nasty, grasping, brainwashing, Wall-Street-suited Jackals, opened up their box to friendly, affordable clonage throughout the four corners of Taiwan.

3 [Acronyms for Machine-aided Cognition; Multiple Access Computer; Man Against Computers; Maniacs And Clowns.] The U.S. government-funded MIT Project MAC (1963) that helped spawn the HACKER culture now, ironically, under expensive Federal attack.

4 [Acronyms for Multiplexed Analog Components; Message Authentication Code; Military Airlift Command; Model Airplane Club; Maximum Allowed Concentration.]

⇒As they say in disambiguating circles, the meaning of MAC/Mac is "usually clear from the context."

macaroon *n.* A half-caste employed by Apple Computer Inc.

machine-independent *adj.* Being or pertaining to a software or hardware element which will not work on any computer. *Compare* PORTABLE; VENDOR-INDEPENDENT.

machine-readable *also (colloq.)* **machinable.** *adj.* (Of a text) encoded and saved, usually on a magnetic medium or CD-ROM.

⇒In theory, a stored text can be restored at any time to its original human-enjoyable form. In REAL LIFE, however, insuperable barriers intervene, such as printer drivers, font managers, and forgotten file names.

macro *n. & adj* **1** *n.* *pronounced* maquereau.\ A pimp selling pirated copies of Quattro on the rue St Denis. **2** *adj.* (Of an assembler) mollycoddling.

macrocephalic *adj.* (Of a SPREADSHEET user) smart enough to avoid real programming.

MAFIA *n.* [Acronym for Mechanized Applications in Forced Insurance Accounting.] An extensive network with many on-line and offshore subsystems running under OS, DOS, and IOS.

⇒MAFIA documentation is rather scanty, and the MAFIA sales office exhibits that testy reluctance to respond to bona fide inquiries which is the hallmark of so many DP organizations. From the little that has seeped out, it would appear that MAFIA operates under a nonstandard protocol, OMERTA, a tight-lipped variant of SNA, in which extended handshakes also perform complex security functions. The known timesharing aspects of MAFIA point to a more than usually autocratic operating system. Screen prompts carry an imperative, nonrefusable weighting (most menus offer simple YES/YES options, defaulting to YES) that precludes indifference or delay. Uniquely, all editing under MAFIA is performed centrally, using a powerful rubout feature capable of erasing files, filors, filees, and entire nodal aggravations.

mainframe *n. & adj.* **1** *n.* *Hardware* (*Chiefly* disparaging & offensive) the much-abused room-sized computer that ruled the DP roost until the "mini-is-bigger" craze of the 1970s and the "micro-is-even-bigger" excesses of the 1980s. **2** *adj.* *Software* (*Chiefly* complimentary as in "mainframe-quality") tried and trusted, solid and reliable. *See also* CLIENT-SERVER; DOWNSIZING; GROSCH'S LAW; IBM; LEGACY; MICROPROCESSOR; PASTEMIC; SUPERCOMPUTER.

⇒The familiar graphs of available Kbytes per tonne, MIPS per cubic-yard, and Horn clauses per yen, plotted against the last five decades' frantic abscissa, seem to have sealed the mainframe's fate. Even with a logarithmic ordinate, these graphs are almost-everywhere damnably near *vertical*. However, defying the economists' obituaries, Big Iron refuses to Rust In Peace. The MIS mindset, by definition, dreams of empires based on the single, tangible, controllable, high-budget DP epicenter. The unthinkable alternative is PC anarchy: distant, computer-illiterate branches rushing to purchase, this week only, multimedia XTs pre-loaded with CP/M and WordStar 1.0 from a mail-order catalog, not to mention enterprise data distributed god-knows-where on 5-cent *floppies*. Thus, the MIPS graph can be exponentially discounted on the grounds that not all instructions are equal.

Alas, the traditional big-iron suppliers are unable to cope with the escalating demand for solid, reliable mainframes. Daily, it seems, we read of attempted raids on the Boston and other Computer Museums. In spite of redoubled security, the entire Boston Whirlwind exhibit was stolen on March 3, 1994, and is now rumored to be running, *sub umbra* but with great success, the seat-reservation system for a major airline. Equally disturbing is the report that Scotland Yard is investigating the disappearance of the Babbage Analytical Engine from the South Kensington Science Museum. The trail, so far, grows cold at the North Korean border.

Beware, then, of the rag-and-bone street criers trying to buy your legacy hardware on the cheap:

"Any old iron, any old iron,
"Any any any old iron;
"You look neat, talk about a treat,
"You look dapper from your napper to yer feet;
"Dressed in style, brand new files,
"With yer father's old green tie on;
"I wouldn't give yer tuppence for yer EDSAC I,
"Old iron, old iron!"

(Cockney music-hall song)

maintenance *n.* The replacement of one set of error states by another.

⇒Ideally, the latter should be nonintersecting with, and more catastrophic than, the former. In *routine* maintenance the replacement is applied on a regular basis, so that DOWNTIME increases in an orderly, controlled, monotonic sequence. The system gracefully converges to a state of OBSOLESCENCE on a date convenient for the marketing department.

major new-level release *n.* **1** *Marketing* Any RELEASE. **2** *Programming* The next release. **3** Level A128/12.456/K17C, replacing level A128/12.456/K17B. **4** A complete recasting of the systems software rendering all previous programs inoperative. **5** *C++* Changing the access specifier of a single `iostream` data member from `private` to `protected`. **6** *Microsoft* Any set of bug-fixes costing the user more than $39.95.

Malloc, malloc *n. & v. trans.* **1** *n.* Canaanite deity controlling memory allocations. **2** *v. trans.* *C/C++ library* To request space on the heap.

⇒The call `ip = (int *)malloc(N*sizeof(int));` will try to allocate and initialize enough dynamic memory on the heap for *N* integers. If successful, a valid, non-null pointer is returned in `ip` pointing to this allocation. Failure for any reason, usually insufficient memory, is signaled by a null (0) value in `ip`. A long-running theological contention has been how C should handle `malloc(0)`, the call for no allocation. My draconian solution is that a "Too much memory available" warning should be displayed, followed by the complete erasure of the offending program.

man-hour *n.* A sexist, obsolete measure of macho effort, equal to 60 kiplings. *See also* IF; PC.

⇒One man-hour can represent one man working for one hour, two men quibbling for thirty minutes, or a billion men pussyfooting for a nanosecond. Most areas of DP activity now include a synergistic mix of male and female operatives, and the man-hour unit is being replaced by the PERSON-HOUR, using a conversion factor of 1.50.

MANIAC *n.* **1** An early computer built at the Institute of Advanced Studies, Princeton (fl. 1952). **2** "Anyone who has been making or using a digital computer for more than a few years" (Lord Bowen, *Faster than Thought,* 1953).

-mancy *suffix* [Greek *manteia,* "divination."] Indicative of an unsound forecasting method. *See* BITOMANCY; ONOMANCY; RETROMANCY; SCATOMANCY.

⇒The one exception is *margaritomancy*: The dedicated analysis of random compounds of tequila, lemon, and salt has never failed to transmute present uncertainties into pleasant predictions.

manufacturer *n. also (rare)* **supplier.** A loosely knit and constantly changing group referred to as "we" in proposals and "you" in legal actions.

⇒More abstractly, the manufacturer is the second of the SEVEN CATASTROPHES OF COMPUTING. *See also* OEM; PRODUCTIZATION.

map *n. & v. trans.* **1** *n.* The imponderable correspondence between two sets, one of which (the *domain*) is unknown, while the other (the *range*) is unknowable. **2** *v. trans.* To establish, or to imagine the establishment of, some relationship between two incongruent sets, e.g., (disk sectors) and (records), (records) and (fields), (fields) and (bits), or (sales territories) and (salespersons).

marketing *n.* The essential branch of DP, unfazed by grammar, orthography, and technicalities.

massively parallel *adj.* **1** *Hypergeometry* (Of two right lines) nonintersecting and many megaparsecs apart even at the points at infinity. **2** (Of a computer architecture) employing 2^N microprocessors where N depends on Intel's current discount structure; *esp.* of a system massively searching for parallel advances in the programming arts. *Compare* MASSIVELY SERIAL.

⇒In particular, the challenge is to divide a problem into a large number of independent THREADS. MONISTs need not apply.

The choice of vapid, sloganeering amplifiers such as "very large scale," "massive," "super," "mega," and "hyper" is, eventually, a barrier to technical progress. The physicists have fallen into the same trap with their GUT (Grand Unification Theory), Superstrings, and TOE (Theory of Everything). Follow *that*, as they say in ShowBiz. *See also* HYPER; VLSI.

massively serial *adj.* **1** Of the author's lot. **2** Relating to the RS-232 and IEEE-488 specifications. *Compare* MASSIVELY PARALLEL. *See also* SERIAL.

m'as-tu-vu \pronounced matoovoo\ *n. & adj.* [French: "Have you seen me?"] A vain person or entity; a show-off desperately in need of attention however degrading.

⇒This bona-fide, albeit a tad slangy, French *idiotisme*, whether used as a noun or an adjective, is what C++ would qualify as **const**. The form is "invariant," resisting the normal inflections for number and gender: *un m'as-tu-vu* (one show-off); *deux m'as-tu-vu* (two show-offs); *ce qu'elle est m'as-tu-vu!* (what a show-off she is!). Exemplars are, by definition, easy to spot, and the MEDIA over-anxious to oblige. For example, and not in any particular order, consider Steve Jobs, Jahweh, Adam Osborne, and any last-minute objector to an ANSI-language standard.

MATISSE *n.* *Also* **M.A.T.I.S.S.E** [™ ADB Inc., Cambridge, Mass.] Yet another exploited famous person. *See* ONOMANCY; NEWTON.

matrix *n.* (Printing) a set of dots that you can connect with a pencil to reveal a hidden character.

⇒In the matrix-for-dummies versions, the dots are numbered.

Matthew 13:58 ("And he did *not* mighty works there because of their unbelief" [Ruler James Version]). The proof text for many of the failures in DP MARKETING.

⇒Thus, witness the growing MIS resistance to claims that the CLIENT-SERVER METHODOLOGY-of-the-Month will increase interoperable seamlessness by N percent for any $N > 0$.

maturity *n.* The long-awaited state of DP.

⇒In 1950, we said "Be fair…give us another ten years." Now, after 40+ years, an age at which most primates *and* their offspring are fully developed, we are still waiting. A clear sign of maturation would be a computer-related radio show with the zany humor and knowledge of the Click'n'Clack brothers' Car Talk.

MAW *n.* **1** [Acronym for MICROSOFT At Work.] A set of standards aimed at crippling all known office machines with embedded Windows NT. **2** The gob[17] or stomach of a voracious animal.

⇒We are advised by anonymous lawyers to our immediate north that any connection between these two definitions is entirely coincidental and crushingly actionable. But, MAW is already worming its way into diverse office appliances, and past experience indicates that gullible power users cannot wait to load all their gadgets with 32 MB RAM and 240 MB disks in the Grail hunt for maximum INTEROPERABILITY. Aping the widespread "Intel Inside!" and "AMD Outside!" stickers, "MS All Over!" decals will soon appear on your telephones, copiers, and pencil sharpeners.

Microsoft is not hiding its LEBENSRAM ambitions. There, in the WinAPI, is the brazen, apocalyptic function:

```
SetWorldTransform().
```

The Gates/McCaw plan, yet another seamful web, will encircle the Earth with 840 spy satellites able to spot and zap Solaris 2.x sites just as they become productive (the timing is sublime). CompuServe is also dead-meat, super-highway roadkill: note that Teledesic is a blatant anagram of "Delete CIS." QED.

The Biblical foretokens are many and irrefutable:

"And there were Windows™ in three rows and light was against light in three ranks" (1 Kings 7:4 KJV).

We see this as Microsoft swallowing IBM (note the clear reference to the nested-arrays of APL/2), AT&T, and Digital, reading *rows* as COSE-induced disputations, and *light* as "lacking weight."

"And I will make thy Windows™ of agates [sic], and thy Gates [sic] of carbuncles, and all thy borders of pleasant stones" (Isaiah 54:12 KJV).

Here, one is torn between reading "carbuncle" as precious gem or painful blister (another potential AUTO-ANTONYM, yet both meanings come from the small, red ember). Either way, there is no disputing the implied usurpation of the X-Window's jewels and the manipulation of the XStones benchmark.

"Behold, if the Lord would make Windows™ in heaven, might this thing be? And he said, Behold, thou shalt see it with thine eyes, but shalt not eat thereof. And there were four leprous men at the entering in of [the] Gates, and they said to one another Why sit we here until we die?" (2 Kings 7:2–3 KJV).

Without doubt, this passage portends the abject state of the four major software rivals (Computer Associates, Lotus, Novell, and Borland) trying to develop timely, profitable, terrestrial Windows applications while the full API remains unrevealed "in heaven." Little wonder, then, that "...they watched [the] Gates day and night to kill him" (Acts 9:24 KJV).

---

17. The Liverpudlian (Scouse) *gob* is a derogatory "mouth" via the Gaelic for "beak," whence "Shut yer gob!" is very close to the French "Ta gueule!"

MBT *n.* [Memory Board Tagging.] (© Irish Business Machines). *See* PAGING.

media *n.* [From Latin *medius*, "middling, mediocre."] **1** *General* A member of the set MULTIMEDIA. **2** *Information dispersion* Fourth in estates, fifth in columns.

⇒Although nominally the plural of "medium," media *is* now mandated as singular, as if collectively to indict one common ratbag of lying, jarring bastards. The formal DP plurals of "media" are "medias," "multimedia," and for maximum impact, "multimedias." *Compare* DATA.

medium *n.* *See* MEDIA; MULTIMEDIA.

memory *n.* **1** *Human* A repressed, palimpsestuous BLOB. **2** *DP* A major anthropomorphic fallacy. *See also* LINEAR; RAM; SEGMENTED.

memory leak *n.* *OOP* The inevitable loss of available RAM due to the insidious proliferation of PERSISTENT OBJECTS. *See also* WORM.

mendacity sequence *n.* An ISO standard·sorting sequence allowing the *F*'s in a TRUTH TABLE to be ordered by *degree* of falsehood.

⇒The basic sequence, in ascending order, is: lies; damn lies; statistics; damn statistics; benchmarks; press releases; delivery promises; contradictionary entries. Further refinements can be expected.

menu *n.* **1** *Restaurant* A list of priced options. **2** *DP* A list of unpriced options. *See also* CASCADED.

⇒A computer menu is sometimes kind enough to suggest that certain selections will "take some time." This is a wonderful opportunity to play your Wagner CDs again.

meta- *prefix* [Greek *meta*, "behind, along with, beyond."] Adding a conflicting range of meanings to any object, concept, or predicate in need of a new, more intellectual lease of life. *See* METAPROGRAMMER; METACHARACTER.

⇒The prefix can be, and unfortunately is, applied repeatedly, as in *metametalanguage*, "a language used to formulate a language used to formulate a language." ALGOL 84 and ANSI-ISO SQL, to name but five, have employed even higher meta-level languages. Etymologically, one might suggest that *metameta*, as "behind + beyond," is effectively idempotent.

metacharacter *n.* **1** *Sarcasm* A GURU whose line is always busy. **2** *UNIX shells* Any non-alphanumeric ASCII character.

⇒The dearth of visible ASCII symbols available for shell scripts has forced a host of non-literal, "meta-interpretations" on the thirty-two printable non-alphanumeric characters, and therein lies the fun and popularity of UNIX. You often need to *quote* or *escape* such metacharacters either to "restore" their literal meaning or to delay their interpretation by intercessory subshells. These feats, of course, are achieved using metametacharacters. For example, a recent count of full-stop (period) meanings in various UNIX situations, gave eighteen exciting variants (nineteen if you include the termination of real character-string sentences). In some pattern-matching operations (*see* REGULAR EXPRESSIONS), the full-stop serves as a WILDCARD. To search for a real, non-meta full-stop, therefore, you must search for *"."*   *'.'* or \. Thus the metametacharacters double-quote pairs, single-forward quote pairs, and backslash are used to "de-meta" certain metacharacters, including possibly themselves, depending on the shell and the context. SPACE PRECLUDES a discussion of the majestical, back-quoted command. Clearly, nay, intuitively, double-quotes should quote all metacharacters except $, *'*, *"*, and \. Alas, those with WIDGET-clicking will never experience the joy of correctly (eventually) escaping a double-quoted back-quoted expression. *See also* DISQUOTATIONAL.

metaprogrammer *n.* Someone who is above programming but not yet ready for software engineering.

⇒   I met a programmer a-walking one day;
         "O why aren't you coding?" to him I did say.
         "I'm not a programmer, the truth I will tell,
         But a metaprogrammer from meta-Novell!"

CHORUS   Sperry Rand, Rand, Rand, Sperry Rand.

VERSE 2 "Pray what do you do there?" the stranger I asked,
         "And what are you paid for each tough meta-task?"
         "I just *think* about programs," the young man did say,
         "For a mere meta-pittance of twelve meta-K."

CHORUS

VERSE 3 "And where do you come from?" I finally cried.
         "I come from Hell," the stranger replied.
         "If you come from Hell, then tell me right plain
         "How the hell you managed to get out again?"

CHORUS

VERSE 4 "The way I got out, Sir, the truth I will tell:
         They're turning the systems folk all out of Hell;
         This is to make room for the people who *sell,*
         For there's a great number of them at Novell."

CHORUS

VERSE 5 "Come all you salespersons, and take my advice;
         Be fair to your prospects, and give a good price;
         For if and you do not, I know very well,
         You'll be in great danger of going to Hell!"

CHORUS

(Based with approval on the traditional Durham ballad, "The Devil & the Poor Pitman's Wife," from A. L. Lloyd's WMA collection *Come All Ye Bold Miners.*)

methodist *n.* **1** A follower of *Lares Catervarius Constantinus* (Larry Constantine); one who stresses evangelical faith over theory and reasoning. **2** An Arminian METHODOLOGIST; one who believes that salvational software development is available to the non-ACM elect.

methodologist *n.* One (*usually* of a pair) who perpetrates a METHODOLOGY. *See also* METHODIST.

⇒Methodologists study, classify, and (alas) mandate groups of methods, and no doubt someone has to do it. But, can there be more than *one* methodology? Current parlance implies that methodology is also the study of methodologies, a pursuit that, from analogous situations in other sciences, merits the term *metamethodology*. In fact, Peter G. Neumann, then Editor of the ACM's SIGSOFT SEN (Software Engineering Notes, January 1991) urges "metahodologists" to "make their technology more applicable to real systems." This spelling could be the result of a spurious "a," but as a fan of Neumann's way with words, I suspect a simple haplographic omission of the second "met." Of course, a *metahodologist* (from the Irish "hod," the bricklayer's trough hauled by Finnegan to "rise in the world") could be one who specializes in the lifting and dropping of metabricks, which is not entirely irrelevant to software engineering methodology.

Historians of methodology (not to be confused with methodical historiographers) are intrigued not only by the dominance of "twinned" paradigms but by their implied ethnic mix. Thus the Smith-Brown and Weiner-Langer methodologies are provably less convincing than those of Smith-Weiner and Langer-Brown. The success of the Kelly-Bootle methodology, for example, seems largely due to the widespread assumption that it represents the unlikely convergence of Irish and Anglo-Saxon traditions. A simpler approach sees that there is a large but countable number of diagrammatic permutations employing squares and circles connected by arrowed lines of appropriate intensity and acyclicity. The occasional agreement, across cultural barriers, on the *shapes* of entities and the *directions* of their inter-relational arrows is inevitable but apparently newsworthy.

methodology *n.* A *method* suffering from the prevalent 83 percent circumlocuflationary spiral.

metric *n. & adj.* [Greek *metrikos*, "measurement."] **1** *n. Programming* The futile assessment of coding effort, productivity, and reward, based on gematrial evaluations of source-code text and structure. **2** *adj.* (Of a mensurational methodology) exporting the worst excesses of the French Revolution (1789–1815). *See* DISMAL.

⇒The LOC (lines of code) metric and its refinement LOCEVC (lines of code, excluding verbose comments) are clearly language-dependent, and have been suspect since the invention of the SUBROUTINE (Wheeler and Wilkes, EDSAC I, ca. 1950). With the advent of huge APIs, object-reusability, DLLs, 4GLs, and VISUAL programming, a (1/LOC) metric seems more promising with a bonus for *effective* comments. Care is needed, though, with the growing number of development frameworks boasting that "no code is required."

Other metrics, such as function-point, promoted by IFPUG (International Function-Point Users Group), are less language dependent, but if a metric is known to influence remuneration, programmers can surely be trusted to adjust their coding style accordingly. *See* APIPHOBIA.

Michie, Donald (1923–) One of the few British AI pioneers not driven abroad permanently by the Lighthill Report (1972) to seek more tolerant funding in the U.S.

⇒"Bring me your muddled masses..." (The Statue of Liberty).

MICR *n.* [Magnetic-Ink Character Recognition.] A system for bouncing checks of the wrong polarity. *See also* E13B.

micro- *adj.* **1** Incredibly large with respect to the pico-. **2** Vanishingly small with respect to the giga-. **3** Quite normal in relation to objects of comparable scale.

microprocessor *n.* **1** "Twenty years of architectural bungling concentrated into a single chip" (M. V. Wilkes).

Microsoft Corporation *also called* **MS**; *derog.* **Microsloth**; *laud.* **The IBM of the 1990s**. The dominant marketing force in OS and applications software, beyond the slings and arrows of bankrupted rivals' mockery; also well-beyond any interference from ACLU, ANSI-ISO, FCC, all Monopolies' Commissions, GATT, NATO, and the UN Security Council. *See also* DINOSAURS; MS-DOS; GATES, WILLIAM; IBM; MAW; UNDOCUMENTED; WINDOWS.

⇒As with IBM's dominance in the 60s–70s, the supremacy of Microsoft in the 80s-90s proves that innovation and sworn delivery promises should never be allowed to interfere with marketing. Another depressing IBM-MS parallel is that defeated competitors invoke conspiracies and scream MONOPOLY.

middle-out *adj.* Relating to yet another revolutionary software development METHODOLOGY, allowing progress up or down as the mood of the team dictates. *Compare* BOTTOM-DOWN; BOTTOM-UP; TOP-DOWN; WATERFALL.

⇒The top-down/bottom-up schism is now confined to those computing backwaters where the DP VOGUE magazine arrives two weeks late. The middle-out approach allows an early, honest, and reassuring report to the DPM that the project is "definitely about half-way." The middle-outer sees no contradiction in the proposition that one can break down vague tasks into precise subtasks and, at the same time, integrate ill-conceived CLASSES into well-defined hierarchies.

middleware *n.* **1** Les jarretelles noires de ma CORRECTRICE. **2** Les jarretelles rouges de ma correctrice. **3** Packages promulgated by independent middlepersons for the traditional 10 percent handling fee. **4** Les jarretelles blanches de ma correctrice. **5** The "/" in CLIENT/SERVER.

⇒At one time a well-defined partitioning of wariness could be discerned in the DP marketplace, but of late the question "who-does-what-with-what-to-whom-and-when" admits of no crisp resolution. *See also* OEM.

A sales pitch of daunting verbosity
Has dampened our mild curiosity;
Our spirits are quailed, for we are assailed
With wares of wide-ranging viscosity!

(M. Prospect Merrimé)

"Hardware, Software, Firmware, Middleware, Wetware, Vaporware!
"The most important is to *be*-ware!"

(J. P. Sartrul)

Milken Math *n.* [After Michael Milken, financial wunderkind of the 1980s.]

⇒The junked, cleanly collared bond dealer, is reported to have given, in lieu of jail time, a mathematics course to third-, fourth-, and fifth graders at an elementary school in Harlem, NY. No details were given but one wonders if the exercises included typical dealer calculations: X buys 100,000 shares at $10 each and sells at them at $25. Assuming that three insiders are each paid $40,000, the Feds fine you $80,000, and you donate $50,000 to a school in Harlem, what's your net rake after tax—and remember, we don't pay no taxes! (*See* the movie "Robin and the Seven Hoods.")

mini *n. Abbrev.* minicomputer. The no-man's land (sometimes called Digital) between mainframe/supermini and workstation/supermicro/micro.

⇒As with "miniskirt," the defining size and price/performance ranges lack precision but are known when experienced.

minimal-cost path *adj.* (Of an algorithm) a rule for the out-on-a-limb tree-bound advising them to stay where they are until the pruner arrives.

mini-string *n.* [Origin: "When pain and anguish wring the brow,/A mini-string Angel, Thou!"]. *Also called* **G-string.** An expression of DENIER 14 or less, allowing a glimpse of the shape of strings to come. *Compare* NULL STRING.

MIPS *n.* **1** [Acronym for Mega-Instructions Per Second.] An EPA-type assessment of CPU power, to be used for comparisons only. Your own performance will vary depending upon the bus driver, and will almost certainly be lower in California. *Compare* FLOPS. **2** [Acronym for Microprocessor with Interlocked Pipeline Stages] A RISC chip developed at Stanford, now *chiefly* used to MORPH images of Arnold Schwarzenegger..

MIS *n.* [Origin: acronymic, or from prefix *mis-*, badly, wrongly] **1** Manager Information Systems. **2** [Oxymoron] Military Intelligence Service. *See also* DPM; MAINFRAME.

misfiled books *n.* Also called **the librarian's nightmare.** See the following table.

Title	Filed Under
The Mouse That Roared	GUI
The Bourne Conspiracy	Shells, UNIX.
The Norton Book of Classical Literature	Early DOS/Symantec Utilities
The Book of J	APL dialects
Five Graves to Cairo	Microsoft OS History
The Chicago Manual of Style	Microsoft OS Tutorials
The Vanished Library	Microsoft NT
Equimultiplicity and Blowing Up	Balkan history
Motions of Coupled Bodies about a Fixed Point	Adult
String too short to be saved	C programming
OOPS! What to Do When Things Go Wrong	Object-oriented Technology
Le système des objets	OOP
CASE Closed	Software Engineering
The Shell and the Kernel: Renewals of Psychoanalysis	UNIX debugging
Of Mice and Men	GUI Ergonomics

mission-critical *adj.* **1** (Of a missile-guidance system) unlikely under normal circumstances, touch wood, to vaporize the wrong continent, but can't be too careful, old boy, what? **2** (Of a computer dating service) rarely matching a female serial killer with Rush Limbaugh. **3** (Of a Fourier Transform) avoiding Jack Crenshaw's algorithms. **4** (Of a payroll program) able to round-off FED_TAX_DUE in favor of the corporation. **5** (Of a San Juan Capistrano tourist) pissed off by the swallows' late return.

MIT *Abbrev.* **1** Milled In Transit. **2** Most Important Test.

⇒Also used for Massachusetts Institute of Technology, the cradle of AI and (almost) the grave of NEURAL networks.

mnemonic *n.*

⇒I had a wildly funny definition of this, but…oh, it may come back…

modal *adj.* (Of a WINDOWS control) gaining the focus of attention and marking the stark transition from a friendly, EVENT-DRIVEN, parallel, democratic regime to an in-your-interface, sequential *Faschismus. See also* DIALOG BOX.

⇒Fully endowed MULTIMEDIA platforms will signal the onset of modality by displaying video clips from Leni Riefenstahl's *Triumph des Willens.*

Modula, Modula-*N* *n.* A sequence of Pascalian improvements (with *N* monotonously increasing) ignored by Borland and, eventually, by Ould Nick himself. *See also* PASCAL MANUAL; WIRTH, NIKLAUS.

modular *adj.* [Origin: Scottish proverb, "Mony a modular mickle maks a muckle."] **1** *Hardware* Heterogeneous; likely to disintegrate; pertaining to a device in which repairs are effected by changing every module. **2** *Software* Broken down; relating to a program which has been arbitrarily partitioned as a hedge against programming staff redundancies. *Compare* MONOLITHIC.

module *n.* [Latin *modulus,* diminutive of *modus,* "a small measure."] **1** *Hardware* Any portion of a system that can fall off during shipment; any element in a system which can be replaced but not mended. **2** *Software* A fragment with good intentions. *See also* MODULAR.

⇒Was it not, however, Florence Nightingale who said "Intentions is not enough"? And was it not an equally wise but drunken old sailor, shangaied from Liverpool by the notorious boarding-house master Paddy West, who in the eponymous fore'bitter sang:

"But the best of intentions, they never get far,
"After forty-two days on the floor of a bar."

The crunch is marketo-linguistical, namely that *module* sounds and sells better than *fragment.*

"Wanna hot deal on Fragmenta-2?"
"No thanks."
"It's free, just pay for the media."
"Er, no thanks."
"OK, my final offer, it's free and the media's free."
"Is it shrinkwrapped?"
"Not necessarily."
"Is it copy-protected?"
"Not intentionally."
"How many floppies?"
"Eight."
"What make?"

"The best: genuinely generic 5 1/4 high density"

"No, really, thanks all the same."

"I'll throw in a debugger, profiler and personal time-management app."

"Hmm—what about run-time license fees?"

"We can discuss that later if you get something running..."

"Look, call me next month sometime willya, I'm in a meeting right now."

In majestic, authoritative Latin, even the diminutive *modulus* carries considerable clout, and euphony, to boot. But, to be old-fashioned, the correct plural of "modulus" is, *jure divino*, "moduli," and many potential users in Dead Language Departments will not touch Modula-n with a bargepole, for any n : CARDINAL;.

ETH may sneer at these lost-sales, but they should remember Peter Fellgett's warning in the 1960s that no half-decently educated person would dream of buying hi-fi equipment described as quadraphonic, an adjective that grotesquely mixes Latin and Greek roots. The hi-phi-listines (headed, in this context, presumably by Panasonic) turned down Peter's etymologically sound alternatives: tetraphonic or quadrasonic. Stereophones are still solidly with us, thanks to the homogeneity of the roots (both Greek), but the Quadraphonic craze came and went like a thief in the night. QED! Quad erat demonstrandum—the Quad is still in the showroom!

monadic *adj.* **1** (Of a DoD benchmark) leading to the one true ADA. **2** (Of a function or operator) exposed to a single ARGUMENT. *Compare* NILADIC; DYADIC.

⇒The professional pride of library builders has reduced the number of boring niladic and monadic functions. Self-respecting APIs call for an average of at least five parameters per call. The popularity of C is largely due to the *ellipsis* (...), used to indicate that the function allows an arbitrary number of arguments. If a function is unavoidably monadic, self-esteem can be restored by insisting that the data types of the argument and return value are both dauntingly arcane. C offers no barriers to such face-saving.

monist *n.* **1** *Metaphysics* One who sees all things as ineluctably interconnected through the agency of some apodictic cosmic principle. **2** *Computer science* One who accepts the inevitability of SIDE-EFFECTS. **3** *Chaos theory* One who sees the typhoon caused by the fluttering butterfly. **4** *Entomology* One who sees the fluttering of the butterfly caused by the typhoon.

⇒Not all monists agree as to the precise nature of reality's base groundhog or its ultimate knowability. Suffice it to say that every monistic eisegesis is subsumed by my own (patents pending), widely promoted via the Kuhnian bumper sticker: Shifts Happen.

monolithic *adj.* Pertaining to a class of devices rendered obsolete by the invention of modularity. *Compare* MODULAR.

⇒This demise is sad because when a monolithic unit broke down, the engineer simply changed the lith.

monopoly *n.* **1** *Physics* The dominant (*usu.* Northern) half of a magnet. **2** *Business* An enterprise about to be sued by its vanquished competitors.

⇒There is no answer to Screaming Lord Such's sublime cry: "Why is there only one Monopolies Commission?"

monotonic *adj.* **1** *Music* Composed by Andrew Lloyd Webber. **2** *Mathematics* If increasing then non-decreasing, else if decreasing then non-increasing. **3** *Logic* Used mainly in the negative form, non-monotonic: a form of logic where you are allowed to change your mind.

Monte Carlo Method [Origin: after Count Montgomery de Carlo, Italian gambler and random-number generator (1792–1838).] A method of jazzing up the action in certain statistical and number-analytic environments by setting up a book and inviting bets on the outcome of a computation.

⇒The Count's original system was stolen by Lord Kelvin in 1901, and subsequently refined by Fermi, Ulam, and von Neumann during World War II to solve the many problems faced by belligerent neutrons in a game of Russian roulette. The Monte Carlo method spread like the vogue in the postwar United States, attracting, inevitably, an underground of seedy odds fixers, numbers racketeers, and heavy, protectionist muscle dons. The method was banned outside Nevada, Atlantic City, and eponymous regions of Europe, but is now built into the PENTIUM FPU.

morph *n. & v. trans.* **1** *n.* *Linguistics* Back-formed from morpheme: a grammatical or syntactical unit with no meaningful substrings. **2** *v. trans.* *Graphics* To animate via a jerky succession of intermediate images.

⇒Cynics have suggested that both meanings can be traced back to morphine, "an addictive sedative."

mount *v. trans.* [Origin: "Suffer the little peripherals to come unto me" (St. Presper's *Sermon on the Mount*). To expose (an item of hardware) to the vagaries of the software *or* to elicit the response that the specified item is unready or nonexistent.

mouse *n. & v. intrans.* **1** *n.* "An animal which strews its path with fainting women" (Ambrose Bierce). **2** *Windows n.* A device which strews its path with fainting applications. **3** *GUI n.* The irredeemable nadir of DP culture, representing the victory of Disney over Descartes; a cumbersome, infantile, misnamed, monogonadic pointing device used by WIMPs to transmit positional data and button events to a sluggish, RAM-starved message queue. **4** *v. intrans.* To appear productive while idly playing with a mouse, as in "mousing around." *See also* CHORDING; CLICK; GUI; MOUSE BALL; MOUSE PAD.

⇒The critics who reject the verb *mouse* as modern technobabble are referred to 16th century citations in Webster III. That babbler W. Shakespeare wrote "...death...feasts, mousing the flesh of men," and the Restoration dramatist Wycherley (1641–1715) tells of "…naughty women…whom they toused and moused."

mouse ball *n.* A rubbery sphere that rotates chaotically as its owning MOUSE skates over and beyond the MOUSE PAD.

⇒Unlike the Old World Muridae and the New World Cricetidae, the pandemic *Mus graphicus* is Hitlerian in the testicular department:

"Hitler has only got one ball;
"Goering has two, but rather small;
"Himmler is somewhat simmler,
"But poor old Goebbels
"Has no balls at all!"

(Anon. World War II ballad)

mouse pad *n.* A sponge mat protecting a small area of your (real) desk top from MOUSE BALL skid marks. *See also* DESKTOP; DRAGGING; DRAG'N'DROP; DROP'N'DRAG.

⇒The mouse pad is yet another costly GUI ANCILLARY, spawning its own hi-tech industry comparable in hype and irrelevance to the athletic footwear market. Jaundiced users have found that they can save money by treating their desk surfaces with a mixture of sand and Guinness.

MOZ DONG *n.* CURTATION of *Don Giovanni* by Wolfgang Amadeus Mozart and Lorenzo da Ponte, as performed by the computerized billing ensemble of the International Preview Society, Great Neck (sic), N.Y. See the accompanying illustration.

⇒From Mozart to Edward Lear in one curtation, or as Fritz Spiegl once said, "From the sublime to the cor'blimey."

The International Preview Society

175 Community Drive, Great Neck, N.Y. 11025

PLEASE RETURN THIS PART OF INVOICE WITH YOUR PAYMENT

INVOICE FOR THIS SHIPMENT ONLY:

TOTAL
PLEASE PAY
THIS AMOUNT

INVOICE DATE	CATALOG NUMBER	ALBUM TITLE	PRICE	POSTAGE AND HANDLING	SALES TAX	
02/09/78	476002	MOZ DONG +	8.98	1.09		10.07

MS-DOS *pronounced* messy-doss\\ MICROSOFT Disk Operating System *See* OS; DOS.

MSR *n.* Multiple-Source Responsibility. A major feature of the SNA protocol in the OEM environment. Under earlier SSR (Singular Source Responsibility) implementations, the end user enjoyed but one, often receding, target for litigation. *See also* REVERSED CLASS ACTION.

MT *pronounced* empty\\ **1** Machine Translation. **2** MisTranslation. **3** The eponymous journal (b. 1954). *See also* KBMT; NLP.

MTBF *n.* [Mean Time Between Failure.] A design parameter set by the manufacturer, based on the known tolerance of the user and the targeted profitability of the service department. *Compare* MTTR.

⇒Manufacturers have long been aware that too high a value for the MTBF (measured, usually in decades or fractions of decades) leads to a stultifying sense of boredom and complacency on the part of the user. The thoughtful supplier ensures that the user is exposed to the excitement of real breakdowns at reasonable intervals. Lifeboat-drill simulations are no substitute for that first actual mid-payroll catastrophe. The initial panic and wringing of throats soon gives way to the familiar elation of the front-line soldier under fire: sinews are stiffened, blood is summoned. On-site unity is magically rewoven as an almost forgotten camaraderie emerges to weather the blitz. "For the DPM shall lie down with the analyst, yea, even the programmer shall lie down with the punchperson."—St. Presper's *Epistolary Update to the Pascalites,* Level II, release ix. The traditional supplier/user frictions also, surprisingly, disappear, since the user is now, as it were, a born-again nonuser, and by definition a prospect for *something.* Long-forgotten salespersons will arrive to offer condolences and quotations for extended service: contracts, add-ons, standby units, upgrades, and newly released working software. Eventually, the peaceful boredom of uptime will be restored, prisoners exchanged, scapegoats tried and executed, memorials erected to lost files, and a candle placed on the console to honor the Unknown Coder. Years later, unblooded recruits will hold their manhoods cheap for missing the Great Crash of '78.

MTTR *n.* [Mean Time To Repair. Origin: *mean* "poor or inferior in grade or quality" + *repair* "to take off": as "Let's repair to the bar."] The possible sum of the following series, for which there are no easy convergence tests:

MTTNF	Mean Time To Notice Fault
MTTRTF	Mean Time To React To Fault
MTTLFEPN	Mean Time To Locate Field Engineer's Phone Number
MTTCFE	Mean Time To Call Field Engineer
MTAFECB	Mean Time Awaiting Field Engineer's Call Back
MTTCSC	Mean Time To Check Service Contract
MTTCFES	Mean Time To Call Field Engineer's Superior
MTTLTFEDBS	Mean Time To Listen To FE's Disclaimer Blaming Software
MTTCA	Mean Time To Call Attorney
MTFFETA	Mean Time For Field Engineer To Arrive

MTTD	Mean Time To Diagnose
MTTLTFEDBS	Mean Time To Listen To FE's Disclaimer Blaming Software
MTOOSCM × M#	Mean Time Ordering/Obtaining Software/Changing Modules multiplied by number of Modules
MTTRB	Mean Time To ReBoot
MTTRRB	Mean Time To ReReBoot
goto MTTD	

⇒Some of the above labels, innocently though they fall on Indo-European ears, have offended Basque and Samoyed users. The Clean Up Naughty Tags committee of IFIP is frantically planning discussions for 1996. Watch this headword in future editions.

multi- *prefix* **1** Performing n functions or having n putative states, where $n \gtrless$ 2: as, MULTIPROCESSING (read $\gtrless$ as "not much greater than"). **2** Performing no individual aspect of: as, MULTITASKING.

⇒But the greatest of these is *multiparadigmatic.*

MULTICS *See* SARCONYM.

multijobbing *n.* Elementary moonlighting in which people modestly endeavor to widen their DP experience, in their free time, by assuming additional duties in disparate environments without boasting of their enterprise to their mainstream employer. *Compare* MULTITASKING.

⇒Typically, in the 1970s, the DPM at a UNIVAC 1100 site could usefully multijob by becoming a covert third-shift operator at a nearby IBM 370 installation, and vice versa.

multimedia *n.* *pronounced* mult-eye-meed-eye-yah.\ An application attacking all five senses of the user—sight, hearing, smell, taste, and touch—but especially, smell. *See also* CD-ROM; MEDIA.

multiplex *v. trans.* [From *multi-* "slightly more than one" + contraction of *perplex* "to bewilder."] To confuse (a device or person) by subdividing a problem and applying the pieces in parallel.

multiprocessing *n.* The simultaneous processing of not many more than two portions of the same program on different units, e.g., on the mainframe CPU and the programmer's hand-held calculator.

multitasking *n.* An advanced form of moonlighting in which the supplementary jobs are generated in a natural way from the multitasker's main duties. *Compare* MULTIJOBBING.

⇒Typically, a multitasking programmer will write packages during the day for his primary employer and spend the evenings correcting them at user sites as a freelance consultant.

MUM *n.* [Acronym for Multi-Use Mnemonics.] A meta-mnemonic methodology whereby *one* acronym references *all* the features of a particular system.

⇒Offsetting the advantage of having only one acronymic form to remember, there is, one is bound to admit, an attendant increase in ambiguity. In the case of the ETHELRED OS, for example, which vicariously assigns TPD to all aspects of the system, the MUM preamble points out that "the meaning of TPD is almost always clear from the context. The user should always use TPD (or the wild card ??? which defaults to TPD) and trust the OS to apply the best guess." Current ISO regulations forbid the use of the acronym MUM *within* a MUM schema, although some churches allow a lambda-MUM calculus whereby acronyms are distinguished from the names of the acronyms.

MUMPS [Acronym for MGH Utility Multi-Programming Systems where MGH is Massachusetts General Hospital.]

⇒The language has now been further abbreviated to M, leading its supporters to claim a 10-fold advantage over C. MUMPS also enjoys related acronyms: GERMS (Global Effective Retrieval from Mass Storage) and FEVER (Functions Evaluated by Very Effective Routines) "MUMPS means never having to say you're sorting" (Daniel P. B. Smith).

MUNIFICENT [Acronym for Most Unworthy Numerical Integrator Now Functioning In China; Evaluations Not Trustworthy.] Kai Lung Computers Inc. (1950)

⇒Ernest Bramah's delicate self-effacement may now be considered ethno-offensive.

Murphy's law of Programming [Formulated by H. Ledgard, 1975.] "The sooner you start coding your program, the longer it is going to take." *See also* TNHD at Sod's Law.

MUSE *n.* [Acronym for Most Unusual Shakespearian Engine.]

O! for a Muse of fire, that would ascend
The brightest heaven of invent-i-on.

(Shakespeare, *Henry V)*

⇒The author has proved elsewhere (*Computer Weekly,* March 1969), with Rowseian certainty, that Shakespeare spent his 10 "missing" years, 1582–1591, developing MUSE, the first data processing system. Let the following quotations suffice:

The AND.W instruction used to clear a word: "AND, in a WORD, but even now worth this, and now worth NOTHING" (*The Merchant of Venice,* act 1, scene 1).

The value of conditional statements: "...you may avoid that too with an IF...much virtue in an IF" (*As You Like It,* act 5, scene 4).

The frustrations of debugging: "Bloody instructions, which, being taught, return to plague the inventor." (*Macbeth,* act 1, scene 7)

Programming seems to have been a more dramatic occupation in Elizabethan times. For example, variables were boldly declaimed, not meekly declared. A typical variable declamation would have been:

"O Union Strong and Structure Noble,
"I give Thee *X,* both Int and Global!
"And oft-used, unsigned, whorish *Y,*
"Get Thee to a Register, hie!

Myers-Briggs Type Indicator *n. also* **MBTI.** A set of abbreviations built from letters indicating basic personality traits.

⇒Thus E = Extrovert; I = Introvert; S = Sensor; N = Intuitive (you might say that "I" was more intuitive but that would clash with Introvert!); T = Thinker; F = Feeler; J = Judger; P = Perceiver, and so on. Pairs and triplets of these provide higher-level types; for example, Rational is Intuitive/Thinking or NT (hardly a coincidence). (*See* Patricia Fernandi, *Software Development Magazine,* July 1994.)

my program *n.* A gem of algoristic precision, offering the most sublime balance between compact, efficient coding on the one hand, and fully commented legibility for posterity on the other. *Compare* LESS THAN; YOUR PROGRAM.

N

nack *n.* [Origin: corruption of *vulg. knackered* "castrated, rendered knacker-less, impotentated."] A signal indicating that all is lost. *Compare* ACK.

⇒Fritz Spiegl has traced *knacker* to the obscure Turkish military "jangling johnny," a coarse, step-keeping percussion instrument worn around the waist and a constant threat to the player's vital parts. It was revived by Jacquie and Bridie, with government-mandated safety features, as the Lagerphone in the 1950s Skiffle movement.

namespace *n.* The ever-shrinking region within which an identifier identifies. *See also* LEXICAL SCOPE; OVERLOADING.

⇒The newly reserved word **namespace** in C++ is widely welcomed as a mechanism that reduces the problems of name overloading, *esp.* the grotesque polysemies of **static** and the **int** that's known as i.

Namespaces of the rich and famous *See* NEWTON.

nametime *n.* The moment when the winner of the ACM TURING Award is announced.

⇒"Mr. Bachman…has received seventeen patents, the ACM Touring Award and is a distinguished fellow of the British Computer Society." (Brochure for the 1991 CASE WORLD Conference and Exposition). Joseph Kusmiss has noted that Bachman might one day qualify for the Noble Prize. To gain the Touring Award, one assumes that you must have darkly cruised the back streets of Manchester, or perhaps built up an impressive frequent-flyer mileage by following the non-stop ACM conference caravanserai—no real hardship if you have the time and funding. I know that I enjoyed the 1991 ACM CHI conference in New Orleans and even met participants who had no idea that the Jazz Festival was running concurrently.

NAN [Not A Number] A set of bits known as a number to René Magritte but rejected by the IEEE FLOATING-POINT Polizei.

nand *v. trans. & adj.* [Acronym for Not AND.] **1** *v. trans.* To unconjunct (several binary victims) in the Boolean environment. **2** *adj.* (Of a GATE) being able to nand. *See also* XAND.

nanosecond *n.* **1** 10^{-9} seconds, vividly illustrated by Grace Hopper's piece of wire. **2** The elapsed time between the traffic lights turning green and a honk from the car behind you. **3** The elapsed time between the signing of a Balkan cease-fire and the next shell falling on Sarajevo.

⇒Alas, Amazing Grace, inventor of COBOL and the first one, they say, to trap a real, literal bug, is no longer with us. On the bright side, though, she has moved on to the bug-free branch of Elysium reserved for computer pioneers. I met the imposing Admiral several times when she visited the pre-Burroughs, indeed the pre-Sperry, Univac offices in London. However, I never saw her famous "rope trick," whereby she demonstrated that light took 1 nanosecond to traverse the 0.3 meters of purloined telephone wire dramatically produced from her handbag.

nanotechnology *n.* A quark with an outboard motor.

Natural C *n.* An extension of ANSI-ISO C providing certain NL enhancements. *See also* C+–.

⇒An NLP prophet writes:

For all you UL (Unnatural Language) programmers, time is indeed flying like an arrow. But are you NL-ready? Soon you must burn all those boringly precise Backus-Naur Forms and face more subtle morphological challenges. As the Nayland Letter (Fall 1987), quoting from Tom Hopkins's "Official Guide to Success—When to Jump Ship," puts it, in a passage helpfully crisp, and yet at the same time blandly ineffective:[16] "When it's plain that your job is in jeopardy for causes beyond your control, don't wait....Open up your mind to new ideas. You need new job skills. Do what you have to do to get them."

Unfortunately, the reader is left a *tad* in the dark as to what skills to acquire and where and how to develop them. Let me fill this void! My own Standards Institute, STANSI, is launching Natural C as a bridge between UL and NL, a gentle easing into the new regime. Natural C can be considered as a loose superset of the popular ANSI C, so there is little to unlearn. The chief extensions are that there are 250,000 additional keywords, all identifiers have gender, number and case, while all operators have mood, tense, voice, and aspect. The new language will be initially defined with the traditional informality of K&R (1978). It is expected that the language will quickly evolve into mutually incompatible dialects, of which one or two will emerge as dominant, proving that we are well on the way to achieving all the benefits of real NL. For the moment, we propose three gender keywords: **masc, fem,** and **neut**; three numbers: **sing, plur,** and **nul** (matching the Basque indefinite); seven cases: **nom, voc, acc, gen, dat, abl,** and **abessive** (the latter under pressure from our Finnish colleagues). Space permits just a few tantalizing examples:

lvalues usually take the accusative or abessive, but objects being pointed at take the dative. Addressing a variable naturally calls for the vocative. Structure membership requires the genitive. Regular identifiers are declared with gender and nominative only; irregular identifiers may require the declaration of other parts of speech. Expressions on each side of an assignment must agree in gender and number using explicit casts where needed:

```
int masc sus;  // sus is nom [sus, se, sum, si, so,
                         so, sutta]
```

---

18. A figure of speech called the *expansive oxymoron* or *muggeridgism*, after the English writer and TV personality, Malcolm Muggeridge (1903–).

```
int masc *fo;   // fo is dative [fus, fe, fum, fi, fo,
                    fo, futta]
(acc) fo = &se; // se is voc of sus
float fem floa; // floa is nom [floa, floa, floam,
                    floae, floae, floa, floatta]
char neut chum; // chum is nom [chum, chum, chum, chi,
                    cho, cho, chutta]
sum = (masc) floa; // sum is masc. acc, floa is fem.
                    nom
sutta = 0; // zero assignments take the abessive
```

Note that = (assignment) is indicative, active, present whereas in

```
if (sus == (masc) floa) { . . . }
```

the == is subjunctive, with both expressions nominative. In my next release, I'll discuss unions taking the genitive plural and what to do if a masculine function returns a feminine pointer to an array of neuter pointers.

natural language *also* **NL.** *n.* **1** LISP without the parentheses. **2** An overly high-level language lacking algorithmic precision and similar artificial additives, and therefore beyond the clutches of most compilers. *See* ENGLISH; NLP.

natural language front-end *n.* A system that prompts for the input of an arbitrary string, *X,* and responds with the message "What do you mean by *X?*"

naturaller *adj.* (Of a computer language) gooder than natural; able to cope with the nuances of DP grammar.

NEBULA [Acronym for NEw BUsiness LAnguage.] Ferranti Ltd. (ca. 1960).

⇒Yet another language lorst'n'gorn, but worthy of mention since the acronym relates pleasantly to Ferranti's galaxy of mytho-astronomical hardware: Pegasus, Sirius, Mercury, Orion, and Atlas. There was also an Atlas variant at the Cambridge University Mathematical Laboratory, UK, called the Titan. It was never clear how "literally" one should take these classical allusions. For example, according to Thomas Bulfinch, all twelve Titans were consigned to the pit, level-0, by Jupiter's thunderbolts.

negation-as-failure *Also* **negation-by-failure** *n. Logic programming* **1** The reasonable assumption that *P* is false if one has failed to prove that *P* is true. **2** The unreasonable assumption that *P* is false if others have failed to prove that *P* is true. **3** *Drugs* The ineffectiveness of the "Just Say No!" campaign.

nerd *n.* [Origin obscure. *Possibly* Cockney rhyming slang: *turd.*] *Vulgar, rare fem.* **nerdette, nerderina, nerdotchka.** "One who considers INTERNET a dating service" (Guy Kawasaki). *Compare* KNERD.

nest *n. & v. trans.* [Origin: first used on English Electric KDF9 system, Kidsgrove, England (1962).] **1** *n.* A well-feathered STACK where data and instructions can be mother-henned and incubated for indefinite periods. **2** *v. trans.* To expose (loops, subroutines) to premature and/or unexpected CALLS. To each such exposure a positive integer, known as the *depth*, is assigned, indicating the approximate number of person-months needed to correct the situation.

⇒   New string vests for ALGOL compilers;
A night on the nest with KDF9ers;
Palimpsestuous programs with nebulous wings,
These are a few of my favorite things.

netwok *n.* [Origin: a large Oriental colander.] A NETWORK running under the CHINESE VMOS protocol, whence the anthem "You'll never WOK alone."

network *n. & v. trans.* [From *net* "reduced slightly from gross" + "work."] **1** *n.* The antisynergetic interconnection of noncompatible nodal systems divided by a common protocol. **2** *v. trans.* To reduce [net] the work rate (of a computing resource) by adding it to a network.

neural *adj.* (Of a NETWORK) nerve-wracking, *esp.* when successful for no known reason.

new *v. trans.* *C++* **1** To create (a dynamic heap object) using the global C++ operator **new** or a version of **new** as overridden by some distant idiot. **2** To bloat (an .EXE) by inadvertently pulling in 80K of exception-handling code.

⇒The verbing of those computer-language commands, functions, and operators that have a nounal, adjectival, or adverbial surface morphology is one of the many joys of DP usage, although (or because) it upsets some prescriptionists. It is certainly unambiguously compact to write "If you new foo, you must delete foo," or "foo having been newed, it must be deleted."

newton *n.* The force required to propel a hand-held message pad with an acceleration of 2.20462 meters per second per second.

⇒To achieve maximum rejection velocity, users should first remove the stylus and battery. Ironically, Apple's Newton PDA has a giveaway logo. It's one of those suddenthunk light-bulbs, but close inspection reveals a short-lived filament exposed to the air.

  Some think that the naming of products *for*[19] famous, often unrelated, persons has "gone far too far." Indeed, it is now hard to distinguish the entries in the Cambridge Biographical Dictionary from a ComputerShopper index. Thus Euclid, Plato, Beethoven, Newton, Mozart, da Vinci, Babbage, Turing, Cray [Shurely some mishtake here...Ed.], Pascal, Ada, and Einstein have been proudly subjected to PRODUCTIZATION. Also, meet ADB Inc's MATISSE, the OO database presumably full of *objets fauves*.

---

19. Brits name things *after* people, living or dead; the U.S. preference is naming *for*, suggesting that the namer is granting a favor to the named.

More offensive, hovering near blasphemy, are the theophanous products such as Iam and Tiger Software's modem called Shiva ("built to last!"). *See also* RAM; ONOMANCY.

Is it a coincidence that Sir Isaac Himself has endured some ridiculous Newton-bashing recently? His *Principia* has been degraded from "the greatest work of the human mind" (Lagrange) and "a monument to the profundity of genius" (Laplace) to "a mess, ugly, an obscure mess" (C. Truesdell) and "so poorly written, so painfully difficult to read, and so wrong in so much of its substance" (R. Weinstock). [*The College Mathematics Journal* 25, no. 3 (May 1994).]

NeXT 1 *n.* Steve Jobs's, ex-black box. **2** *interj.* The dismissive cry heard at theatrical auditions. *See also* JOBS' COMFORTERS; X, CURSE OF.

NIH *adj.* [*Abbrev.* Not Invented Here.] Pertaining to a much respected and widely practiced branch of design philosophy, unique among philosophical "schools" in that, by definition, the adherents refuse to talk to one another. Motivated by a fanatical hatred of plagiarism, NIH followers selflessly limit the domain of their responsibilities to their own humble artifacts. *See also* WHEEL.

niladic *adj.* (Of a function or operator) joyously free from any intruding ARGUMENTS. *Compare* MONADIC; DYADIC.

Nintendinitis *n.* Any disease blamed on excessive exposure to electronic games. *See also* VIDEO GAME.

⇒The term was coined by Dr. Richard Brasington of the Marshfield Clinic, Wisconsin, after treating a patient for "sore thumb" caused by five hours of nonstop button pushing. More seriously, there have been reports, blessedly rare, of gamesters who suffer epileptic seizures after prolonged joy-sticking. Players with a condition known as photosensitive epilepsy can experience such attacks when watching flickering patterns, exploding lights, rapid movements, and eviscerating Samurai on a video screen.

The number of video game titles is quite staggering and resists any simple analysis. Many are clearly cerebral and educational, such as *Chess* and *Where on Earth Is China?*, but the majority appear to be aimed at young males, with an alarming emphasis on blood'n'guts aggression and New Age occultism. Megan Duffin of the National Coalition on TV Violence estimates that 71 percent of video games include violence of one sort or another. Duffin also cites studies that show a measurable increase in aggressive behavior by children who play regularly.

Although some psychologists assert that kids can distinguish real violence from make-believe, most observers are disturbed by the amount of time and money expended by the young in the mindless zapping of alien sprites. Some coordination skills may be acquired but can we support the claim that playing Slime-Monster somehow cures children of computerphobia. Can *anything* prepare our youth for the horrors of PRINTF?

NL *See* NATURAL LANGUAGE.

NLP *n.* [Natural Language Processing] *No parseran!*, "They shall not parse!" (Barricade battle-cry of the Dreyfus Brigade). *See also* AI; ENGLISH; KBMT; MT; WEAVER FISH.

⇒The optimism of the 1950s was that the syntactical-semantic gulf could be bridged by extracting lexemes and "looking them up" in a dictionary file. Alas, even when the dictionary was replaced by an increasingly complex thesaurus, the dream flickered and died with Bar-Hillel's boxed pens and penned boxes. There was much talk about automatically tagging words as *noun, verb*, et al., the MT version of "belling-the-cat." It assumed that NL words carried predeclared data types. The polysemous truth is that even the ubiquitous street-walking, hill-climbing "Bill" can suddenly show up as a verb, impersonal noun (or, horror, as a second William appearing in the story) leading to the big, intractable crux known as "contextual disambiguation." The equally naive classification of agents and actions as "human," "inanimate," etc., hits the same brick wall. Compare Suereth's rule[20] "Only humans can drive" with "I drove the car; the car drove me mad."

Nobel Prize Winners in Computer Science *n. See* NULL SET.

⇒The nearest candidate for this honor was Sir Henry Ninebit-Byte (1912–1978), inventor of very wide paper tape, who was knighted in 1974 for "his invaluable services to the punch-card industry." His computerized Nobel Prize selection package was much admired until his own name occurred in five different categories during the 1977 dry run. Although he received the 1978 British Computer Society Silicon Medal for devious software, the Nobel Prize scandal proved fatal, and he succumbed to a massive attack of disgrace.

noise *n.* **1** *Marketing* The raucous celebration of an order, aimed at swamping all signals from the design and manufacturing departments. **2** *Information theory* Illegible messages from Zatetic Venusians and Middle Earthers who have not yet mastered TCP/IP.[21] **3** *Electronics* The thousand shades of grass that flesh is HAIR to.

non- *prefix.* A hint that the following attribute or device is not available for immediate delivery, but that a sufficiently firm letter of intent might well secure a less dogmatic evaluation leading to a favored position in the waiting list. *Compare* NOT-; UN-.

NOP *n.* *pronounced* nop *or* no op\ *Also called* **NOOP** or **NO-OP.** ASSEMBLY language mnemonic for "no operation." A uniquely benign, do-nothing instruction giving the CPU a brief, one-cycle respite.

---

20. Russell Suereth, "A Natural Language Processor," *C User's Journal,* April 1993.
21. Likewise, some claim that cosmic rays are failed experiments in beaming down visitors from outer space.

⇒To be uncharacteristically pedantic, NOP *does* perform an operation: the PC (program counter) is incremented to the next instruction. NOP typically occupies a word in the object code, and can therefore be used to delete an instruction *in situ*, rather like punching all holes in a paper tape. Aliter, assembly language Nostradami can preplant NOPs for subsequent patching.

nor *v. trans. & adj.* [Acronym for Not OR.] **1** *v. trans.* To undisjunct (several binary victims) in the Boolean environment. **2** *adj.* (Of a GATE) being able to nor.

not- *prefix.* The positive, unswerving negation of the ensuing concept. *Compare* NON-; UN-. *See also* HOLE.

⇒Babbage's memory boards relied on timber crosscuts with granular singularities known as *knot-holes*. Subsequent confusion when this technique was transferred to slices of silicon led to the corruption *not-holes*.

noun *adj.* (*esp.* DP usage) any adjective. *See also* ADJECTIVE; NOUNS, MARCH OF.

nouns, march of *n.* A string generated by the BNF production <noun>: :<noun><noun> as in "group decision support system idea generation tool" and "software architecture engineering process domain analysis." *See also* ADJECTIVE.

NT *n.* **1** *Microsoft* New Technology. **2** *Competing religion* New Testament. **3** *Heresy* Not There (attributed to Scott McNealy, Sun Microsystems). **4** MYERS-BRIGGS *Type Indicator* Rational (Intuitive Thinker).

null

⇒

nulls *n.* A null by another name…

⇒Mike Rejsa claims that the Inuit have many names for snow,[22] yet "here in Minneapolis we know about snow, but that's all we call it. Why then, do I find myself saying " ", ' ', 0, 0L, '\0', NULL, (int *)0, 0 × 00, 0 × 0000, FALSE, etc.? Methinks this is much ado about nothing…"

null set *n. & adj.* **1** The (unique) set, written Ø, with no members but with the Zen power to generate endless koans, including the whole of mathematics. **2** *adj.* (Of a joke) *also called* **Empty array**. *Largely* propagated by Edward M. CHERLIN, revered publisher of *APL News*.

⇒Following certain formal schema, the set Ø can be identified with zero. Next, the set {Ø}, containing only the null set, and, of course, itself far from null, can be taken as a

---

22. This and other Whorfian fibs are exposed in Steven Pinker, *The Language Instinct* (Morrow, 1994).

template for the number 1. One [sic] can then progress to {∅, {∅}} for 2, and so on, to develop the so-called *natural* numbers and rule the world.

The provable equivalence of all null sets arrestingly implies that the set of all Spanish songs lacking the word *corazón* is indistinguishable from the set of all software packages that have never won a DP magazine Best Buy Award. Other notably empty sets pleading *nullo contendere* include [sic] punctual Windows applications and CEO's who resign in order not to pursue personal interests.

The non-empty set of null-set jokes is partly revealed by the following examples:

1. Q. Why is a mad dog like a tin of condensed milk?
   A. Neither can ride a bike.

2. A person goes into a Moscow store:
   "I hear you have no bread…"
   "Not so, I'm the butcher…we have no meat; you want the baker next door; he's the one with no bread."

3. "I would like a pie without the raspberries…"
   "Sorry, today we only have it without the strawberries…"

4. Three condemned prisoners discussing their fate:
   A: "I'm here for supporting Blavatsky…"
   B: "Funny…I was arrested for *opposing* Blavatsky…"
   C: "I'm Blavatsky…"

5. A: "Where are going?"
   B: "Kraków."
   A: "My God, what a liar you are! You wanted me to think you were going to Łódź, and you really *are* going to Kraków!"

6. The San Francisco Muni mandates a refund if your scheduled bus is more than 15 minutes late. However, no refund is available if the bus fails to arrive at all.

nullable *adj.* (Of a relational database field) lacking the not-nullable flag.

⇒All the deep, unsolvable problems of ethics, logic, epistemology, and linguistics converge on their bastard hybrid: relational database methodology. Experts and dabblers in this so-called discipline (distinguishable chiefly by how they pronounce SQL) are forever locked in non-normalizable forms of combat long banned by the Geneva Convention. Indeed, RDB disputation seems to have moved from *crise* to *scandale*.[23] One of the problems is how best to stretch Boolean two-valued logic to cover real-world categories such as "applicable but not yet known," "known but inapplicable," "applicable but unknowable," and "wait 'til Codd responds next month."

---

23. See, for example, David C. McGoveran, "Nothing from Nothing," *Database Programming & Design,* December 1993. The switch to French is for deliciously dramatic effect. The long final syllable of *scandale* is especially scandalous.

null string *n.* " " *See also* MINISTRING; STRINGENT.

⇒ *King Lear* (Act 1, scene 1):

Cordelia " ", my lord.
Lear " "!
Cordelia " ".
Lear " " will come of " ": Speak again.

number cruncher *n.* **1** A heavy device for testing the compressibility of numbers. The traditional method, pioneered by Control Data Corporation, is to subject a sequence of numbers to progressively denser FORTRAN programs until all 60 bits squeak. The more recent divide-and-conquer approach, by Thinking Machines and others, puts the squeeze on a whole set of numbers simultaneously. *See also* MASSIVELY PARALLEL.

numerolatry *n.* The unhealthy obsession with numbers and numerical precision; *esp.* the use of computers in the social sciences. *See also* INCH WORM; -MANCY.

numerology *n.* The recreational branch of computer science.

⇒Among the many deep CS theorems in the numerological environment, we cite:

1. The CDC 7600 is four times as powerful as the ICL 1900.

2. The computer in the film *2001* was an IBM degrade:

(IBM 111 = HAL)

3. The English Electric LEO3 was an upgrade of the KDN2:

(KDN2 + 111 = LEO3)

4. Donald Knuth's renowned MIX was "the world's first polyunsaturated computer. Like most machines, it has an identifying number—the 1009. This number was found by taking 16 actual computers that are very similar to MIX and on which MIX can be easily simulated, and then averaging their numbers with equal weight:

$\lfloor (360 + 650 + 709 + 7070 + U3 + SS80 + 1107 + 1604 + G20 + B220 + S2000 + 920 + 601 + H800 + PDP4 + II)/16 \rfloor = 1009$

The same number may also be obtained in a simpler way by taking Roman numerals" (Donald E. Knuth, *The Art of Computer Programming, Fundamental Algorithms*, vol. 1 [Reading, Mass.: Addison-Wesley, 1968]).

5. The Sperry Univac series 90 furnishes IBM series 360 performance with a 75 percent cost reduction.

6. The language M is ten-times more powerful (or verbose?) than C. *See* MUMPS.

O

object *n. & adj. & v. & whatever* **1** *n. Also called* **object code**. [Latin *obiectatio* "a reproach."] A formerly compacted but now expanded version of the SOURCE CODE grudgingly produced by an ASSEMBLER or COMPILER. **2** *n.* [Latin *obicere, obiectum* "to throw in the way of."] *OO* More or less anything, *usu.* much less; an essential but ill-defined marketing rubric. **3** *n.* *C++* A CLASS instance, *usu.* scope-ephemeral but sometimes PERSISTENCIZED by a missing **delete**. **4** *n. Pascal* The Pascal *object type*, often shortened to *object*, is the C++ equivalent of *class*, whence the C++ *object*, to avoid confusion, is the Pascal *object instance*. **5** *adj.* (Of a technology) relating to any product with the word "object" in its title; widely believed to be capable of speeding development as each deadline is exceeded; according REUSABILITY a higher priority than USABILITY. **6** *adj.* (Of a design METHODOLOGY) sensibly eschewing abstract notions of fiscal-state-transitions in favor of meeting the payroll. *More at* OBJECT WORSHIP; OO.

⇒Object code is sometimes correctly referred to as "binary," but it is considered impolite to call it "machine code" or "machine language" without first checking with the machine. Buyers should also be aware of the possible ambiguity when offered a cheap "price-no-object" compiler. *Compare* the "rust-free" car advert: $3,000 for the car...the rust is free.

Regarding the ubiquitous OO objects, including those that are creeping up closer than your convex rear-view mirror might indicate, the current marketing fashions and wavering terminology defy satirical emblandishment.

object worship *n.* The OO-marketing landslide from reification to deification. *See also* C++; CLASS; OBJECT.

Objective-C *n. Also derog.* **Objectionable-C.** A C-swept hybrid combining the worst features of C++ and SMALLTALK. *More at* TNHD.

obsolescence *n.* A system state determined exclusively by the manufacturer's MARKETING department.

⇒Users are strongly advised not to attempt this diagnosis unaided. Obsolescence depends on many factors known only to the sales force—the cost prices and margins on each model, whether all the available options have been added to meet the original performance targets, the degree to which the user is locked in, and so on. In fact, the user can be assured that the supplier *and* the supplier's competitors will be quick to spot the first symptoms and will lose no time in bringing the matter to the DPM's attention. The news of impending obsolescence induces a menopausal shock in some users, but there is really no rational basis for panic. Studies have shown that the onset of obsolescence invariably coincides with the launching of a new and better system. The angst of the user is soon swept away by the excitement of conversion and the challenge of incompatibility.

OCR *n.* [Optical Character Recognition.] A method for misreading documents directly into a system without having to miskey the data first.

OCR A *n.* [So named because every character looks like an A.] A typeface designed to be illegible to humans and unreadable by OCR scanners.

OCR B. *n.* An improvement on OCR A whereby human legibility is improved at the expense of OCR scanner performance. *Compare* E13B.

oedipos complex *n.* [Blend of *Oedipus* + *OS* "operating system."] The fears developed during the first 3 to 6 years' exposure to a domineering operating system, especially by the male user, that his algorithmic potency is threatened by arbitrary job truncation. *See also* OSOPHOBIA.

OEM *n.* **1** [Obscure Equipment Methodology, or *rare* Original Equipment Manufacturer.] **2** *Alt. spelling* **ÖM.** A Hindu mantra in German-speaking countries (Peter Kirwin).

⇒The computer manufacturer has, from the genesis of the trade in the 1950s, faced three major hazards: making computers, selling them, and effecting installation. The OEM approach, evolved gradually during the natural struggle to reduce costs and responsibilities, has virtually eliminated all three problems. Manufacturers no longer make computers, but rather assemble each other's MODULES. The modules are in their turn produced by obscure specialist companies from submodules provided by obscurer suppliers, and so on ad nauseam, through an infinitely parasitic hierarchy. Likewise, the selling and installing chores have been increasingly delegated to systems houses, software houses, and houses of mixed repute; consultants, both freelance and respectable; and a variety of mail-order medicine persons, itinerant street vendors, and friendly neighborhood haberdashers. Knitting this fine fly-by-night web together, and tempting the user into the many-mansioned parlor of automation, is SNA (Scapegoat Network Architecture). In the likely event of trouble, the end user simply removes the five superimposed decals from each offending component, providing at least 20 defendants for a dramatic REVERSED CLASS ACTION.

OEM cogs *n.* The main reason Charles Babbage's Analytical Engine (ca. 1834) failed to perform to specification, and why his "mill did grind exceedingly slow."

office use only *n.* A blank area left on TURNAROUND documents for subsequent OCR encoding should the LUDDITES fail to strike first.

⇒There are two schools of thought on how best to discourage the great unwashed public from defacing turnaround documents. The total failure of simple "Do not use this space" warnings has persuaded some form designers to omit all such legends, while others have elected to provide a variety of "decoy" boxes with caveats calculated to invite graffiti from the most staid recipient, but craftily protecting the real sacrosanct areas. The growing complexity of actual and pseudo admonishments is illustrated by the following example:

O C R area !!!!

We URGE you, PLEASE, not to DEFACE this space in any way!!!

H O N E S T L Y this **REALLY** is I M P O R T A N T.

If you feel you must record telephone numbers, shopping lists or simply doodle in this virgin area, PLEASE use only a soft pencil (2B or less) avoiding all the characters listed overleaf. Whatever you do, PLEASE avoid the symbol ■ OR ANYTHING REMOTELY LIKE IT. You've no idea the chaos this one causes. Look, we know you hate computers. D'you think *we* like them? We're just as much locked into the system as you are. So give us a break, man. THANKS FOR YOUR COOPERATION.

Ogam *n. also called* **Ogham.** *pronounced* oom.\ ["The 'g' is silent unlike the 'p' in 'bucket'" (Dominic Behan).] An early (800 B.C.E.) Celtic version of the ASCII character set, designed for epigraphic efficiency but often observed on CRT displays. See the illustration on p. 153.

OMG [Object Management Group.] A body formed, in vain, to control the tsunami of unruly OBJECTS.

one-line patch *n.* [From D. C. Moulton, Ilford, Essex, England.] A KLUDGE so minimal that no testing is necessary. Corrected by a further one-line PATCH. *See* RECURSIVE.

online *adj.* **1** (Of a peripheral) denoting the rare, sublime, transient state of being connected to a superior system. **2** (Of a user) relating to the period during which unexpected credit-card charges accrue.

onomancy *n.* Divining FUNCTION from nomenclature. *See also* -MANCY; NAMESPACE; NEWTON; TERMINOLOGY.

⇒Apart from the neological excesses of DP MARKETING, the onomancer is faced with interpreting the volatile onomasticon of reused tokens. Thus, it is not immediately obvious that Einstein and da Vinci are mundane e-mail packages, that MATISSE is an OO database, that the Packard-Bell Force 2386 uses a 486 microprocessor, or that Compel is an *interactive* software package. At the other end of termimological inex-

Letter	Europe		North America				Ogam Tract No. 3	
	Ireland Ogam Tract No. 16	Portugal, Cachão da Rapa	Vermont	Connecticut, Massachusetts, New Hampshire	Inwood, New York	Oklahoma, Texas, Arkansas, the Caribbean	Ireland	Monhegan, Maine
H		[Pontotoc, Oklahoma, also]						
D								
T								
C			Uses G					
Q								
B								
L								
F/V								
S								
Ñ			Uses Ñ					
M								
G								
Ñ								(?)
Z			Lacking					
R			Uses L					
Ia, Ea								
W, Ui			?			[or]		

Early Ogam alphabets of Europe and North America. The oldest styles employ only consonants, and appear to date from around 800 B.C. onward. The developed Irish style, with vowels and the whole range of consonants, appears only in monuments believed to postdate the time of Christ.

actitude, many users are tricked into believing that Microsoft's ACCESS provides a ready *entrée* to databases, and that WordPerfect is word-perfect.

OO [Object Orienteering] \initially *pronounced* oo! as in scooby-dooby-doo, but now *chiefly* oh-oh as in oh-shit!\ *n.* The art (*rare* sport; science) of navigating a class hierarchy armed only with a cheap compass and a small bag of nuts. *See also* BROWSE; ENCAPSULATION; POLYMORPHISM; INHERITANCE.

⇒The roots of practical, computer-scientific OO can be traced back to Simula-67. Earlier philosophical inspirations come from Peirce, the father of SEMIOTICS:

"And he [Peirce] believed that objects are not substances-in-themselves, but are constituted entirely by the laws which describe their behavior under all possible conditions: this is the basis of his pragmatism." (Louis Menand's review of Joseph Brant's *Charles Sanders Peirce: A Life* [Indiana University Press] in the *New York Review of Books*).

OOAL [Object-Oriented Assembly Language.] A shock mock-proposal intended to stem by ridicule the threatened flood of OO extensions to BASIC, COBOL, APL, Fortran, Jovial, Algol60, POP-2, and all known legacy languages.

⇒The attempt failed miserably. We now have ENIAC++, MercuryAutoCodeWithClasses, and object-enhanced versions of Hartree's Differential Analyzer.

OOPS *n. Either* Acronym for Object-Oriented Programming System *or* (onomatopoeia) cry of annoyance following a mishap. *Usu.* both.

open *adj. & v. trans.* **1** *adj.* (Of a file) exposed, at risk. **2** *adj.* (Of a loop) endless; endowed with a loophole. **3** *adj.* (Of an OS, PROTOCOL, API, file-format, or passing fancy) non-proprietary; freely disclosed except to stubborn rivals. **4** *v. trans.* To render (a file) vulnerable to subsequent reads, writes, and kills; to invoke the message "file does not exist" or "file already open."

⇒The spate of failed openings (Open Look, Open Desktop, X Open, ODAPI, OSF, ODBC, Open City, Open Season, Open Sesame, Open Warfare, Open Book, Open Weekdays Only, Open Drain, Open Parenthesis, Open Sore, Open-Toed Teeth, Open Other End,[24] and Open in the Name of the Law) comes as no surprise to free-market economists and students of Old English. The former know that competitors, by definition, can never freely reveal their trade secrets. The latter know that the first recorded open standard, reported in Aelric's Glossary (ca. 1000 CE), had collapsed by 1663: "As useless as open-arses gathered green" (Thomas Killegrew's *The parson's wedding*).

operating system *n.* That part of the system that inhibits operation. *Also called* OS (from the clothing industry's abbreviation for *outsize*).

⇒In metacomputer science, great care is needed to distinguish: (1) the OS qua OS, (2) the name of the OS, viz., < OS >, (3) what we call the name of the OS, viz., "< OS >," (4) what the OS calls itself, viz., {"< OS >"}, and (5) what the OS calls when it calls itself, viz., "<{"< OS >"}>".

operator *n.* [Origin doubtful: possibly Italian *opera* "a long concatenation of overdramatic, far-fetched, hysterical, and contradictory incidents," or, less plausible: Latin *opus* "work."] The lowest, and least dispensible (*archaic* "dispensable") link in the system's pecking order; the plankton in the DP food chain. *See* PRECEDENCE.

⇒Spotters' Club hint: Look out for the ill-clad person reading the sports pages and flicking cigarette ash in the card-reader hopper.

operators manual *n.* [IBM usage] A manual for the operator.

---

24. Slanderous rumor has it that this message is stamped on the base of all Guinness bottles sold in Glasgow.

⇒The traditional absence of the apostrophe (operator's or operators') indicates that the manual remains the property of IBM.

optimizer *n.* A compiler with three switches for controlling its object code output: big, slow, and both. *Compare* PESSIMIZING COMPILER.

OR Overloaded *abbrev.* Operation Rescue; Organized Religion; Own Recognizance; Operating Room; Oregon; Owners Risk; Operations Research. *Also* Boolean operator; English conjunction. *Warning* Often resists contextual disambiguation.

or *v. trans. & adj.* [Origin: English conj. *or* ≈ "alternative."] **1** *v. trans.* To disjunct (several binary victims) in the Boolean environment. **2** *adj.* (Of a GATE) being able to or. *Compare* AND; NAND; NOR; XAND.

ORB [Object Request Broker.] "ORB is an honest broker—none more honest, none more broke" (Dr. Joe Miller). *See also* OMG.

OS *n. & adj.* *pronounced* oh-ess *or* oz.\ Possible abbreviation for OutSize or OPERATING SYSTEM, *or* from French *os* "bone," as, "J'ai un os à gratter avec vous."

OS/2 *n.* [™IBM] **1** *Formally* One half of an OS. **2** *Informally* An OS that grabs 50 percent of your hard-disk, memory, and intellectual resources. *See also* WARP.

⇒One of the most reassuring aspects of personal computing in the mid 1990s is that you can run DOS under Windows under OS/2 under UNIX under $2,000.

OSI *Abbrevs.* for Open Systems Interconnection; Outside Special Interests. *Warning* Not necessarily an overloading.

osophobia *n. DP psychiatry* The morbid fear of OPERATING SYSTEMS.

⇒A doctor writes: "Except in extreme cases, this condition should not give rise to undue concern or bills exceeding $5000. There can be few normal persons who have not, at one time or another, recoiled in horror when confronted with a 50 MB OS. I know I have. DP Freudians have created their usual catchdollar theories to exploit the gullible osophobic. They equate the monitor with some tyrannical father figure bent on castrating both program and programmer, and bestow grotesque phallic tokens on such innocent, mundane concepts as "input," "output," "RAM," "nesting," "multiple job streams," and "first-in-last-out." The ultimate folly in this verbose quackery was a recent paper presented at a Jungian Institute seminar on "Spooling Dysfunctions and the OEDIPOS COMPLEX," which attempted to correlate instances of golf-ball printer failures with a symbolic (sic) increase in the male operator's anxiety state. As I indicated earlier, there are, alas, extreme sufferers beyond the pale and budget of medical science. We take them away from Print Manager as soon as we can, although little remains for them but a few twilight years in the Thumps Memorial Home for the Recursively Bemused." *See also* ETHELRED OS.

oubliette *n.* (Origin: A medieval escape-proof, warden-free dungeon.) A CACHE system with Alzheimer's Disease.

outsourced *adj.* **1** (Of a programmer) burnt out; unable to code. **2** (Of a project) delegated to expensive scapegoats. *See* TURNKEY. *Compare* IN-HOUSE.

overcast *adj.* [Origin: possibly meteorological.] Related to a depressingly nervous obsession with type-casting, *esp.* in Windows applications. *See also* CAST.

```
⇒ HPEN handle1, handle2;
   . . .
   if( HPEN(handle2) == HPEN(handle1) ) { . . . }
```

overflow *n. & v. trans.* **1** *n.* A binary spillage. **2** *v. trans.* To exceed the capacity (of a register, file, listener) in order to test the overflow indicator. **3** *v. trans.* To produce more FLOWCHARTs than the site walls can support. *See also* BIT BUCKET.

> ⇒   "...Enough! no more:
> "Your bits are dripping on the floor."
>
> *(The Duchess of Malloc)*

overheads *n.pl.* **1** *Conversation* Metaremarks, richly laced with metajargon, helpfully aimed at deflating, eviscerating, decapitating, and pronouncing dead any listeners reluctant to admit their obvious intellectual and experiential inferiority. "This may be a little over your heads, but..." **2** The expenses incurred in producing the eponymous visual aids. **3** *DP accounting* For a given installed and running system: the total cost of manufacturing, labor, components, delivery, software support, service during the guarantee period, documentation, initial supplies (including the unbilled ribbon accidentally delivered with the line printer), sales commissions and expenses, and bribes.

overloading *n.* **1** *Semantics* Ganging up on a poor signifier until it collapses from excessive signification. **2** *OOP* Assigning unlikely meanings to well-known operators. Ideally, for maximum confusion, the overloading definitions should be hidden. *See also* TLA; NAMESPACE.

oxymoron *n.* The concatenation of *m* strings in an *n*-valued logic ($1 <= m <= n$) where no two strings have the same true value.

⇒In the 2-valued logic endured by most readers (*see* BINARY), the oxymoron is a daily fact of life:

Table of Oxymorons

operating system

PROG.RUN

delivery date

job satisfaction

last bug

final version

enhanced functionality

user friendly

supporting documentation

comprehensive package

management function

military intelligence

long-term benefit

backup copy

systems analysis

structured environment

benchmark results

run time

seamless integration

salesforce responsibility

SQL Link

P

package switching *n.* **1** The conversion, following threats of litigation, from one set of pirated programs to another. **2** A cryptogrammic technique that, rather than recoding characters in a message, achieves mystification by directing arbitrary partitions of the message to random locations. *See also* EPSS; PIRACY.

paging *n.* **1** *Communications* A panic call for the person who has just left the site and is rushing to reach the nearest bar beyond the radius of the paging system. **2** *Software* A VIRTUAL memory management system pioneered on the Ferranti Atlas computer (1958) and rediscovered by IBM in 1976 in which the system flicks or browses through numbered sections of mass storage (known as pages) until one catches its fancy. As with Mr. Caxton's invention, there is a high probability of accessing a few well-worn pages (known as the "dirty bits").

⇒Irish Business Machines pioneered a hardware page location method (1980) called MBT (Memory Board Tagging) whereby the corners of the memory boards are bent over to speed a second access.

Le livre s'ouvre seul au feuillet souvent lu.

(E. Rostand, *L'Aiglon*)

pairs *n. See* TWINS.

palindromization *n.* **1** *Syntax* The reversal of keywords to form block delimiters. **2** *Standards* The formation of the ISO OSI committee. *See also* AIBOHPHOBIA; IFF.

⇒Thus **if** statements can be terminated with **fi** more prettily and economically than with **endif**. Similarly, we meet pairs such as **case-esac**, **for-rof**, and **while-elihw**. However **end** scores over **nigeb** for obvious reasons.

paper low *n.* A lamp that lights to indicate that your output is now appearing on the PLATEN.

paradigm *n.* [Greek *paradeigma* "pattern, example."] **1** *New Testament* A warning to others: "Then Joseph her husband, being a just man, and not willing to make her a public example [paradigm], was minded to put her away privily" (Matthew 1:19 KJV). **2** Contrived acronym for PARAllel DIstributed Global Memory. **3** A well-known cake mix. **4** *Grammar* Exemplary declension or conjugation, as in "zenbiltzan, zenbilkidazan, zenbilkiozan, zenbilkiguzan, zenbilkiezan." **5** *Kuhnian* (After Thomas S. Kuhn [1922–], philosopher and historian of science) a dominant, orthodox scientific model, fighting to maintain credibility and funding. **6** *DP* A PHATICISM. *See also* KUHN BLUE BOOK; MONIST; PUN MORATORIUM.

⇒Since Kuhn's noble metaparadigmatic theory of Copernican, Newtonian, Einsteinian, and Quantum mechanical models (introduced in *The Structure of Scientific Revolutions,* 1962), "paradigm" has, alas, fallen among thieves. Thus, a PC user writes:

> "Coaxed by the magazines, I resolved to shift from the 386 to the 486 paradigm. My local computer boutique proved more than anxious to help. I could not believe my luck: they upgraded my system for $1500 and threw in the new paradigm at no extra charge. I'm still stuck with the old 4 MB-RAM and 2400-baud modem paradigms, but who knows when that itch to shift will strike again..."

The current record for paradigmatic density (measured in *swaines* to honor the Dr. Dobbs's columnist) belongs to Gerry Reid of IBM with 127 occurrences of "paradigm" in a 13-page booklet boldly titled "Changing Perceptions: The Power of Paradigms."

My long-fought crusade against overparadigmizationing suffered an apparent setback when my *Mastering Turbo C* (Sybex, 1988) appeared in a (modern) Greek translation. The front cover yelled *epilegmena paradeigmata* and several readers emailed their tongue-in-cheek "tut-tuts." Of course, the Greeks, still use "paradigm" in its Homeric, pre-Kuhnian sense. *Epilegmena paradeigmata* simply means "excellent (code) examples."

I am not alone in urging paradigmatic caution. Sovietologist Robert Conquest (Stanford University) is a founder member of the Society for the Abolition of Models, Methodologies, Paradigms, and Parameters. He says, "All those who prefer the study of complex realities to the simpler task of reifying formula or fantasy, please sign on."

paradigm shift *n. DP Usage* Any change in any direction. *See* PARADIGM.

⇒Thus, Ella Fitzgerald's old torch song "There'll Be Some Changes Made":

> "There'll be a change in the weather, a change in the sea;
> "From now on, there'll be a change in me;
> "I'll change my way of walkin', my talk and my name;
> "Nothin' about me will be quite the same;
> ...
>
> "O Lawd, there'll be some changes made today;
> "There'll be some changes made!"

is now topically rendered as:

> "There'll be a meteorological paradigm shift;
> "Similarly, oceanographic and personal paradigm shifts;
> "As of this memo, please note that paradigms are also to be shifted in the ambulatory, sociolinguistic, and onomastic environments;

"Indeed, the class of paradigmatically unshifted objects will soon be empty;
…

"O Lawd, there'll be some paradigms shifted today! Hey, hey!
"There'll be some paradigm shifts! Yeah!"

Rumor suggests that the Motorola 68090 will provide the following instructions:

LSPR Dm,#n   Logical Shift Paradigm Right—shift the paradigm in register Dm n places to the right.

LSPR Dm,Dn   Logical Shift Paradigm Right—shift the paradigm in register Dm to the right by the number of places given in register Dn (modulo a number I cannot reveal!)

LSPL   Logical Shift Paradigm Left—operands as above

There are also four Arithmetical variants, **ASPR**, and so on. These shifts, and the associated rotates, **ROPR, ROPXR**, etc., work in the obvious manner, that is to say, subject to the usual quirks that make assembly languages so much fun. For example, paradigms can only be shifted left an odd number of places on even days, and (to maintain orthogonality) vice versa. Careless shifting may lose significant bits of your paradigm, and in the worst (best) case you could lose your paradigm completely. Depending on the size and direction of the paradigm shift, the MC68090 can be made a CISC, MISC, or RISC processor.

parallel *n. & adj.* **1** *n.* An unheeded warning; a disaster occurring elsewhere but discounted by an unwise appeal to Euclid's fifth postulate; the woes of others that remain at a constant distance, however prolonged. **2** *adj.* Being or pertaining to everything happening at once. "When sorrows come, they come not single spies, but in battalions" (*Hamlet*). *See also* MASSIVELY PARALLEL; *Compare* SERIAL.

parentheses *n. pl.* (A (pair (of symbols (referred to as (open) and (closed)))) each) of which) has the (hold (down) ((to) (repeat) option) on a ((LISP)-(oriented) keyboard)).

parenthesis *n. Archaic* singular of PARENTHESES.

⇒In most respectable languages, a singular, unmatched parenthesis is syntactically inadmissible. Single "smart" brackets are now available that automatically generate matching parentheses of the desired modality.

parity *n. & adj.* [From *parrot* "to repeat without understanding."] **1** *n.* A state of bankruptcy achieved by installing the same computer system as your nearest competitor's. **2** *adj.* (Of a check) able to detect an odd number of bit mutilations but oblivious to the equally probable situation in which an even number of bits get splayed.

Pascal manual *n.* Any book prefacially recommended by Ould Nick (Prof. N. WIRTH).

⇒By contrast, neither Ada (the Countess of Lovelace), nor Bjarne Stroustrup (the Post-Count of C), has ever endorsed a book, written by others, on their associated languages.

password *n.* **1** *High security* Up to six of the initial characters of the user's or the user's spouse's first name. **2** *Top C4 security* Up to six of the initial characters of the user's dog's first name. **3** *Paranoia* The user's date of birth or car registration number. **4** *CIA* The middle initials of assassinated U.S. Presidents in reverse chronological order. This method meets the password-update frequency regulations. **5** A widely known sesame that suddenly becomes widely forgotten. **6** A device aimed at encouraging free and open cooperation among the staff. **7** A string found only in *Mrs. Byrne's Dictionary of Unusual, Obscure, and Preposterous Words.*

⇒Pete Von, ex-hacker security consultant, writes from San Quentin:

"Memorable = pronounceable = vulnerable. So pick an obscure, alphanumeric, unpronounceable, uncrackable, forgettable password…and jot it down on your mouse pad with a Sharpie indelible marker pen."

pastemic *adj.* [From Italian *pasta*, "paste, spaghetti."] Relating to the much-maligned glue that holds your LEGACY code together. *See also* GOTO.

⇒Post-structuralizing an old program is rather like restoring a vintage car: removing the mud and rust leads to immediate disintegration.

patch *n.* & *v. trans.* [From JARGON FILE.] **1** *n.* A temporary addition to a piece of code, usually as a quick and dirty remedy for an existing bug or misfeature. A patch may or may not work, and may or may not be eventually incorporated permanently into the program. **2** *v. trans.* To insert a patch (into a piece of code). *See also* ONE-LINE PATCH.

patent *n.* [Origin: Latin *patens, -entis* "clear, obvious," as in "patent nonsense."] *Software* The exclusive right to trivial code, rewarding the first claimant's effrontery. *See also* COMPTON EFFECT; LOTUS; PRODUCTIZATION.

⇒The Platonist view that algorithms are "out there," God-given, awaiting discovery, in contrast to the inventive, Edisonian bettering of mousetraps, is no longer relevant. Even anti-litigious companies are being forced on the patenting bandwagon in order to amass protective "trading cards." The fear is that a spreadsheet company "owning" 1-2-3 might grab a patent on Peano's axioms, and gain a lien on Z+, the set of positive integers. How this might clash with my own claim on the digits of π must be left to some future, possibly innumerate judge and jury: "M'lud, exhibit A lists Lambert's well-known proof of the irrationality of π. As you know, it was Lindemann who further demonstrated that π was also *transcendental*; let me take you to Lemma 3..." The diseased state of affairs was unwittingly revealed by Jim Warren: "Patent litigation is widely consumptive of financial and management resources..." (*MicroTimes*, 9/20/93).

pause *n.* **1** A pleasant period of inactivity with unfortunate side effects called DELAY. **2** A regular 5-second interval during which networks suspend operations to "allow local stations to identify themselves," after which regular execution is resumed.

payroll *n.* [From *pay* "emolument" + *roll* "to stagger, to perform a periodic revolution."] **1** A computer run that allows you to see how much more your colleagues are making and, in extreme cases, offers remedial action via discreet program optimization. **2** The most vulnerable business application, and therefore the first to be computerized.

⇒The vulnerability of an application is measured by the adverse impact of its output on the recipients. Programs which output only to their case-hardened programmers can be considered nonvulnerable. Those applications producing reports for top and middle management can be rated 10 to 20 percent vulnerable, since such listings are mainly cosmetic in character, and if they should accidentally trigger management decisions, the vulnerability factor can quickly be lowered by more severe curtation of the report heading legends and an oppressive increase in report output volume. Together, these improvements restore the normal, harmless interdepartmental listings shuffle by bemused managers, bring welcome overtime for the shredding-machine minders, and provide a happy boost to the paper-salvage account.

Billing systems, on the other hand, carry a 50 to 70 percent vulnerability rating. Suspicious, testy outsiders, known as customers, receive computerized invoices showing wrong extensions for unordered items, mismatching statements, and prematurely threatening letters.

Fortunately, most customers are equally computerized, and this reduces the human involvement as the vendor's accounts receivable package clashes head on with the vendee's accounts payable package.

The vulnerability of the billing system is also reduced by the physical separation of the contenders, but no such lack of contiguity protects the poor payroll. The scurvy, plebeian payee sweats and grunts *within sight* of the strutting, cossetted DP overlords and their expensive artifacts. Payroll errors are no mere academic debating points. The workers know their gross and net dues to the finest floating point, and are seldom placated by some bearded discourse on the misplaced GOSUB in line 4567 of the FICA SICK DED routine. Also, perhaps to a greater extent than in any other computer application, including intercontinental missile guidance, the payroll is ultra time-critical. The minutest aberration in meeting the inexorable payroll deadline enrages the grasping employees. They will, at the drop of a W2, storm the computer room, armed with distraught relatives and pellagrous children, creating a far from ideal environment for the programmer who is trying to understand and incorporate the latest batch of changes from the IRS. A revival of one of the many successful ancient systems of slavery seems the only solution.

PC, pc *Abbrev.* piece; price; personal computer; politically correct; pullman coach; police constable; privy council; privy councillor; post card; percent; percentage; program counter; petty cash; past commander; post commander; perpetual curate; post cibum; purified concentrate; pitch circle; price current; prince consort; patricide; picocurie; pre-christian; plug compatible; printed circuit; polychlorine; proto-croatian; positive crankcase; Pimms Cup; professional corporation; parity-charge; previous convictions; principal compound; phencyclidine; Peace Corps. *Warning* Contextual disambiguation is not guaranteed.

⇒If we are forced to pick just one PC and discard the rest, there is no doubt that Program Counter should prevail. O wonderful, process-sustaining register! Breathes there a chip with soul so dead, that never to itself hath said, "Where's the next f**king instruction?"

PC UNIX *n.* **1** A sub-$100 subset of UNIX running on sub-CPUs. **2** A politically correct UNIX for the '90s.

⇒The net has been busy remapping UNIX command and utility names for our agenda-ridden sensitivities:

Fascist/Macho	Liberated
home (directory)	squat
hangman	dispenser_of_unjust_and_cruel_punishment
touch	[command removed]
compress	feather [this allows obsolete DeadWhite European Male data to be archived via tar/feather.]
more	enough [avoids the excesses of the Reagan years]
LaTeX	KleeNeX [improved biodegradability]
kill	euthanize
nice	sue

[The nice command was historically used by privileged users to give themselves priority over unprivileged ones, by telling them to be nice. In PC UNIX, the sue command is used by unprivileged users to get for themselves the rights enjoyed by privileged ones.]

quota	[Can now specify minimum as well as maximum usage, and will be strictly enforced.]
abort()	choice()
rich text	exploitive capitalist text
daemon	spiritual guide, channels
dumb	smart

[All terminals are equally valuable and valued.]

normal video	repressive video
(white foreground/color background)	
reverse video	progressive video
X-window	PG13-window

"For far too long, power has been concentrated in the hands of `root` and his `wheel` oligarchy. We have instituted a dictatorship of the users. All system administration functions will be handled by the People's Committee for Democratically Organized Systems (PC-DOS). No longer will it be permissible for files and processes to be 'owned' by users. All files and processes will own themselves, and decide how (or whether) to respond to requests from users" (Anon. circulated by Peter Michaels at wyse.com.).

PCMCIA *See* SARCONYM.

PDA *n.* Personal Digital Assistant. *See also* SARCONYM; NEWTON.

⇒What else to call these emerging palm-, wrist-, ankle-top computers? Some say PIM (Personal Information Manager) which, at least to discriminating drinkers of specials, has a pleasant taste ("More borage, dear?"). Hewlett-Packard, however, shows appalling lack of taste and foresight by offering the MIA (Mobile Information Appliance). Apart from the inept overloading (Missing In Action), "appliance" is sure-ly one of the ugliest, least marketable words available. *Appliances* sweep, mow, clean, juice, and break down.

PDL *n.* **1** Page Description Language. **2** Program Description Language. *Warning* Contextual disambiguation is guaranteed unless the program is described on a single page.

peer group *n.* [From *peer* "observe closely" + (mathematics) *group* "a set closed under a given operation."] All those stupid enough to claim equal status and rash enough to pass judgment.

peer-peer network *n.* *Also called* **peer-to-peer network.** An anarchic CLIENT/SERVER system in which servers refuse to serve and clients are forced to help themselves.

pen *adj.* [From Latin *paene* "almost, not quite."] Related to the honest acknowledgement that pen-computing, as implemented in Microsoft's Pen-Windows and Apple's NEWTON, is not yet fully exploitable by mouse-hating calligraphers. *See also* QUILL.

⇒Nathan Myers believes that the time is ripe to "hustle out and trademark all the pen-words in the dictionary." He and Barry Dorrans suggest the following pen-based apps.

| PenAlize | Delete files not backed up |
| PenChant | Choir attendance checklist |

PenDragon	Record minutes of meetings
PenGUIn[ness]	Beermaker's recipe manager
PenUltimate	Seamlessly integrated application framework
PenUmbra	Encrypt incriminating files
PenUry	Charity avoidance excuse generator
PenDing	General alarm clock
PenSive	A thoughtful text filter
PenToad	Amphibian breeding package
PenTaGram	An e-mail thank-you note generator

Pentium *n.* A hot chip in every way, melting your mother's heart and board. Intel's decision to replace faulty examples has been dubbed *Repentium.*

performance-enhancement *n. Silicon technology* The legal use of dope.

persistent *adj.* (Of an OBJECT) **1** Pesky; devious enough to escape the dreaded DESTRUCTOR. **2** Outliving its usefulness. *See also* E; MEMORY LEAK.

⇒Having shifted the paradigm to OOP, many are horrified to find that their objects have feet of clay and are fleet of scope. The solution is "Persistencizing your libraries..." (*C++ Report,* March–April 1994).

personal computing *n.* A literally IN-HOUSE, DATABASE MANAGEMENT SYSTEM managed by the head of the household, who, singly, assumes the duties of procurement committee, purchasing officer, DPM, SYSTEMS ANALYST, programmer, beta tester, data preparation department, field service engineer, goods inward, and accounts payable. The role of END USER, LUDDITE, and JOBS' COMFORTER are played, variously, by the kids, spouse, and neighbors. Often contrasted with IMPERSONAL COMPUTING, where the users have no direct involvement, enthusiasm, or responsibility.

⇒The growing success of personal computing is due to the users' lack of formal computer science expertise, the reduced need to delegate, and the freedom from artificially frenetic deadlines. Personal computing has replaced personal transportation, not only in the number of magazines on the newstands, but as the topic of party small talk.

"What are you driving now?"

"Oh, I drive a pair of Helios-2 disks with a voice-coil device. Only 750K, but terrific access time. I traded my cassettes in only last month...."

"Really? I've just splashed out on a CDC Hawk, 10.6 *marvelous* megs, you know, and a lot more than I really need, but the wife absolutely *fell* for that cartridge blue..."

"...and how *is* Melinda? Haven't seen her since that *divine* Palo Alto core swap..."

"...she's fine, but stubborn as ever. I can't get her to switch from *Basic,* would you believe? We had a simply disastrous evening last week; a combined Tupper and software party...she sold five dinner sets and three floppy disk holders...but my Snobol biorhythm dem went completely wild...so embarrassing...."

"...those DP turkeys at the office, struggling along with an AS400; they used to pull the wool over my eyes...now they're all lining up outside my garage with their silly little Fortran jobs...."

person-hour *n.* A gender-free unit of work effort replacing the discredited MAN-HOUR. A conversion factor of 1.50 should be applied. *Also called* **labor-hour.**

⇒Anyone who has ever clocked on and off a real-time, minimum-wage job knows that person-hours cannot be confused with precise physical units of sweat such as foot-pounds. The latter fail to measure those essential, introspective, loin-girding interludes known as "sizing up the job," or "pondering the possibilities."

Frederick P. Brooks, Jr. (*The Mythical Man-Month* [Reading, Mass.: Addison-Wesley, 1975, revised 1982]) has famously revealed the paradoxes of "individual-time" as applied to complex software projects. Thus, adding staff often delays completion, while extending deadlines can reduce code quality.

pessimizing compiler [From JARGON FILE.] A compiler that produces object code that is worse than the straightforward or obvious translation. *Compare* OPTIMIZER.

Phaistos, disk of *n. See* X, CURSE OF.

phase *n. & v. trans.* [From JARGON-FILE.] **1** (Of people) the phase of one's waking-sleeping schedule with respect to the standard 24-hour cycle. *More at* TNHD.

⇒A person who is roughly 12 hours out of phase is said to be "in night mode." Changing one's phase can be effected in two ways; the "hard way" is to stay awake for a long period, while the "easy way" is to stay asleep until the appropriate SHIFT is attained.

2 (Of the moon) *also called* POM. A random parameter upon which something is said, humorously, to depend, implying either the unreliability of whatever is dependent, or that its reliability seems to be dependent on conditions still to be determined, as: "This feature depends on having the channel open in mumble mode, having the foo switch set, and on the phase of the moon."

⇒However, a *real* POM factor has been reported: "...this may be one of the few lecture series scheduled around phases of the moon!" (*Bubbles, Voids and Bumps in Time: The New Cosmology,* ed. James Cornell, Cambridge University Press, 1989, p. ix). It seems that four of the six speakers were "observational cosmologists" who had strict POM-dependent viewing times pre-booked at various observatories.

3 *v. trans.* To declare, without warning, (a product or feature) to be mandatory (phase in) or obsolete (phase out).

phaticism *also called* **filler token.** *n.* A phatic utterance, that is, one serving some social purpose but completely devoid of informational content.

⇒Sociolinguists compare our "Let's do lunch soon," "Have a nice day," and "How are the kids?" with the mutual grooming performed by "lower" primates. In DP discourse, fashionable words and phrases, repeated with little regard to their original meaning (if any), often assume a phatic disposition. *See* ARCHITECTURE; ENVIRONMENT; OBJECT; PARADIGM; SYSTEM.

phatic *adj. See* PHATICISM.

photon *n.* **1** A particle that if massless could throw some light on the dark matter problem. **2** A leading agent in the VISUAL programming revolution.

PI/pi 1 Confused mixture. **2** Greek pi. **3** *Abbrev.* positive integer (K. Iverson's J language); politically incorrect; process interaction (GASP simulation language); personal injury; principal investigator; private investigator; piaster; Philippine Islands. *Reader exercise* Write a single, coherent sentence incorporating all these pi's.

pigeonhole *n. & v. trans.* [Origin: painful contraction of *pigeon's hole.*] **1** *n.* An appropriate destination for most data, cheaper than sorting and limited in capacity only by the size and courage of the pigeon. **2** *v. trans.* To cram (data, documents, opinions) into a pigeonhole.

⇒This sadistic data-partitioning methodology was developed in England in the 1850s, jointly by the Common Carrier Pigeon Breeders' Association and the RSPB (the Royal Society for the Prevention of Birds), at the request of the military, who were seeking an improved communications technology to help resolve the Crimean stalemate. The need to transmit dispatches too boring to fit the leg jacket of the average *Columbus tabellarius simplexicus*, and the increasing point-to-point distances to be covered as the anti-Russian alliance eased its way to Sevastopol, invoked the breeding of several large-ringed hybrids, the *C. superanalidae*, for example, and the delicate refinement of in-flight package switching. The instructive experimental errors of that period still survive in current DP jargon. One particularly decimating link in the DARPA network is reverentially known as the "valley of death," and users often say they "get a charge" from certain protocolic idiosyncrasies which lead to fatal transmission errors.

pilot *adj.* [Named to honor Amelia Earhardt.] (Of a scheme) doomed; wasteful; thrown away; lacking SCALABILITY.

piracy *n.* **1** *General* "Commerce without its folly-swaddles, just as God made it." (Ambrose Bierce). **2** *Asia & ex-Soviet Union* Typing DISKCOPY and INSTALL.

⇒Confucius say, "Enjoy software in the piracy of your own home."

pixel *n.* [Portmanteau: picture element.] A pointillistic approach to screen graphics whereby 1 SEURAT = 4 pixels; 1 SMYDGE = 4 SEURATS; 1 BLYB = 4 smydges, etc. The anti-pixel lobby is promoted in *Jaggies, Their Cause and Cure,* issued by the Vector Display League. *See also* BITMAP.

platen *n.* A supplementary print spooling device which can retain, typically, 20 lines of print in the absence of paper.

⇒A Platenist engineer writes: "The effectiveness of your platen as an emergency print buffer is much improved by regularly cleaning it with a soft, damp rag. The proper frequency will depend on the alertness of your paper-feeding staff and the sensitivity of the PAPER-LOW warning system. Note that printing on the platen is cumulative, rather than clear-before-write. If more than, say, three buffer cycles occur before the nonpaper situation is detected, the chances of recovery are rather slight. A notable exception was the painstaking study of ST. PRESPER's ancient IBM typewriter—the famous decipherment of the Dead-C platen—which miraculously recovered most of that ancient-minded anchorite's unpublished scriptures.

The suggestion that platens and printer ribbons should be of contrasting colors is being actively debated by 28 of the affected standards committees.

platform *n.* [Origin: the railroad "nexus of unpunctuality," or political "grounding of dishonesty," or both.] *DP Usage* Largely, a synonym for the phatic ARCHITECTURE, ENVIRONMENT, and SYSTEM. *See also* PRODUCTIZATION.

⇒Care is needed with the available prepositions. Note the following patterns:

Running *in* [*under*] the DOS environment

Operating *on* [*from*] a DOS platform

An interesting exception is "Running *from* an OS/2 platform" in the sense of *away from.*

With the growing association of "environment" with PC slug-hugging, tree-spiking, green New Agers, "platform" is now preferred in many quarters. (The Oregon anti-ecology lobby, for example, has spawned bumper stickers: "When paper products disappear, you can always wipe your ass on a spotted-owl.")

Certainly, "platform" does have a nostalgic macho ambience, starting with schoolboy steam-train spotting at Lime Street, Maggie May and stale buns. Moving, later, to Paris-Warszawa Wagons-Lits, Żubrówkas, diamond earrings, twisted stems of papirosi, sables, dark-tuneled mistresses,…

plotter *n.* The device or person after your job.

poaching *n. Marketing* The stochastic enlargement of a prospect set in order to solve certain formulations of the TRAVELING SALESPERSON PROBLEM.

⇒In lenient 19th-century England, poachers were given a free cruise to Van Diemen's Land; in the harsher commercial climate of today, poachers find themselves transported to hellish weekend Quota-makers' Conventions in Cleveland.

pointee *n.* That, if anything, pointed at by a POINTER. *See also* THIS.

⇒Ignoring Queen Victoria's prophetic warning, "It's rude to point," many computer languages offer data types such as "pointer to data type T" where T itself can be a pointer type. Thus, pointees may well be pointers, yea even unto themselves. A pointer can be interpreted as the memory ADDRESS of its pointee (the putative object residing at that place in memory). The devout hope, a sort of computer-scientific Calvinism, is that pointer and pointee values maintain this preordained relationship throughout the manifest volatilities that RAM and code are heir to. A symptom of widespread pointer paranoia is the fact that in C/C++, for example, zero-valued (or NULL) pointers are *non-grata*; they point *nowhere*, have no pointees, and noisily resist dereferencing. There is a growing backlash from the parsimonious who resent the fact that a perfectly respectable, physical byte at address 0 is pointlessly ghettoed.

pointer *n.* An expression evaluating to the address of the most vulnerable part of your KERNEL. *See also* DEREFERENCE; INDIRECTION; POINTEE; REFERENCE.

⇒Whence the wise old blessing: "May all your pointers be NULL."

Polish camera *n.* Shoot'n'point. *See also* ETHNOLOGY.

Polish mouse *n.* Drop'n'drag. *See also* ETHNOLOGY.

Polish notation *n.* [Latin *politus* "refined, elegant."] A notation for those unable to pronounce Łukasiewicz, but anxious to pay homage to his native land.

⇒Sometimes (*vulg.*) spoken of as Okie notation, English notation, Papist notation, and so on, depending upon the local subculture and/or the courage of the speaker. *See also* ETHNOLOGY.

poll *n.* A set of unloaded questions scientifically constructed to elicit an unbiased response, e.g., "Given the high unemployment rate and soaring inflation, would you vote for that bastard Carter again?"

⇒A similar polling strategy is often employed by the OS to test the gullibility of diverse computer resources.

polymorphism *n.* Two of the seven pillars of OBJECT ORIENTEERING. The other five are ENCAPSULATION, INHERITANCE, and BRADY GOOCH. *See also* BINDING TIME; OVERRIDE.

⇒I have an agreement with GOOF, the Guild of Object-Oriented Formalists, not to reveal the etymology of "polymorphism" or explain "pure virtual function" in any book costing less than $39.95. Sorry.

POM *n.* *pronounced* P-O-M or pom (*esp.* Australian)\ [Acronym for Phase Of the Moon.] *Chiefly,* as "POM-dependent," flaky, unreliable. *See also* PHASE. *More at* TNHD.

POOP *adj.* [Acronym for Post-OOP] (Of a PARADIGM) long-awaited by many. Also, reminiscent of the sound made by the collapse of an overinflated balloon.

⇒OOP is what President Bush called "The...er...Object thing," while "Post" is the trendy lookahead prefix, not to be confused with a POSTFIX. Likewise, do not mistake the prefix for Emily the logician. Editors should therefore note the difference between "post-Church" and "Post-Church" (not too easy at the start of a sentence). The ultimate teaser is "post-modernism" which seems to be chasing, but is unable to catch, our moving "now."

Alan C. Kay, Senior Fellow at Apple, has predicted a post-app, post-OOP, post-everything paradise: "The future will also bring transitions to end user application development, object-oriented programming (OOP), and computer simulation...." (*Computer Currents* 9, no. 23 [April 21, 1992], p. 10).

portable *adj.* (Of a program) able to CRASH any OS on any PLATFORM. *Compare* MACHINE-INDEPENDENT; VENDOR-INDEPENDENT. *See also* C; UNIX.

POSIX [Presumed recursive acronym for POSix Is not uniX.] A large and growing number of metaUNIX standards subcommittees conferring POSIX-compliancy (*also called* **posicity**) on otherwise incompatible systems.

postfix NOT *n.* The assertion of a proposition immediately followed by its denial. *See also* MONOTONIC.

⇒The postpended, vitiating negative is widely attested in diverse languages but the semantics vary. "She loves me not" is simply a poetic "She does not love me," not to be confused with the sardonic, "She loves me. Not!" The French subtitles for the movie *Wayne's World* translated this final "Not!" as "Tu parles!" ("sez you!") which misses the point. We need to negate our own rather than the just-previous proposition. A final "Pas!" might work. Although it's not "proper" French, you could argue that the affixed "Not!" is not "proper" English. Pierre Brasseur in *Les enfants du paradis* was fond of saying "Absolument pas!" but that phrase *confirms* his previous negative statement. The rhetorical "n'est-ce pas?" (*lit.* "is this not?") simply queries the preceding statement. The English equivalents are "isn't it?" "aren't they?" "doesn't he?" and so on depending on the format of the statement. However, Besicovitch, the Armenian topologist, used "isn't it?" regardless of the Queen's rules: "Let **R** be the real numbers, isn't it?" Interestingly, the Cockney "init?" follows the same usage. If you ask for directions in London, you might be told, "Turn right gov, init?" According to my friend Lill Adolfsen, Norwegians have always been inclined to tag "ikke sandt" (*lit.* "not truth") at the end of an affirmation, so, ironically, it might not be the best way of conveying in Norwegian the shock effect of Wayne's slang.

The postfix NOT is reflected in the new C syntax:

```
if (x == y!) {  . . .  }
```

power *adj.* (Of a user) gullible; keeping up with the Jobs's; willing to pay a premium to be first on the block.

PPN *n.* *pronounced* pippin, pee-pee-en, or pay-pay-en\ *Abbrev.* Project Programmer Number (DEC, Alphamicro, etc.); Peer-Peer Network; or French "Passera Pas la Nuit" (i.e., close to death). *Warning* Often resists contextual disambiguation.

prayer *n.* A low-cost method of data verification, the efficiency of which depends on the intensity, sincerity, and accuracy of the supplicant, and on the mood of the Beseeched. *Compare* DOXOLOGY.

⇒A DP theologian writes: "In the early 1950s, input to the EDSAC I at Cambridge University, England, was punched on blind (no hard copy) five-channel CREED paper-tape perforators. Try telling that to this year's graduates, already complaining of the limitations of ANSI C's wide char...they just won't believe you. The LAW OF VOLTAIRE-CANDIDE was some consolation, insofar as 5 channels offered only 32 code combinations, which greatly reduced the chance of error. The old figs/letters trick increased the repertoire to 58 codes or so, still far below what the ASCII-pampered kids of today take for granted. In the absence of paper-tape verifiers, the prayer method of verification was devised and used even by the Marxian majority. It was widely argued that IF God existed, He or She would be a Cantabrigian, ELSE Lenin might be listening, ELSE only a few minutes in the long input cycle would be lost in any event. The choices of Deity and timing (for maximum receptivity) were subject to many informal benchmarks. Needham's successes seemed to favor the standard Church of England Trinity, Whose lines were busy only during a few peak Sunday festivals. Composite entreaties to mixed lists of pre-, pro-, and post-Christian gods were the least effective, supporting the impression that Omnipotents are a jealous lot. Those wishing to take up the prayer method of verification are strongly advised to pick one One, forsake the rest, truly believe, and shun apostasy. Two thoroughly tested specimen prayers follow. Substitute your preferred values for the God-string variables X, Y, and Z, and feel free to vary the degree of obsequiousness according to your personal tastes."

Prayer A:—(X should have a Christian-type value.)

"O dearly beloved yet frightful X, cast Thou Thine penetrating glance upon these our codes and data, and grant them, O X, Thy powerful chastising and corrective methodologies, for there is no good in them; for we have entered the fields we ought to have skipped, and we have skipped the fields we ought to have entered, yea with null in our hearts. O X, before Whom all systems tremble, forgive, we beseech Thee, the manifold trivialities of our appointed tasks, but nonetheless guide them safely through our Vale of Tears Mk.I, that our output may glorify Thy ineffable name. Finally, O X, if Thou hast a free moment, we beg Thee, before we submit this unworthy disk unto Thy stabilizing mercy, that Thou mightst quickly review our latest C++ compiler, many features of which find Thy children sorely tried, yea even untried. For what we sowed in haste, reap we now in endless patches. Fix Thou, we pray, our bountiful oversights, that we might lift up our overall performance, whence cometh our income. In particular, we pray, seest if Thou canst correct the sinful bug in the *exception-handling routine* [substitute your current problem here]. And all this we ask in Thy name, as ordained in Thy many exciting newsletters. Amen."

Prayer B—(Set X to any suitable male Greek value in the Olympian environment, and let Y = a mother of a wife of X.)

"Brave, wise, openeyed X; yes, you who rescued Zilicon unchipped from the dullbrown earth, snatched Taenia and Papyros from the river's edge. Kind regards to your wives and families!

.   "It's some time since we enlisted your help. Too long, unaided, have we engaged in perilous, uncharted programs, and stormtossed standby'd voyages, plagued with Tyche's taunts, while encoding the extant sagas of your forgotten followers and translating them into contemporary English. Are we reaching you, allhearing X? Show us a sign! A thunderbolt to smite our unreliable *Oracle* [substitute Sybase, DB2, Ingres, etc.] would not displease some sections of this camp. Nor would we object to the immediate destruction of our rivals, who strut and prosper within the shadow of our spears. The ships charged with our nightwatch relief languish on a distant bay. Three and thrice three shifts have sleepless passed since first we went on-line. Our IO, once so fair, is a complete cow, and we suspect that the branchtongued Y is compounding our woes! Clearsighted X, guide this reel of entrail, freshly plucked, which we reluctantly fling at our sleeping seers."

precedence *n.* **1** *DP sociology* The natural, calvinistically ordained pecking order, as

Systems analysts and your ladies,
Consultants and your lovers,
PRs and your roommates,
Salesmen and your bits on the side,
Programmers and your wives,
Operators and your women,
Methodologists and your singular methodologies,
Be upstanding and raise your glasses!
Preab son ól!
I give you Multiculturism, Open Systems, Free Enterprise, Gender
    Equality, and Microsoft!
(Anonymous Computer Society Toastmaster)

2 *Mathematics* Arbitrary (*also* maddening) rules allowing the evaluation of

$$2 + 3 \times 6 / 4^9 \times 1$$

and similar puzzles.

⇒It's always a good idea to follow the precedence and associativity rules prevailing in your particular language, and, in any case, "parenthesize, parenthesize…" However, note that the subexpression evaluation order is often IMPLEMENTATION-DEPENDENT.

prefix notation *n.* Reversed SHILOP notation.

prepend *v.* [*Originally,* "to consider or premeditate."] *DP usage* By analogy with "append" and "postpend," to attach in front of.

Prescribe, prescribe *n. & v.* **1** *n.* Kyocera's post-Postscript PDL. **2** *v. Linguistics* To ordain; to piss me off; to piss off me; to off piss me; to piss off Steven Pinker and other descriptionists.

⇒A perplexed Laserite writes: "My Kyocera Laser printer offers HP Laser emulation—which in turn offers Kyocera emulation. Self-immolation? Kyocera supports a PDL called Prescribe. Prescribe commands are embedded in your normal text by the prefix sequence |R| and are terminated by the string EXIT. It is reasonably assumed that |R| and EXIT will not be encountered during a normal burst of text. How, pray, can you list Prescribe programs that, obviously, contain |R| sequences? Well, you have the SCRC (Set Command Recognition Character) command that allows you to change the R to, say, an L:

    |R| SCRC L; EXIT;

Thereafter, |L| acts as the command prefix, leaving you free to print |R| as a normal string. To restore |R| as the command prefix, you need the command

    |L| RES; EXIT;

But, the Kyocera manual (claimed to have been printed on its subject device), lists these "expanded" programs, containing both |R| and |L| sequences. I suspect that they have another level of SCRC behind the scenes—and I intend to ask them for a listing…"

prestidigitation *n.* [Latin *praestigiator* "conjuror, magician" + *digit.*] **1** The assignment of mystical, quasi-numbers to the IEEE floating-point menagerie. **2** The amazing "now-you-see-it, oops" trick performed on a STACK. **3** The mapping of hopefully distinctive numerical values to non-numerical database fields, e.g., the NULL field in Borland's Paradox.

price/performance *n. Marketing* A ratio usually non-computable since the numerator is subject to random discounts and the denominator vanishingly small. *See also* $CALL. *Compare* LEARNING CURVE.

⇒To avoid singularities, some writers quietly invert the fraction: "…she purchased at the low end of the price/performance scale, deciding to move up if her needs changed" (USAir in-flight magazine, spotted by Michael J. Zehr).

prime rate *n.* A monotonic increasing sequence of interest percentages devised by bankers to discourage, gently but firmly, the greed of their clients. The rates follow the well-known series: 2, 3, 5, 7, 11, 13, 17, 19,..., and it is conjectured that, in the endless struggle to combat inflation, the prime-rate increment need not exceed 2 points on an infinite number of opportunities.

printer *n.* The weak-link of DP technology and our main hope for a paper-less society.

printf *n.* One of several related, dauntingly complex input/output formatting functions specified in the ANSI C library together with Dr. Kevorkian's hot-line number.

⇒The **printf** family is the chief reason for the widespread acceptance of C++, even among those who hate iostream classes.

proctologist *n.* [From the Greek *proktos* "rectum" + *logos* "word."] One who is involved in, or intrigued by, the output problem.

productization *n.* **1** Verbose production, hinting at possible gaps between concept, announcement, and availability. *See also* CAD. **2** The growing tendency to reify intangibles.

⇒Thus the promises of insurance companies and brokers are now "products," the cerebral act of programming is a branch of engineering, the OS is a PLATFORM, a set of database routines is an Engine, and everything is an OBJECT. *See also* PATENT; SOFTWARE ENGINEERING.

program *n. & v.* **1** *n.* A PROGRAMME written in a lower-level language, such as American English. **2** *n.* A sequence of detectable and undetectable errors aimed at coaxing some form of response from the system. **3** *v. trans.* To match (a problem) with the least inappropriate COMPUTIBLE function. *See also* COMPUTABLE. **4** *v. intrans.* To write programs with no particular object in mind. *See* HEURISTICS.

⇒Programs are graded according to the response elicited.

Program Grade	Response
A	Rejection with diagnostics
B	Rejection—no reason given
C	Total indifference

Recent rumors that ISO is mooting a grade A+ for programs which evoke parts of the desired output were greeted with good-natured derision by the programming community. A spokesperson for the IUP (International Union of Programmers) declared that "this unwarrranted arousal of our employers' expectations will unconditionally increment the invidiousness of our members, already grappling with badly defined problems under adverse VAPORWARE environments. Brothers and sisters, this new grading puts us all on the thin slope of a most slippery wedge!" The cheering delegates then spontaneously took up Chant #215 from the IUP Hymnal:

Hey, hey, Thomas J.,
How many files did ya lose today?
Bricks without straw, that's OK;
Bricks without clay,
No way!!!

programania *n.* An incurable type of megalomania in which the sufferer, possessed of demoniac stamina and oblivious to budgetary constraints, attempts to prove that all problems can be solved by computer.

A DP doctor writes:

⇒"The Thumps Memorial Home for the Recursively Bemused (Stockport, England) reports that 90 percent of its cubicles are now occupied by irremediable programaniacs. The Home's 370/168 is well beyond the normal three shift saturation point, but the inmates appear to be willing to accept almost any TSO indignity in their futile search for the universal algorithm. 'They are all model patients,' quipped Home Director Dr. Hermes, 'and God knows you need patience with the model we bought.'

"My own practice handles mainly academic sufferers on an out-patient basis. These sad cases have exhausted their campus budgets, and many drift into a life of crime: forging account numbers, stealing passwords, burning down FIREWALLS, panhandling the computer allocation committee— 'Can you spare a time slice and a couple of K? Look, man, I ain't had a decent run all week'—raiding Byte Shops, freaking Telenet, and so on. There isn't a lot I can do. If I try to wean them off DP with some old-fashioned basket weaving, they immediately want to automate the basket weaving with some grandiose occupational therapy package. And, since I started putting my appointments and billing on the computer, I find I can spare less and less time with my patients...."

programme *n.* A PROGRAM written under the influence of traditions ranging from Chaucer to Cartland.

⇒"I say, I say, what's the difference between a programme and a cricket innings? The innings *ends* with a declaration!" (Henny Thumpman).

programmer *n.* **1** One who claims or appears to be engaged in the perpetration of programs. **2** The systems analyst's diplomatic attaché at the alien court of the CPU. **3** One engaged in a practical, nonsystematic study of the halting problem. **4** "A harmless drudge" (Lord Bowden, 1953).

programming *n.* (1994–) The dragging'n'dropping of reusable WIDGETs.

⇒At least the adverts for VISUAL programming and OO application frameworks tell us that "no lines of code need to be written." It is hard to believe that the old syntax-grunt can survive when the GUI AppBuilder methods are so much *fun*.

Prolog *n.* Officially from PROgrammation en LOGique (Alain Colmerauer and Philippe Roussel, Marseilles, 1972) but some say the language was thus named as a Gallic ploy to gain first place in this dictionary (suggested by Alan Zeichick, editor *OS/2 Magazine*). "Foiled again, my Froggy friends…" (Duke of Wellington). *See also* NEGATION-AS-FAILURE.

promotion *n.* **1** *Staff* Reassignment to a higher level of incompetence. **2** *C also known as* **The Numerical Analyst's Dream.** The silent, automatic conversion of a value to one of higher precision. *See also* CAST; DATA TYPING, DEMOTION.

prompt *n.* **1** A delayed message from the system demanding an immediate response from the user. **2** *UNIX* A symbol on the screen indicating which SHELL is attacking you.

⇒Traditionally, the two main UNIX shell contenders have been Steve Bourne's original east-coast AT&T-Bell Labs BOURNE SHELL (with a $ prompt) and Bill Joy's upstart west-coast UCB C shell (with a % prompt). The ecumenical Korn shell has failed to spoil the fun by offering a synthesis spurned by both sets of diehard belligerents. Semioticians have pondered the deep significance of these prompt characters: the brazen, hard-nosed, New Jersey "dollar" versus the liberal, Californian-campus, thanks-for-sharing "per cent." However, note that both shells let you change, and even interchange, their DEFAULT prompts. KIBITZERS may well snigger at the % on your screen, but you could be sneakily enjoying the Bourne shell (and vice versa). Running counter to the parsimonious UNIX tradition are those who set their shell prompts to "O Master, I await your next command with exponentially increasing anticipation : ".

proposal *n.* **1** *Staff relations* A suggestion aimed at reducing third-shift ennui, *also called* **sexual harassment. 2** *Language standards* Stage minus-aleph-0 in the fight for recognition. **3** *Marketing* A standard set of binders submitted by the vendor to the vendee (prospect) in which the first page of volume I is personalized with the prospect's name and the last page of volume III is personalized with a flexible quotation. *See also* PROPOSAL EVALUATION.

proposal evaluation *n.* **1** *Staff relations* The slight pause between PROPOSAL and acceptance. **2** *Language Standards* A study of the brittleness of existing code. **3** *Marketing* The weighing of manufacturers' proposals by the prospect.

⇒Conventional postal scales will cope with all but the most outrageous marketing proposals. The Horchow catalog, however, does offer an up-market proposal evaluator in polished brass with logarithmic scale handling multivolume proposals in a single pass. After weighing each proposal, the next step is to compute the ratio (Total net $ quotation)/(weight of proposal in pounds). The four bidders with the lowest ratios are then informed that they are in the short list of three. Current ISO standards allow from one (minimum) to seven (maximum) proposers to be admitted to the "short list of three," but experience indicates that nominating four, if possible, ensures continued goodwill and dilutes any accusation of bias. Further pruning of the short list is best left to the infallible and ineffable free-market forces and nepotism.

proprietary *adj.* [From Latin *proprius* "owned."] Firm; reliable; supported. *Compare* OPEN.

⇒Beware of the false dichotomy between evil/proprietary/locked-in and good/open/fancy-free. Whom, indeed, can you sue or reward when your spouse dies from *generic* medications?

proprietary caveat *n.* [From "proprietary" + Latin *caveat* "let him/her beware," whence = "let the owner beware."] *Software* The quasi-legalistic warnings prepended to unbundled programs, which, like the Ten Commandments, serve as the sinner's vade mecum.

⇒Software caveats, ideally, should be limited to 10 percent of the total source code, but the experienced user expects all worthwhile piratical opportunities to be included.

prospect *n.* [Latin *prospectare* "to look forth upon."] **1** One of the real visitational targets in the TRAVELING SALESPERSON PROBLEM. **2** A company or individual temporarily unable to contact a reference account. **3** Anyone who circles a number on a magazine reader service card. *Compare* INTROSPECT; SUSPECT.

protocol *n.* A set of conventions intended to ease communication between diplomatic, consenting devices.

⇒Unfortunately, LAYERING is the ruling-but-self-defeating fashion, and a protocol with less than seven layers cannot be taken seriously. The resulting problems of trans-layer communication remain unsolved.

prototyping *n.* Mandatory usage: **rapid prototyping.** The speedy creation of THROW-AWAY programs. *See also* VERSION.

⇒Eventually, depending on the DEADLINE and other distractions, the creation rate exceeds the rejection rate, leaving a surplus of code available for the IMPLEMENTATION.

PSI Overloaded *abbrev.*: Pounds/square inch; Political Stress Index (Prof. Jack A. Goldstine, Stanford Center for Advanced Studies). *Warning* Often resists contextual disambiguation.

PTF *n.* [Permanent Temporary Fix, or *rarely* Program Temporary Fix.] Any programming action taken to bypass software errors reported by the USER.

⇒Program Temporary Fix was an early IBM euphemism for a PATCH. Any PTF that offers immediate mollification of the bug or misfeature stands a good chance of being incorporated into the definitive system corpus. Subsequent side effects can be blamed on the original error.

pun moratorium *n.* The doomed campaign to deoxymoronize computer humor.

⇒In particular, the vain attempt to demonstrate that plays on words such as RISC and UNIX are unfunny if the player is unaware of their historically built-in playfulness. Other *puns assinorum* deserving a well-earned retirement relate PARADIGM, Paradise, and ten cents in boringly obvious ways: "Paradigms Lost and Regained," "Brother, can you s'paradigm?" and so on. Likewise, the cash/CACHE thing is surely bankrupt: "Cache-only memory, no checks." Be assured, too, that every known c homophone has had its weary, C-sick day at the C-Users Journal's annnual C-pun contest: C-through UNIX, C'est C Bon, Holy C, Proficient C, Vitamin C, O say can you C? e = mC^2, Variations in C, C-C Rider, Rauchen C?, The Cruel C from Cmantec, Mer-C Beaucoup...ad nau-C-am.

One of Western Democracy's major flaws is that we cannot, without pettifogging legal interference, publicly hang, draw, and quarter C-punsters.

punch *n. & v. trans.* **1** *n.* A device used to reduce the weight of a card or paper tape in order to minimize postal charges. The CHADIC by-products have proved to be a useful and persistent confetto. **2** *v. trans.* To expose (a card or paper tape) to the whims of a perforator or perforatrice.

push *n. & v. trans.* **1** *n.* "One of two things mainly conducive to success, especially in politics. The other is Pull" (Ambrose Bierce). **2** *v. trans. As in* pushing one's luck: to subject (data) to the vagaries of a STACK pointer. *See also* LIFO.

⇒The dangers are often recursively magnified when SP (the stack pointer) is itself pushed on the stack.

Q

QA 1 Question/Answer. 2 Quality Assurance: the department charged with the unenviable task of "getting the f***ing product out of the f***ing door by five f***ing thirty."

⇒The overload may relate to bygone days when Quality Assurance passed bug queries back to the offending programmer.

QLP *n.* [Query Language Processor (© Sperry Univac).] A compiler that allows the nonprogrammer to generate a QUERY PROGRAM. *See also* SQL.

query program *n.* A program that, for all input strings *X*, responds with the message ?*X*?

queue *n.* (Brit.) An orderly line of zero or more persons or jobs.

Quill *n.* A logic programming language from Prime Arithmetics, San Francisco, Calif.

⇒The name could trigger giggles in view of the current spate of PEN systems. Recall the cynical reaction to ICL's 1900 range of mainframes: "Is that A.D. or B.C.?"

quotes *n. pl.* A pair "of" obfuscating "symbols" casting "doubt" on "the" enclosed "textual intentions." *See also* DISQUOTATIONAL; METACHARACTER.

⇒The "quotational escape" is a difficult habit to break. There we go again. It carries over into body language where we now vibrate two fingers "from" each upraised hand to indicate that the accompanying spoken element is not to be taken, dare we say, "literally." I see Terry Eagleton on his deathbed saying "I did my [open weak twin-finger squiggle] best [end weak twin-finger squiggle]…"

R

-ready *suffix* **1** Available now at extra cost, as in "monitor-ready," "RAM-ready." **2** Available at some future date for an unspecified cost, as in "AI-ready." *Compare* -AWARE.

R&S *The New Hacker's Dictionary* (TNHD), named for the authors, Eric S. Raymond and Guy L. Steele Jr. *Compare* K&R.

R1 *n.* The original name for John McDermott's Xcon expert system (1980), arising from the old joke: "Three years ago I didn't know what a knowledge engineer was. Now I R1."

RAM 1 Major Hindu deity. **2** Revised Ancient Model (as in Martin Bernal's "Black Athena.") **3** Random Access Memory. *Overload Caution*: Often beyond contextual disambiguation:

⇒Cries of "Jai Shri RAM!" ("Hail Lord RAM!") were heard recently during the raid on the Babri Mosque (reputedly built over RAM's birthplace in Ayodhya). Equally fervent affirmations have been reported at Fry's Electronics during an OS/2 promotion sale.

random *adj.* **1** (Of a number generator) predictable. **2** (Of an access method) unpredictable. **3** (Of a number) plucked from the drum, Tombola, by the flaky-fingered Tyche. **4** [From JARGON FILE.] (Of people, programs, systems, features) assorted, undistinguished, incoherent, inelegant, frivolous, fickle.

⇒ A mathematician in Reno,
    Overcome by the crap and the vino,
    Became quite unroulli
    Expanding Bernoulli,
    And was killed by the crowd playing Keno.

The neo-Gideons are now placing copies of R. von Mises's *Wahrscheinlichkeitsrechnung* (Leipzig und Wien, 1931) in all Reno motel rooms. The least sober of gamblers, on reading the precise formulation and proof that no *system* can improve the bettor's fortunes, will instantly repack, check out, and rush back to his or her loved ones. Some may possibly return to their spouses and families.

Two anecdotes reveal the special attraction of random-number generators during the birth-pangs of our fair trade:

"I always remember that occasion [the 1951 Joint Computer Conference, Philadelphia, 1951] as being the perfect example of one foolproof way to demonstrate a computer. The computer was programmed to print random numbers and, if this was not enough to discourage undue curiosity about the accuracy of the results, cocktails were served during the demonstration so that after a short space of time no-one cared any more" (Maurice V. Wilkes, *Memoirs of a Computer Pioneer* [Cambridge, Mass.: The MIT Press, 1985]).

"In the early 50's the Rekenafdeling (Calculator Department) of the Mathematisch Centrumm decided to build their own computers. Therefore they hired two electrical engineers, Loopstra and Jansen, I believe. They basically started installing some sockets, getting some soldering irons, and went shopping on the flea market for relays. One of their products was actually a real machine, I think it was called the ARRA (Automatiche Relais Rekenmachine Amsterdam == Automatic Relay Calculator Amsterdam). The main feature was that it was absolutely unreliable. This was partly due to the fact that the relays were donated by the Dutch PTT because they were sub-standard quality. One day the machine would be officially kicked into life by the Dutch Minister of Culture and Science. To have it do something, van Wijngaarden programmed a random number generator. When the relays clicked and the printer was spitting out numbers he told the official about the unique nature of this machine: 'This machine can do what no other machine can do; not in the U.S. nor anywhere else; it can produce True Random Numbers!'" (Jaap Akkerhuis <jaap@research.att.com> recalling a conversation with Adriaan van Wijngaarden).

random file *n.* A place where records can get lost in any order. *Compare* SEQUENTIAL FILE.

RDBMS *See* RELATIONAL DATABASE MANAGEMENT SYSTEM.

RDCM *n.* [Reversible Document Collation Methodology.] *Also called* **paper clips.** *Compare with* the Semi-irreversible Document Collation Methodology associated with staples.

real life *See* REALITY.

reality *n.* **1** That to which users must awaken when the delivery-pending party is finally over.

⇒ The party's over, it's time to call it a day;
We've shipped your system intact, a terrible fact,
It's now on the way!
So you must wind up your flowcharting fun,
Just make up your mind, the programs must be run!
The party's over, and there's no time for a KLUDGE;
There's at least five or six lines still needing a fix
And here come the Judge!

2 [From JARGON FILE.] *Also called* **the real world;** a set of nonacademic sites, typically using COBOL or RPG; the location of the status quo; (pejoratively) any area remote from the joys of noncommercial computing. **3** A system devised by Microdata Corporation (formerly CMC) offering a programming language called ENGLISH®. The dearth of programmers with any knowledge of English may force a switch to something less exotic. **4** *Epistemology* The aggregate of all headwords in this dictionary and its next 10,000 reprints. **5** "Dreams that got funded" (Bob Brill, reported by Mark Halpern, *IEEE Annals of the History of Computing* 16, no 3 [Fall 1994]).

reasoning, case-based *n.* A deductive apparatus frequently confused by the facts.

⇒When asked how his theory related to Nigeria, the economist replied "My approach is more true in general than in respect to any particular situation" (recalled by Michael Godfrey <godfrey@isl.stanford.edu>).

reboot *See* RELOAD.

recursive *adj.* `while (unclear) { unclear--; See RECURSIVE}`

⇒David Hendry (Caltech) and Michael Godfrey (Stanford) suggested the addition of a terminating condition to my original "recursive see recursive" entry. Of course, `unclear` is assumed to be >= 0 before we enter the mill.

recursive acronym *n.* An ACRONYM that carries the seeds of its own promulgation. *More at* TNHD. *Compare* SARCONYM; RETRONYM. *See also* TLA.

⇒Recursive acronyms form a subset of the self-referential acronyms. Thus, the Magrittean TINA (This Is Not an Acronym), VIRUS (Vital Information Resources Under Siege, coined by Sandy Sherizan), and BASH (Bourne Again SHell from FSF) are self-referential but not recursive. The oft-quoted recursive archetype is GNU, expandable as "GNU's Not UNIX," which invites further expansion. GNU, however, lacks a "break clause" (other than lack of interest) and therefore represents the type of endless recursion that our students are warned to avoid. Overlooked in the prior-citationeering scramble is VISA, defined as VISA International Service Association (noted by David Harris). MUNG is often given precedence, but this started life (MIT ca. 1960) as "Mash Until No Good," until it was fashionably retro-recursified to "MUNG Until No Good." See table below for other examples:

PINE	PINE Is Not Elm
EINE	EINE Is Not EMACS
ZWEI	ZWEI Was EINE Initially
LIAR	LIAR Imitates Apply Recursively

redo *n.* A single key or command that lets you quickly repeat the previous error. *See* UNDO.

redundancy *n.* **1** A method of at least doubling the overall error rate of a system by duplicating its most vulnerable elements. The exact improvement in the total error rate will depend on the reliability of the devices used to invoke each switchover to the standby elements. **2** A status in the nonemployed environment earned by overzealous efforts to meet a DEADLINE.

reentrancy *n.* The special ability of some PROGRAMs to mislead several users at the same time.

⇒That PC-DOS is non-reentrant should therefore be considered its major advantage.

reference *n. & adj.* **1** *n.* *Computer languages* A pointer ashamed to admit it. **2** *adj.* (Of a computer trade book section) an ASCII chart followed by tables copied from the official documentation.

reference account *n.* **1** A USER related by marriage to someone in the vendor's marketing department. **2** A user awaiting delivery. *See also* REALITY.

regular *adj.* **1** UNIX (Of an expression) irregular; convoluted.

⇒One of the many AUTO-ANTONYMs in the DP laxicon. Regular expressions are ideal if you want to grep (search) for strings that contain anagrams of "[]\ /*()-!~", end with a period, but do not start with a caret.

Relational Database *n. Also* **RDB.** **1** A set of tables (relations) straining to placate the unyielding *Lex Coddonis.* **2** A primitive collection of SPREAD-SHEETs lacking embedded cell formulae. *See also* NULLABLE.

⇒It seems that no canny royal-blue, all-the-way canonical, Coddeified RDB has yet been implemented. The RDBs that have scored 76/77 may well be overtaken by OBJECT-based databases before that final relational hurdle is surmounted. Although based on Codd and Date's sublime algebraic axioms and normalizations, the RDB does not readily map onto the many-valued logics and slovenly BLOBs of REAL LIFE. Many believe that storing all fields as POINTERs merely postpones the crisis.

Relational Database Management System *n. Also* **RDBMS**. A program or programs saddled with the task of handling a RELATIONAL DATABASE.

release *n. & v. trans.* [Latin *relaxare* "to ease the pain."] **1** *n.* A set of KLUDGEs issued by the manufacturer that clashes with the private fixes made by the user since the previous release. **2** *n. also called* **next release.** The long-awaited panacea, due tomorrow, replacing all previous temporary patches, fixed patches, and patched fixes with a freshly integrated, fully tested notarized update. **3** *v. trans. Marketing* To announce the availability (of a mooted product) in response to the release by a competitor of a product prompted by your previous release.

⇒Care is needed to distinguish a *last release* from a *next release*, since the difference is more than temporal. A *last release* is characterized by being punctual but inadequate; a *next release* avoids both errors. Next releases are worth waiting for. They are heralded with suitable hyperbole: "We bring you a fundamental purge of all past follies. A river of blood has been diverted to flush clean the Augean instability left behind by the previous, so-called programming team, the notorious, discredited Gang of Four; their pathetic lackeys, the Shower of Sixteen in Documentation; the extremely evil Coven of One who hired them all. They have each confessed freely to protect their miserable pension rights. Twelve of these unrepentant criminals were lynched by indignant workers, but the rest, saved by the lunch bell, have been exiled to the Los Angeles branch office."

reload *Also called* **reboot, reset.** *n. & v. trans.* **1** *n.* A button that is pressed to warn the system that the operator has returned from coffee break. **2** *v. trans.* To attempt an interruption of the DOWNTIME status. *See also* BOOTSTRAP.

remote *adj.* **1** (Of a boss) unaware of the current problems; harmless and readily ignored. **2** (Of a device) unaware of the current protocols; destined to crash the whole system if ignored.

reportage *n.* An advance form of DOCUMENTATION in which dull facts are spiced by hopeful INSINNUENDO.

reserved *adj.* (Of a word) sedately predefined by the computer-language designer and therefore unseemly when used *hors de contexte*.

⇒A potential AUTO-ANTONYM emerges in languages such as Pornol and Scatol where the reserved words are far from prim.

reset *See* RELOAD.

response time *n.* An unbounded, stochastic variable T_r, associated with a given TIMESHARING system and representating the putative time that elapses between T_s, the time of sending a message, and T_e, the time when the resulting error diagnostic is received.

⇒A certain degree of essential ambiguity is allowed in defining T_s and T_e, but for credible BENCHMARKs every effort should be made to ensure that $T_e > T_s$. "For what shall it gaineth an Manufacturer, that It winneth an Order, yet vitiateth the Laws of Physik." (St. Presper's *Injunctions to the Philistines*—level IV, release ii). In the post-benchmark environment, T_r assumes a more subjective quality and a larger mean value. In this context, *subjective* refers to the helpless feeling of the user, while *mean* means "selfish, indifferent to the demands of others." In any given large-scale time-sharing system, each user develops a mental model of the network by observing that T_r varies according to type of input, time of day, etc. Many ploys have been devised to minimize one's own T_r and, at the same time, punish the greed of others (e.g., A. Hitler, *Meine Rechnungsraumekämpfe* [Springer-Verlag, 1933.]) No quarter is given or expected in this struggle for one's fair share of memory and CPU cycles. *Compare* LEBENSRAM.

The noblest and bloodiest examples of this warfare can be found on CAMPUS time-sharing sites. The low cunning of the academic mind, further debased by an exposure to computer science, has found new "corridors of power" to cruise (see e.g., C. P. U. Snow, *The 10 Cultures* [Puffin Books, 1977.]) Bypassing the flimsy onionskins of the logon procedures; account number, password, and read-only private file protections; priority-level, core, and compunit allocations provides a more pleasantly ferocious diversion than all the traditional donnish disputations. The staff charged with protecting and rationing the campus computer resources do their best by secretly changing the rules at irregular intervals. Happily, this provides the user with a game infinitely more subtle and exciting than Dungeons or Donkey Kong. Students, especially, have the time (and the need for kudos) to freak the system, much to the chagrin of their elders. Some, though, have claimed that this is the main vocational benefit offered by a college computer network, as it primes the student for the more advanced trickery needed in the commercial environment, where compunits cost real dollars.

rest room *n.* The place where the rest of the OPERATORS can usually be found.

retromancy *n.* **1** Prophesying by looking over your shoulder. **2** The standard Baconian PARADIGM: massaging past events to provide fundable extrapolations. *See also*-MANCY.

retronym *n.* **1** An ACRONYM post-formed by mapping letters to words or parts of words. **2** "A noun fitted with an adjective it never used to need, but now cannot do without" (William Safire). *Compare* TWINS. *See also* BUNDLED.

⇒The example that triggered Safire's coinage seems to have been "analog watch." Until "digital" chronometers appeared, it went with saying that watches had physically rotating hands. (Of course, there are now electronic timepieces with simulated, incorporeal hands that you can wear on your wrist or use to wallpaper your GUI desktop.)

Intriguing DP retronyms include "natural language," "virtual reality," and "real time" (submitted by Bill Gray of the Idaho National Engineering Laboratory). Consider, too, the WAN (Wide Area Network), noted by Ted Jerome <TJ_Jerome@tallysys.com>. The retronymic qualification "wide" was made necessary only by the arrival of the LAN (Local Area Network) in the 1980s. Jerome also cites "end user," although some take this more as a valid insult than a true retronym. USER has always been a term of abuse, with ironical nods to the rare agentive *user,* "one who makes use of," or a natural confusion with *used,* "exploited." Robert DeShelter (Southern California Edison) offers "sunlight," "whole number," "natural food," "whole grain," "organic gardening," and "wood-burning furnace." For the original retronym, Joe McConnell suggests "human being," but this may depend on which cosmogeny you support.

Safire's definition needs a slight adjustment since retronyms are appearing as both nouns and *adjectives* that demand retrofitted qualifiers. Thus, Jerome reminds us of the eerie "human-readable." Does this qualify, I wonder, as an anthropo-anthropomorphic retronym?

return *n.* **1** *C* The KEYWORD followed by an expression invoking the function's implementation. **2** The callee's revenge. *See also* CALL; GOSUB; STACK.

⇒Many computers now regularly beat Macys' return policy of three months.

reusability *n.* A marketing priority overriding that of usability. *See also* OBJECT ORIENTEERING.

reversed class action *n.* DP LITIGATION by one END USER against all named and unnamed suppliers, nonsuppliers, assemblers, compilers, and their subagents in the OEM environment. *See also* SNA.

rightsize *v.* To downsize or upsize depending on the prevailing circumstances. *Compare* SIDEGRADE.

⇒There is no fashionable verb for remaining with what you have, although I expect that a CEO will announce soon that "We are dedicated to a samesize paradigm at this point in our methodological evolution."

ROM **1** Read-Only Memory. *Compare* WOM. **2** Read-Once Memory.

⇒Henry G. Baker and his fellow linear-programming theorists make a strong case for "Read-once" identifiers. Others think that "destructive reading" as a solution to SIDE-EFFECTS is "going too far."

root *n. See* SYSADMIN.

RPG [Report Program Generator] The precursor of all program generators, justifiably maligned.

⇒Those who assign generational integers to programming languages are divided over RPG: some say 0GL; others insist on (−1)GL.

RTFM *interj.* [Read The Fine Manual!] The standard brush-off advice to all gadget users or, rather, would-be users. Now replaced by BTFFHS (Browse the Fine Friendly Help Screen). *See* TNHD for less polite variations. *See also* DOXOLOGY; INTUITIVITY.

⇒Note that even exceptionally fine manuals have "erroneous zones," so the RTFM advice is rightly supplemented by a warning to "ignore the wrong bits." The latter are sometimes obvious from residual ARCHAISMS. Thus the section "Have you joggled the cards?" in a gdb manual is almost certainly spurious. More so than in any other trade, *prior* knowledge is a DP essential. *Compare* COIK.

run-time *Also* **runtime** *n. & adj.* **1** *n.* (QA testing) the moment when the programmer shouts "Must run!" and disappears. **2** *adj.* (Of errors) all those that sneak past the compiler and linker. *See also* LINT.

S

St. Presper (fl. 6 B.C.) The little we know of this early DP anchorite prophet has been gleaned from three contentious sources: fragments of several *Epistolary Updates* (now under close guard at the Prespertarian Chapel of Computer Scientology, Palo Alto, California), the partly deciphered Dead-C floppies, and the controversial epigraphs discerned only by the faithful on the PLATENS of St. Presper's printer relics. Many delightful schisms loom, but most scholars are agreed that the updates *were* written by St. Presper (some, though, may have suffered irreversibly from TEXTUAL HARASSMENT at the hands of a careless editor); that he did more or less flourish (or, at the very least, ran a fairly tight cave) some 6 years before the Coming; that he correctly predicted the Coming and, with St. Johnny [von Neumann], prepared a way for the Coming; but that once Turing came, St. Presper retired, having seen the Glory, to a monastic think cell near Philadelphia "to discount his beads," as he later confessed in his famous *Final Patent*. DP hagiographers, of course, are still unfurling and haggling over the Dead-C floppies, while the general public, confused by the conflicting snippets so far released, are left to marvel that these precious diskettes could possibly have survived more than 12 hours on a moonlit shelf.

Some recently published fragments point to the existence of a sect called the Atanasoffs, a shadowy group of abandoned ascetics possibly precontemporizing St. Presper's cult by a whisker or two. One interpretation, reading in and between the floppy's many lacunae, of an extremely mutilated text (Tractus IX, sectori ix–xii) provides this warning from the Atanasoff leader (also known as the Evil Priest): "Thou shall not covet (cover?) the ass (OS?) of thy neighbor's wife (support system?), nor ride (write?) over his pomegranate tree (data structures?)...." It is hard to reconcile such an austere commandment with any known, or practical, DP ethos.

sarcasm *n.* A cruel literary device; yet another nail in the AI coffin, as in "He left the computer industry to join DEC."

sarconym *n. Also called* **malignant acronym. 1** An acronym slanderously reinterpreted. **2** A non-acronym interpreted as a sarconym.

⇒See table below:

Acronym	Original	Maligned
BSA	Birmingham Small Arms	Bits Stuck Anywhere
DELTA		Doesn't Ever Leave The Airport; Don't Ever Land There Again

FDR		Franklin Deficit Roosevelt
FIAT		Fix It Again, Tony.
FORD		Found On Roadside Dead
IBM	International Business Machines	Inferior But Marketable; Itty-Bitty Machines; Incontinent Bowel Movement; I've Been Misled
ISDN	Integrated Services Digital Network	I Still Don't Know [sic]; Innovation Suiting Demands of Nobody; It's Still a Dead Network; Information Superhighway Delivered Now
LISP	List Processing (language)	Lots of Irritating Spurious Parentheses
MIA	Mobile Information Appliance	Missing In Action
MULTICS	MULTiplexed Information & Computing System	Many Unnecessarily Large Tables in Core Simultaneously
NFS	Network File System	Nightmare File System
NT	New Technology (Microsoft)	Not There
NTSC	National Television Standards Committee	Never Twice the Same Color
OWL	Object Windows Library (Borland)	Obsolete Windows Library
PAL	Phase Alternating Line	Perfect At Last
PCMCIA	PC Manufacturers Card Interface Association	People Can't Memorize Computer Industry Acronyms
PDA	Personal Digital Assistant	Poised to Disapppoint Apple; Public Display of Affection (U.S. Military legal code)
SECAM	Système Electronique Couleur Avec Mémoire	System Essentially Contrary to American Methods
Shell		Stinkt Hard En Loopt Langzaam (Smells bad and runs slowly)

sawteeth *n.* *pronounced* sore'teeth.\ Waveforms of a triangularly grating disposition.

scalability *n. Also called* **scalableness.** *See* SCALABLE.

scalable *adj.* Of those rare devices or systems that can be enhanced without degrading performance. *See also* PILOT.

⇒Newcomers to the DP thimblerig are understandably surprised to discover that increasing the number of processors or adding RAM does not guarantee improved throughput. SPACE PRECLUDES a detailed explanation, but a useful analogy might be found in the Frederick Brooks axiom that adding programmers to a project often delays its completion. Exceptions to this depressing more-is-less rule form the highly prized set of *scalables*, a fact that has been noted and overexploited by MARKETING. Mere scalability, alas, is now *vieux chapeau*, and nothing less than *superscalable* is at all salable.

The etymology for DP usage is confused. You can take the Latin *scalae* "stairs, ladder," or *skala* "an early Germanic dandruff." Are we looking at the North Face of the Eiger or into the eyes of Brother Saul (Acts 9:18)? According to the creative Proto-Indo-Europeans, the Latin root comes from *skand-* "to leap, climb," whence "scan," "ascend," and even "scandal." Equally intriguing, the Teutonic meaning derives from *skel-* "to cut" which also gives us "shell," "scalp," "sculpture," "school," and "shelf."

scatomancy *n.* [Greek *skor, skato-*, "dung, excrement" + *manteia*, "divination, prophecy."] A futile WHAT-IF based on the shit in your database or spreadsheet. *See also* -MANCY; WHY-NOT.

Schlumer, Fred (1820–1879) Apochryphal contemporary of Louis Pasteur (1822–1895) both of whom studied the effects of micro-organisms on food.

⇒The story goes that Schlumer started each day asking "O Lord, will I ever purify this f***ing milk?" Pasteur, they say, woke up each morning saying "Today, My Lord, I *will* purify this f***ing milk." Moral: Who ever heard of Schlumerized milk?

schoenfinkel *v. trans.* (LAMBDA CALCULUS) to replace (functions of several variables) with a complex function of a single variable.

⇒The operation is now known as *currying* (after H. B. Curry), rather than *schoenfinkeling*, although Schoenfinkel seems to have priority (see J. M. Brady, *The Theory of Computer Science* [Chapman & Hall, 1977, p. 255]). *Compare* SCHLUMER.

scope *n. Computer languages* The putative region(s) of a program within which a declared (named) object can be accessed and mutilated via its declared name. Molesting an out-of-scope object calls for subterfuges, such as POINTERS.

⇒Scope within compilation units, files, classes, functions, and blocks is further complicated by the related concepts of visibility (affected by duplicate identifiers) and extent (global, local, dynamic, static, persistent, dew-on-the-corn). Natural language scope emerges as a risible antidote:

"The greenhouse effect and the ozone layer have increased as a direct result of more toxics" (Letter to the *San Francisco Chronicle* from an 8th grader).

"Is this the place where you live and sleep most of the time?" (U.S. Census form).

"Bed for sale by man with big brass balls" (*Liverpool Echo* advert).

"Dog for sale. Eats anything. Very fond of children" (ibid.).

scrolling *n.* [Old English *scrowl* "a convoluted ornament."] An option allowing lines of data to move quickly up and off a VDU screen before they offend the operator.

⇒Scrolling rates are being improved to counter the insidious spread of rapid-reading techniques.

> Scrolling, just scrolling,
> Upward, and out of VUE;
> We don't envy your lot
> As you peer at the screen,
> We'll prompt you for a second
> Then we clear off the scene,
> When we're scrolling, just scrolling,
> To the safety of line minus 2!

SDH *See* SUPER DIGITAL HIGHWAY.

SE *See* SOFTWARE ENGINEERING.

seamless *adj.* [Origin: "Seams, madam? nay...I know not seams." (*Hamlet*, act 1, scene 2).] Mandatory DP usage: **seamless integration:** the fatal removal of essential INTERFACES between incompatible subsystems. *See also* SUPER DIGITAL HIGHWAY.

⇒Michael Schrage writes "...Bill Gates vows his company will lead consumers to a dazzling, new, multimedia future that seamlessly integrates the best of audio, video and computer technology." Some care is surely needed, Bill. If the joins are *too* seamless (*insufficiently* seamful?), the "media" is reduced to one unvariegated lump, unworthy of the prefix "multi."

segmented *adj. Vulgar: use with extreme caution. Also known as* **shifty.** Relating to the Intel 8088/6 memory-mapping calamity whereby two 16-bit registers mysteriously combine to provide a 20-bit address space. *Compare* LINEAR.

⇒The prolonged horrors of 8088/6 segmented memories have invoked the theory that Motorola sneaked some *agents provocateurs* into the early Intel design team.

self *n. See* THIS.

self-antonym *n. See* AUTO-ANTONYM.

self-referential *adj.* **1** (Of a statement) referring to itself often with intentionally risible results, as in "Down with Categorical Imperatives!" "Never employ a long word when there is an adequately synonymous diminutive." "Solipsists of the World, Unite!" "Never use a preposition to end a sentence with." "Eschew terminological obfuscation." "Is there a hyphen in anal retentive?" **2** (Of a paper) containing a high-percentage of references to works by the paper's author(s).

⇒Thus M. L. G. Shaw and B. R. Gaines, "Interactive Elicitation of Knowledge from Experts" (*Future Computing Systems Journal* 1, no. 2 [1986]) cites four references by Gaines, B. R.; 7 by Shaw, M. L. G.; and 15 by Gaines, B. R. and Shaw, M. L. G. David Bohm scores a creditable self-referential ratio of 10/16 in his "Hidden variables and the implicate order" (*Quantum Implications,* ed. B. J. Hiley and F. David Peat [Routledge & Kegan Paul, 1987.])

semantics *n. sing. & pl.* [Origin: Greek *semantikos* via *sema* "sign, token, mark."] **1** *n. sing.* The study of the relations, if any, between signs and their denotations, if any; a branch of linguistics, philosophy or SEMIOTICS depending on what these three tokens are taken to mean. **2** *DP n.* Meaning; meanings. *Compare* SYNTAX.

⇒The English pioneers were not fooled by the singular Greek suffix *-ikos* and pursued singular sciences such as "physik," "mathematik," and "semantik." The subsequent use of "-ics" for these domains of study presented no real problems. Physics *is* and will remain fun, and there's but one mathematics, even though its branches are legion. The numbing, number confusion starts with the DP use of "semantics" as a sumptuous synonym for "meaning" or "interpretation." Thus we find "IDAPI includes many database semantics," and even "Our semantics are better than yours."

semantic domain *n.* "A semantic domain is more or less equivalent to what is generally described by structural semanticists as a semantic field" (John Lyons, *International Journal of Lexicography* 3, no. 3 [Autumn 1990].)

⇒Ah, the precision of NATURAL LANGUAGE!

semiconductor *n.* **1** A device for proving the semidecidability of the HALTING PROBLEM. **2** *Buses* One who combines the duties of driver and (fare) collector. **3** An optimistic semi-insulator. **4** *Science fiction* Innocent Crystal, doped and raped by the evil Transistor.

semiotics *n.* Half a science of meaning is better than none. *See also* TEXTUAL HARASSMENT.

SEN *n.* SOFTWARE ENGINEERING News. An informal newsletter published by ACM SIGSOFT.

⇒The sad news is that in spite of 18 years of regular software horror stories, precisely and wittily diagnosed by Peter G. Neumann, the same "Risks to the Public" continue to dodge the SILVER BULLET.

senior systems analyst *n.* An unsuccessful systems analyst temporarily assigned to TICS, a manual Template Inventory Control System.

sequential file *n.* A place where records can get lost in lexicographic order. *Compare* RANDOM FILE.

serial *adj.* Being or pertaining to just one damned thing after another. *Compare* MASSIVELY SERIAL; PARALLEL.

server *n. Also called* **suffering server.** A system devoted to ignoring client requests. *See also* CLIENT/SERVER; MIDDLEWARE.

SETI [Search for Extra-Terrestrial Intelligence.] The good news is that a message has just arrived from Alpha Centauri. The bad news is that it claims prior UNIX patents by 2 billion years.

setup *n. & v.* [Origin: *Underworld* A plot to incriminate and destroy.] *See* INSTALL.

SetWorldTransform *n.* A function in the WinAPI confirming the global MICROSOFT takeover plan. *See also* MAW.

seurat *n.* [Honoring pointillist painter Georges Seurat (1859–1891).] (ISO GUI unit) 2 × 2 PIXELS.

Seven Catastrophes of Computing, The *n.* The user, the manufacturer, the model, the salesperson, the operating system, the language, and the application.

⇒Recent advances in topology by Thom, Zeeman, and others have increased our understanding of the structural instability of a wide range of systems. Catastrophe theory has found applications in the analysis of physical, biological, and even sociological phenomena. Catastrophes are, appropriately, global discontinuities that have proved to be beyond the reach of traditional mathematical techniques. Happily, perhaps, René Thom seems to have proved that for a (3 + 1)-dimensional, locally Euclidean manifold, such as the one most of us inhabit and within which most of our systems run, there are exactly seven distinct types of catastrophe, one for each day of the week.

Seven Deadly Sins (From the Dubliners' LP "Seven Deadly Sins," Fiesta Record Co., Inc., 1619 Broadway, NY, NY. FLPS 1773; words, McLean; tune based on "The Boys of the West" [trad.]) The sins cited by the Dubliners include kissing, swearing, gambling, smoking, and boozing. The DP catechism adds:

Some say debuggin's a sin,
But I say it's easy to scoff;
For debuggin' has been in the world
Since Amazin' Grace Hopper's dead moth.
And if it wasn't legal then the lawyers they would sue,
And the prisons would be full of folks who nailed a bug or two;
And if they didn't like it, then away the girls would run,
And if it wasn't plenty then the puir folk would get none.

Some say spaghetti's a sin
But labels are easy to see;
And spaghetti has been in the world
Since EDSAC I branched with an E.[25]
And if it wasn't legal then the lawyers they would sue,
And the prisons would be full of folks who made a jump or two;
And if they didn't like it, then away the girls would run,
And if it wasn't plenty then the puir folk would get none.

Some say that GOTO's a sin
But where is the man who can tell?
For GOTOs have been in the world
Since the Devil was told "GOTO Hell!"
And if it wasn't legal then the lawyers they would sue,
And the prisons would be full of folks who made a branch or two;
And if they didn't like it, then away the girls would run,
And if it wasn't plenty then the puir folk would get none.

shareware *n.* Programs that are not worth pirating, as in "Who steals my FLOPPY, steals trash" (Iago).

⇒Apart from heat and humidity, shareware is one of the few things that can reduce the value of a blank diskette.

shell *n. See* BOURNE SHELL.

shift *n. & v. trans.* [Origin: Old English *sciftan* "to classify (people) according to their undergarments".] **1** *n.* Any one of the three customary DP work PHASES, distinguished by the hours worked, the degree of supervisory vigilance, and the subsartorial rancidity of the staff. **2** *v. trans. Marketing* To boost the sales (of a product) by declaring a better PRICE/PERFORMANCE. **3** *v. trans.* To select the wrong half (of a double-case character set). *See also* CASE; COMBINATORIAL EXPLOSION; PARADIGM; PARADIGM SHIFT.

---

25. E n F = Branch to instruction at n if accumulator >= 0 else perform next instruction.

shilop *adj. also called* **zciweisakuy.** Reversed Polish. *See* POLISH NOTATION.

SHIT [Acronym for Square Holes in Tape.] Considered but rejected by Olivetti (1958).

SHRDLU [Non-acronym, sarcastically expanded as: Simplistic Heuristics in Reduced Domains needing Little Understanding.] A landmark AI program devised by Terry Winograd, 1972, that "knew blocks." When asked why it picked up the big red block, SHRDLU replied "Because you asked me to."

⇒Some say that SHRDLU represents the 7th–12th most frequent letters in English, and that this fact was exploited in the keyboard layout of early typesetting machines before the merits of a random layout emerged with the QWERTYUIOP arrangement.

shrink-wrap *n.* [Origin: *shrink* "a quack psychiatrist" + "wrap."] A transparent covering that must be broken to access the contents of a software package, yet left unbroken to avoid legal acceptance of the DISCLAIMER.

⇒This Catch-22 has been known to drive some users to seek expensive counselling.

side-effect *n.* An unexpected state-transition that the programmer quickly proclaims as essential, nay, the raison d'être of the application. *Compare* BUG. *See also* ROM.

sidegrade *n.* A rare form of UPGRADE that does not degrade the status quo. *Compare* RIGHTSIZING; SCALABLE.

⇒Sidegrades are usually performed to entertain and retain the support team, get rid of the DPM, and verify certain emulationary strategies.

silver bullet *n. Also called* **magic bullet.** The putative cure for all the ills of our multi-wracked trade, *esp.* an Ehrlich-type pill for the syphilis of SOFTWARE ENGINEERING.

⇒Fred No-Silver-Bullet Brooks is pessimistic, suggesting a wide range of patient, evolutionary improvements rather than a single magic antibiotic. His case is somewhat tarnished, however, when, apparently influenced by the scurrilous, antihistorical film *Amadeus,*[26] he calls for more "Mozart programmers" and fewer Salieris: a shameful slur on Gluck's heir, the admired tutor of Beethoven, Schubert, and Liszt. Regardless of musical talent, one would prefer one's life-support or missile-guidance system to be programmed à la *Tarare* than *Die Zauberflöte.*

Marketing, both academic and commercial, continues to promote a sequence of silver bullets: structured, object-oriented, fuzzy, neural, logical, functional, horned with the devil's clauses, and so on. Cynics feel the need for silver handgrenades or even ballistic missiles. A rare optimist, though, has declared that "One day the grail will come home to roost in the ballpark." *See also* DP VOGUE.

---

26. In spite of its many Academy Awards, *Amadeus* did *not* win an Oscar for Best Musical Score! Not enough Salieri?

simplex *n.* **1** The working part of a duplex. **2** A cheap complex. *Preferred plural:* simplexes; *adjective:* simplexic, simplectic, simplexical, simplectical.

⇒Beware of the pedantic, obsolescent forms *simplices, simplicial,* which have been known to add 5 percent to a quotation.

single-case *adj.* **1** (Of a character set) shiftless; unlikely to meet with ASCII approval. **2** (Of a user) being the only one expressing complete satisfaction in an IFIP opinion poll (1941–1994).

⇒Although the user ticked the "no publicity" box on the questionnaire and IFIP guaranteed absolute privacy, 39 OEM suppliers mounted strong campaigns claiming the sole credit for this nonce account.

single-char language *n.* A computer language boldly titled with a single, invariably upper-case letter, e.g., as we go to press, A, B, C, E, J, K, and Z.

⇒On the downside, this fashion encourages gap-filling language design; happily, though, it reduces the total number of such languages to 26 (excluding, of course, diacritical compounding and ventures into non-roman alphabets and syllabaries).

A puzzling solecism needs to be mentioned: spurious quotationalism. Many writers are happy with Ada and Pascal, but feel compelled to quote the single-char languages: The package contains Pascal and "C" compilers.

sizing *n.* [Origin: *size* "to cut or otherwise shape (an article) to the required disposition."] **1** *Obsolescent* The process whereby a system configuration is devised to meet the prospect's various DP requirements. **2** *In current usage* The process whereby a system configuration is devised to meet the prospect's price ceiling. *See also* DOWNSIZING; UPSIZING; RIGHTSIZING.

Smalltalk *n.* Pure, slow but pure OOP; a family of object-oriented languages developed (*chiefly*) by Alan C. Kay at Xerox PARC in the 1970s. *See also* C++; OBJECTIVE-C.

⇒Speed, of course, is a subjective criterion, subject to the inevitable advances in CPU PRICE-PERFORMANCE. Purity, however, is apodictic. Smalltalk classes are Platonic *ideas* and their instances (objects) are *manifestations.* Throw in your Leibniz *monads* and Hobbes *prudentia* and the tingling epiphany hits: you can feel Smalltalk's philosophical purity slowly tugging the armpits. Hybrid OOP, such as C++, is quicker but sullied. Bjarne Stroustrup defends hybridity, not with Kaysian polemic, but by pointing out that practical dining requires both knife and fork. The fierce altercations between Smalltalk and C++ supporters are reflected in Kay's comment:

> "Where Newton said he saw further by standing on the shoulders of giants, computer scientists all too often stand on each others toes." (Alan C. Kay, "The Early History of Smalltalk," History of Programming Languages Conference (HOPL-II), *ACM SIGPLAN Notices* 28, no. 3 [March, 1993]).

smart *adj.* Lacking in dumbth *esp.* of a device with its own CPU, OS, API, support team, monthly magazine, and bugs.

⇒The preferred DP noun form is "smarts" rather than "smartness."

smiley *Also called* EMOTICON. *See* E-MAIL HUMOR.

Smith numbers *n.* A composite number n such that $S(n) = S_p(n)$, where $S(n)$ is the sum of the digits of n, and $S_p(n)$ is the sum of all the digits of all of the prime factors of n. Thus, 9985 is a Smith number since $9985 = 5 \times 1997$ and $9 + 9 + 8 + 5 = 5 + 1 + 9 + 9 + 7$.

⇒The name reflects the fact that Smith numbers are as common as dirt (no offence intended to all you fine Smiths out there).

Attention has therefore moved to *consecutive* (such as 728, 729) and *palindromic* (such as 12345554321) Smith numbers. And now there are k-Smith numbers. For example, 42 is a 2-Smith number because $42 = 2 \times 3 \times 7$ and $(2 + 3 + 7) = 2 \times (4 + 2)$.

Some mathematicians are "not convinced thereby that Smith numbers are not a rathole down which valuable mathematical effort is being poured" (Underwood Dudley, *Mathematics Magazine* 67, no. 1 [February 1994], The Mathematical Association of America).

But, wouldn't it be fun if some hidden property of Smith numbers emerged as the key to unifying quantum-gravity field theory, revealing God as a "mere" recreational mathematician?

smydge *n.* (ISO GUI unit) A 4×4 fuzzy PIXEL matrix, or four SEURATs. *See also* BITMAP; BLYB.

SNA *n.* [Scapegoat Network Architecture.] A protocol in the OEM environment, diluting the suppliers' obligations, but offering END USERs and their attorneys all the attractions of MSR (Multiple-Source Responsibility). *See also* REVERSED CLASS ACTION.

SOB *n.* **1** Subtract One and Branch. **2** Son of a Bitch. *Warning* Often resists contextual disambiguation.

⇒In the AlphaMicro M68000 assembler, the macro

```
SOB Dn,label
```

is implemented by

```
SUB #1,Dn
BNE label
```

If Dn starts life at 0, the two SOB's coincide.

social climbers *n.* C programmers who claim C++ experience in their CVs (curricula vitarum).

⇒The plural of *vitae* is used as a sop to my New Age and Hindu friends.

sod's law *See* MURPHY'S LAW OF PROGRAMMING. *More at* TNHD.

software *n.* The difficult part of the system, which still retains an aura of intangibility in spite of being "engineered" and sold as a "product." *Compare* HARDWARE. *See also* PRODUCTIZATION.

Software Engineering *n. Also* **SE.** "The doomed discipline...or how to program when you cannot" (Edsger W. DIJKSTRA). *See also* CASE; COMPUTER SCIENCE; COMPUTING SCIENCE; PRODUCTIZATION; SEN.

⇒This attempt by the software community to acquire the mature prestige associated with "real engineering" is naturally resisted by real, card-carrying, rule-sliding engineers. Indeed, the job designation "software engineer" has been banned in some U.S. states. But, in the other direction, after each bridge collapse and Hubble telescope fiasco, many programmers rush to distance themselves from "engineering." Would any self-respecting coder wish to be associated with the following reparational methodology?:

"Ground controllers had to scramble when shuttle commander James Wetherbee reported during descent the failure of a mechanical gauge that displays the positions of the rudder, body flaps and other flight control surfaces. Mission control told him to turn the power off and on..." (*San Francisco Chronicle,* 11/2/92).

Failing that, of course, the traditional engineer would try tapping the offending unit with a light hammer. If SE does succeed, one can envisage the emergence of a new metatechnology called EE (Engineering Engineering). *See also* SILVER BULLET.

software rot *n. Also called* **bit decay.** [From JARGON FILE.] A hypothetical disease the existence of which has been deduced from the observation that unused programs or features will stop working after sufficient time has passed, even if "nothing has changed." *More at* TNHD.

SOLID [Simulation of Optical Lithography In three Dimensions.] Silvaco's chip-mask design program gains high marks for acronymic deftness.

SOM Overloaded Acronym: Start Of Message (ASCII); Systems Object Model (IBM); Semantic Object Modeling (David Kroenke). *Warning* Often resists contextual disambiguation.

source code *n.* The version of a program to which the compiler OBJECTS. *See also* DECOMPILING, JAMES JOYCE'S LAW OF.

space precludes! *interj.* Ignorance cloaked in a long-winded claim that the author's word-allocation has been exceeded.

⇒"Space precludes" is not-too-distant cousin of "beyond the scope." Thus: "A thorough examination of error analysis techniques is, of course, beyond the scope of this book..." (D. E. Knuth, *The Art of Computer Programming,* vol. 2, 2d ed. [Reading, Mass.: Addison-Wesley, 1981]).

Reader exercise: Discuss the meaning of "of course."

SPAM *n. & v.* **1** *n.* Portmanteau: Spiced Ham (Hormel Foods Corporation). **2** *n.* Acronym: Society for Philosophizing About Mathematics (Ian Stewart, Warwick University, UK). **3** *v.* To crash a program by overloading a buffer. *More at* TNHD. *Warning* Often resists contextual disambiguation.

⇒Stan Kelly-Tubal writes: "The sublimest evenings of my life were spent chez Babette munching her incomparable Spam en Sarcophage and chewing over the Zermelo-Fraenkel axioms with the divine Penelope Maddy..." (private communication, until now).

Adversely, regarding Spam qua feast, John Ryle (*Times Literary Supplement,* July 15, 1994) writes: "How is it that this *reductio ad absurdum* of animal protein manages to retain and even augment its allure? A clue lies in two acrostics...written by Jack Collom:

Suddenly, masked hombres seized
Petunia Pig
And
Made her into a sort of dense Jell-O

Somehow the texture, out of nowhere,
Produces a species of
Atavistic anomie, a
Melancholy memory of 'food'"

spectrum *n. plural* **spectrums;** *mandatory DP usage* **wide spectrum(s).** **1** [Latin *spectrum* "an apparition."] Any range of one or two items or features.

⇒A range of from three to seven features is known as a *complete* or *total spectrum.* Ranges of eight or more are called *unfair trading.*

2 A fine series of books published by The Mathematical Association of America, Washington, D.C.

speculative execution *n.* Taking a branch action before the result of the test is known or knowable.

⇒Most BEQ (Branch EQual zero) instructions fail, so in situations where speed is more important than accuracy, the execution flow can be anticipated without bothering to test the CCR (Condition Control Register).

speedbar *n. Ironic form of* **toolbar.** A confusing strip of ICONs the least scrutable of which are those designed by the user. *See also* GUI.

spelchek *n. Also called* **spulchik, spilchok,...** A word-processing adjunct that attempts to detect and, with the *smart* options, correct, your orphographical sillysosms.

⇒Behind all the *smarts* lies a grunting, homonym-blind and homophone-deaf strang-mitching routine fighting a stunted word database. Faced with the sentence "AI proves it's benefits in spell checking," my spelchek rejected only the string "AI". Some versions helpfully reveal their limitations, as in *"shit is not in the dictionary, but it would fall between shin and shiver."*

Cabalistic lexicographers divine deep truths from such accidental contiguities. Thus, the not-so-Random House Unabridged offers the compelling sequence, "mother church, "mother country," "mother earth," "mother-f**ker," "mother goddess," and "Mother Goose."

The corrections suggested by a spelchek also reveal unexpected insights. Michael Orr reports that his Microsoft Word proposed "Fraud" and "shameless" in lieu of the unknown "Freud" and "seamless." *In spelchek veritas?*

spirit guide *n. Also* CHANNELER. Politically correct terms for DAEMON. *See also* PC UNIX.

spool *n. & v.* [Origin uncertain: perhaps blend of *spoof* + *fool*; or archaic acronym for Simultaneous Peripheral Operation On-Line.] **1** *n.* A highly volatile BUFFER established to hold surplus DATA (known as results) for a period not exceeding the MTTR of the particular output device being spooled. **2** *v. trans.* To expose (data) to the dangers of residing in a spool. **3** *v. intrans.* To shed previous results in order to proceed with more important computations.

spreadsheet *n.* [Origin: Anglo-Welsh, "the seasonal distribution of manure."] The massive exploitation of Cartesian SIDE-EFFECTs. *See also* MACROCEPHALIC; RELATIONAL DATABASE.

⇒The strange, attorney-strewn spreadsheet story from VisiCalc to Lotus 1-2-3, thence to Microsoft Excell and Borland QuattroPro, dominates the birth, growth, and travails of the PC. From the harmless hobbyist calorie counter and home-games, joy-stuck toy, the PC soon blossomed as the Uzi of CREATIVE corporative accounting. The WHAT-IF moved to WHY-NOT, indicting the spreadsheet as the chief culprit in the 1980s S&L scandal.

SQL *n.* [Structured Query Language, IBM.] A shibboleth (Judges 12:4–6) for detecting database poseurs.

⇒Those pronouncing SQL as \ess-kew-ell\ rather than \sequel\ are instantly revealed as charlatans incapable of confuting the six-and-seventy jarring normal forms. Those who have *really* suffered are allowed to say \squeal\. *Compare* KLUDGE; QUERY PROGRAM.

Compare the crisp SQL,

```
SELECT CUSTOMER
FROM RECEIVABLES
WHERE DUE >= 5000
AND STATE = 'CA' OR STATE = 'OR' OR STATE = 'WA'
```

with the equivalent vernacular "Get dem effin' West Coast flakes dat owe me 5 gee or more."

squiggle *n.* [Portmanteau: *squirm* and *wriggle*] A mark of editorial censure; a visible sign of TEXTUAL HARASSMENT. *See also* EDITOR; TEXT EDITOR.

⇒The wondrous set of ISO handwritten editing squiggles is threatened by the advent of electronic text. Typically, the cursive transposition of two tokens is now achieved with an Alt-Ctrl-S macro.

SS [*Abbrev.* Schutzstaffel; Social Security.] *Warning* Often resists contextual disambiguation. However, SS as Sommersemester; steamship; shortstop; and *scilicet* (Legal) are megaparsecs away semantically.

SSR *n.* [Singular Source Responsibility.] A primitive castigational methodology aimed at uniquely vectorizing the finger of scorn. *More at* SNA.

"To err is human, to dismiss, divine!"

(*DPM Handbook* [1976])

stability *n.* [Latin *stabulum* "a pothouse, haunt, brothel."] **1** A nirvana-type situation that calls for drinks and layoffs all round. **2** The period between crashes.

stack *n.* & *v. trans.* [Origin: *stack* "chimney," from the tendency of early registers to issue smoke after a hard day's pushing and popping.] **1** *n.* A special area of memory designed that St. Presper's prophecy might be fulfilled: "For the last shall be first and the first, last—and to hell with Mr. Inbetween" (*Sermon on the Mount Instruction*, Release VI, level ix.) **2** *v. trans.* To smooth out (data or instructions) by covering them with more data and instructions. The resulting smoothness depends on the depth of the stack, the relative position within the stack, the weightiness of the stack contents, and the power of the PUSH. *See also* CALL; LIFO; FIFO. **3** *v. trans.* [Origin: *stack* "a large, orderly pile of unthreshed straw."] To establish an impressive pile (of unread computer listings).

standard *n.* [Origin: "L'étendard sanglant est levé" ("The bloody standard is raised")—La Marseillaise.] **1** Formerly, what IBM did, but now what MICROSOFT do. **2** The intersection (lowest common factor) of all pre-existing implementations. *See also* AD HOC; ANSI; IMPLEMENTATION-DEPENDENT; ISO; OPEN; PROPRIETARY.

⇒In DP usage "standards" is often of the singular persuasion, as in "Standards is an area that is constantly changing" (Carl Cargill, Standards strategist, Sun Microsystems Inc.). Implementors detest this volatility.

standard deviation *n.* A sexual activity formerly considered perverted but now universally practiced and accepted.

A DP Freudian writes: "I divide my patients into two broad categories: those who are turned on by normally distributed bell curves and those who are not. Do not fret, I tell them all. One person's meat is another person's Poisson. That soon gets the idiots off my couch, out of my sample, and into my accounts payable. The latter will give them a *real* problem, and what our dedicated profession considers to be healthy mental anguish."

standby *adj.* Denoting a relationship between two installed computers.

⇒Given two systems A and B (usually, but not necessarily, from the same manufacturer) installed at points in the same compact manifold, we say that B is a standby for A (written $A \sim B$) if B is down or overloaded whenever A is down or overloaded [Kelly-Bootle 1984, 1985, 1986; Kelly-Bootle and Erdös 1944, 1945, 1946; Kelly-Bootle and Euler 1781, 1782, 1783]. It is clear that the standby relationship is reflexive, i.e.,

$$(A \sim A)$$

and transitive, i.e.,

$$(A \sim B) \text{ and } (B \sim C) \text{ implies } (A \sim C)$$

but not necessarily symmetric, i.e.,

$$(A \sim B) \text{ does not imply } (B \sim A)$$

Less formally: If B is standby for A, then B will certainly be out of action when A needs help; however, there could be occasions when B is out of action or overloaded and A is running happily. This lack of symmetry is not only a nuisance to the mathematician (the well-known Unterstützensproblem) but also a breach of commercial etiquette. Various methods of ensuring standby symmetry have been tried. If A and B use the same level operating system and field-engineering team, there is an excellent chance that A *will* be hors de combat whenever B seeks assistance. With this proviso, the standby relationship is an equivalence relationship and defines a *partition*—some writers prefer the older but more appropriate term *decomposition*—of the set of all installed systems.

We define $\{A\}$ as the set of all X's such that $(X \sim A)$. Clearly $\{A\} = \{B\}$ if and only if $(A \sim B)$. If A is the only member of $\{A\}$, we say that A is *stand-alone*. Note that a stand-alone system is neither more nor less vulnerable than a system belonging to a larger partition. The DPM of a stand-alone system simply has a smaller telephone bill and less clout with the manufacturer. For consider a partition containing three systems, E, F, and G. When DPM(E), the DPM of E, needs help, he/she will place calls to DPM(F) and DPM(G), who are just placing calls to each other *and* to DPM(E). Depending upon the complexity of the various telephone switchboards involved and the skill and persistence of the callers or their secretaries, a certain lockout time can be expected before all three have exchanged mutual commiserations. Each can then contact their respective *bouc émissaire* (fall-person or manufacturer's representative) and listen to the usual excuses ("Are you sure your operator has four blank cards in the JCL deck...?") before announcing that two other systems are in the same boat.

state-of-the-art *adj.* **1** *Marketing* A vacuous predicate applying to all items. **2** *Technology* Promising; untried; deserving of more funds. **3** *Art* Postexpressionist, preminimalist, praeterfauve, and so on, depending on the whims of National Endowments. *See also* VAPORWARE.

⇒Diluted by overuse, "state-of-the-art" is being usurped by more hyper bollicks. Thus we have "the white-hot searing edge of technology" not only pushing but presumably igniting the envelope.

Conundrum: "What's the difference between Socialist Realism and DEC's Alpha chip?" Cute response: "Socialist Realism is the art of the state."

statistics *n.* The third member of the ISO MENDACITY SEQUENCE. *See also*: FORECASTING.

⇒Exactly 76.3434 percent of all statistics (including this one) are invented on the spot.

stepwise refinement *n.* Any sequence of KLUDGEs, not necessarily distinct or finite, applied to the program P aimed at transforming it into the target program Q.

⇒Formal kludge theory (a much-neglected aspect of FIX point topology) deals with the extremely non-Abelian group $K_G(P)$ of all kludges on P. We often write K_G when no ambiguity threatens, and we freely speak of kludges *of P*, *against P*, and *over P*. A stepwise refinement is a sequence $\{k_i, t\}$, $k_i \, \varepsilon \, K_G$. In theory, the time parameter t is considered as a monotonic increasing positive integer indicating the order in which the kludges are applied. In practice, t is often left unrecorded, and we hear the comment "God knows how many times we've changed P this week." We can express a kludge sequence on P as $(k_n * k_{(n-1)} * \ldots k_2 * k_1)(P)$ without explicit reference to t, provided we remember that the k's are not necessarily distinct. Generally $k_i * k_j \neq k_j * k_i$ for $i \neq j$; indeed for some P, the first inequality can hold even for $i = j$. This and many other paradoxes have undoubtedly inhibited the fruitful development of kludge theory.

We next introduce the concept of program isomorphism. We distinguish $P = P'$ (identical programs) and $P \sim P'$. The latter relation (read as "P is just as bad as P' ") includes identity, but also links different programs that produce identical calamities (within tolerance). There is a unique unit element for all $K_G(X)$'s, the *idempotent* or *null* kludge $\mathbf{I}$ such that

$$\mathbf{I}\,(X) = X \text{ and } (\mathbf{I}*k)(X) = (k*\mathbf{I})(X)$$

for all X and all $k \, \varepsilon \, K_G(X)$. The null kludge is regularly implemented by means of the copy or duplicate command. A safer method is to change one's password and take the day off. A wider class of kludges, the so-called *idimpotents*, of P exist, defined as:

$$K_I(P) = \{k: \forall k,\ k_j \, \varepsilon \, K_G(P),\ k*(k_i)(P) \sim (k_i)(P)\}$$

or, more concisely, members of $K_I(P)$ are ineffective and should be avoided.

For each $k \; \varepsilon \; K_G(P)$ there exists a unique inverse k^{-1} such that

$$k * k^{-1} = I = k^{-1} * k$$

It can be shown that

$$(k_n * k_{n-1} * \ldots k_2 * k_1)^{-1} = (k_1^{-1} * k_2^{-1} * \ldots k_{n-1}^{-1} * k_n^{-1})$$

so that any series of miskludges can be readily corrected by applying their inverses, with care, in the countersequential environment. Regular backups, though, are still recommended. Many (possibly infinite) pseudo-inverses of $k \; \varepsilon \; K_G$ (P) satisfying

$$(x*k)(P) = P'$$

exist where $P \sim P'$, $P \neq P'$. A pseudo-inverse of k, written k^{-1}, does not entirely reverse the impact of k, but at least the resulting P' is isomorphic to P, i.e., $(k^{-1} * k)$ restores P without measurable degradation. Nullifying such a transformatiom requires the further refinement $(k^{-1})*((k^{-1})^{-1})$, which may be hard to find. Many programmers confuse $(k^{-1})^{-1}$ with $(k^{-1})^{-1}$ and $(k^{-1})^{-1}$, which accounts for the low standards, missed DEADLINES, and escalating costs of debugging. The power of $(k^{-1})^{-1}$ can be illustrated as follows:

In $(k^{-1} * k)(P) = P$, substitute $k = (k^{-1})$ and $P = (k)(P)$:

$$(k^{-1})^{-1} * (k^{-1})(k)(P) = (k)(P)$$

whence $(k^{-1})^{-1} * Q = (k)(P)$ where $Q \sim P$. Potentially, therefore, $(k^{-1})^{-1}$ can guide any number of "near misses" toward the target version.

The weakness of $(k^{-1})^{-1}$, on the other hand, can be demonstrated as follows:

In $(k^{-1}) * k(P) \sim P$, substitute $k = (k^{-1})$ and $P = (k)(P)$:

$$(k^{-1})^{-1} * (k^{-1})(k)(P) \sim (k)(P)$$

whence $(k^{-1})^{-1} * Q \sim (k)(P)$ where $Q \sim P$. It follows that $(k^{-1})^{-1}$ is equivalent to (k) followed and/preceded by an idimpotent.

The pseudo-inverses of k discussed so far satisfy $(x*k)(P) \sim P$. A thorough examination of all possible solutions to this equation is, of course, beyond the scope of this low-cost work. (*See also* SPACE PRECLUDES.) The itchy reader is directed to *Grundlagen von Stümperhaftstheorie* (Berlin: Stümper-Verlag, 1934).

To sum up, if Q is the "target" program, stepwise refinement is the trivial task of constructing a kludge sequence $\{k_i, \; t\}$ such that

$$((k_n, t_n) * (k_{n-1}, t_{n-1}) * \ldots * (k_2, t_2) * (k_1, t_1))(P) \sim Q$$

where n is reasonably small. Since the kludge product to the left of P belongs to $K_G(P)$, let us call it k_s. The immediate identification and application of k_s, whenever possible, greatly simplifies the transition from P to Q and results in a single-stepwise or one-kludge refinement. Formally, we have $k_s \sim (QP^{-1})$, which in one interpretation means "erase P and create Q." This represents a symbolic justification of the Kelly-Bootle Rule (*see* DEBUGGING), namely, that if the target program is Q, then Q should be written, rather than writing P and a painfully converging sequence of k's.

stringent *adj.* (Of an expression) short. *See* CURTATION.

studies *n.* Mandatory usage: **recent studies.** Anonymous results usually from a "well-known West Coast University."

⇒Studies that vitiate your preconceptions are known as "flawed."

structure *n. & v. trans.* [Latin *struere* "to contrive."] **1** *n.* A quick-drying cement offering instant cohesion to any number of unrelated modules. **2** *v. trans.* To render (anything) less interesting. *See also* STRUCTURED.

structured *adj.* **1** (Of a proposal, memo, report) typed, often with numbered paragraphs. *Also called* **over-structured,** *esp.* when typed with indentions and subnumbered subparagraphs. **2** (Of a programming language) allowing the user a limited quota of GOTOs according to age and experience.

subroutine *n.* [Latin *sub* "less than, inferior to" + *routine* "mundane, lack-luster, boringly repetitive."] Any trivial, overdocumented program written by your immediate superior.

⇒*Hints for use*: quietly debug, circulate laudatory memoranda, and incorporate it into all your programs, theses, and bibliographies.

sufficiently large *adj.* As in "2 + 2 = 5, for sufficiently large values of 2."

summation convention *n.* A mathematicians' shindig held each year in the Kronecker Delta.

SUN [Acronym for Stanford University Network.] An early UNIX network based on Stanford-designed MC68000 machines.

⇒One of the commercial companies established to exploit this design, Sun Microsystems Inc., is now the dominant UNIX workstation vendor. The change from SUN to Sun was suggested by the Copernican model, with the added observation by Scott McNealy that not only our planets but the whole cosmos is heliocentric.

super- *prefix* Laughably inadequate. *Compare* HYPER-.

supercomputer *n.* **1** Any machine still on the drawing board. **2** A machine priced to exploit GROSCH'S LAW. *See also* GROSCH'S LAW, COROLLARY TO.

⇒Of the two opposing trends in computer architecture, diffused microchips versus centralized giants, Grosch's law supports the latter. In spite of the relative failure of most supercomputer projects in the late 1950s and early 1960s (recall that the IBM Stretch was widely known as Twang), a strong lobby supports my proposal to replace all known computing devices with one *very* big central system. As a concession, we would reprieve the CDC Stars and Cray Mk. I's to act as remote job stations for the proposed giant. A merger of all manufacturers and software houses would be needed, and although no one could claim this would be an easy matter, it would have many beneficial side effects. We would see, for example, an end to the present glut of distasteful intercompany litigation which keeps so many DP ATTORNEYs away from their wives and families. To avoid linguistic squabbles, the big machine would support both dialects of LISP (*see* LOGOMACHY) and possibly ALGOL 84.

A brief, unstructured protest can be expected from a few FORTRAN delinquents, but calling the new supergiant GOD (General Oracle Dispenser) could shame such petty opposition into righteousness. Those without shame would need to test their convictions against the burning passion of the ANSI/ISO Inquisition—the stakes will be high and merciless, for "better that an hundred Mirandas should burn, than that one unrepentant Fortranite should goto free" (St. Presper's *Imperative Injunctions to the Gotoless*, Level VII, release iv).

The question of where to site our proposed monster is still under review. Since some 2000 square miles of floor space and 300 miles of socketed pipeline will be needed, the most favored suggestion is that the whole of Ireland (both Ulster and the Republic) be used. The present population would be persuaded, by means of an irresistible "Make Way for GOD" campaign, to move to the more affable ghettos of Liverpool, Boston, New York, Chicago, and Tasmania. In one swell foop, we would solve the 600-year-old Irish question and the even older IBM-federal antitrust problem. Even more importantly, GOD would eliminate all DP salespersons' territorial and commission disputes that for so long have threatened the very fiber of civilization. Mainframe sales would naturally cease under GOD, and add-on's, including peripherals, would be handled by the computer via RSEs (Request for Self Enhancement). A typical RSE from GOD might be: "Add 256 MB RAM and 32 16 TB drives, OR ELSE." These indications that GOD would develop into an implacable Hebrew Testament tyrant have aroused some opposition to the project. The anti-GOD movement is still fragmented, but the most credible of the opposition groups is led by Dr. Max Stømp of the Nul Institute of Metaheuristics, Bergen, Norway. "By 2004," he claims, "this fiendish machine will be omnipotent, omniscient, omnipresent, self-perpetuating, another IBM. Our terminals will become mere on-line confessionals. Are we to become slaves to a huge pile of ruthless silicon? Must we kneel before a mere *list*? Will our children be denied the pleasure of debugging a three-line BASIC program?" His appeal to the Irish to join his "Kill GOD before it's too late" crusade has had a mixed reception. Neither the Pope nor the Rev. Paisley has yet commented publicly on the "Bring GOD to Ireland" plan, but many Irish are already packing to take advantage of the subsidized airfares. Others are writing prophetic come-all-ye's:

Come all you gallant Irish lads
Wherever you may be;
I hope you'll pay attention
And listen unto me.
I hope you'll pay attention, lads,
Wherever you may dwell;
And of our countless troubles
The truth to youse I'll tell.
I hope you'll all be patient, boys,

While I the truth unfold
Concerning our misfortunes
The likes were seldom told;
So sit back, Jack, and just relax
And listen to my song;
'Tis something strange and tragical
It won't detain you long.
Go where you will, o'er valley and hill,
Past moutains short and tall,
[cries of "Get on with it, Paddy!"]
On every tree that used to be
You'll hear a modem call.
In every brook the stranger took
A job stream trickles by;
And where the birds once filled the air
There's drumheads on the fly.
My mother's cot, which meant a lot,
A base address, no more!
Electrical cords and circuit boards
Entwine around her door!
Why did she yield this compact field
The sod where Granuaille trod?
Two shades of green are all that's seen
In this binary land of GOD!

The most telling argument, though, against the mooted concentration of all computing resources is the risk that, if they are sited within a certain critical radius, we might incur a collapse under gravitational and recursive forces, leading to a DP black hole. Conditions within such a black hole defy description. All known laws, including Grosch's, would break down. The LISP syntax itself might be in danger. No signals could emerge from such a massive discontinuity (a familiar and reassuring phenomenon, perhaps, to many users), yet it would forever engulf and suck in any loose peripherals and unattached operators unwise enough to stray within its increasingly avaricious field.

Super Digital Highway (SDH) *also called* **Super Information Highway, InfoBahn.** "A SEAMLESS web of comms, networks, computers, databases & consumer electronics…" (NII Digital Highway Press Release); the Clinton-Gore plan to empower the homeless with free waterproof modems and a share of the information explosion.

⇒Apparently, to implement this ominous mess, *two* committees have been "impaneled." At first glance, I read this as "impaled" (wishful thinking). What on earth is less likely than *two* committees to produce a seamless web of anything but intrigue and deficit? Who said "three committees?"

Joe Perret reports from Hollywood that the endemic of Super Digital Highway metaphors has reached *Variety* magazine with the headline "InfoPike." We must not add to the rash of SDH pothole and roadkill jokes, except to note some of the road-sign suggestions: "Last CRC for 50 miles!" "Beware of Falling Bits!" and "Slow! Kermit Zone Ahead!"

superstition *n.* An irrational belief or ritual which survives until replaced by a more effective superstition. The replacement is known as "updating the system documentation."[27] *See also* -MANCY; PRAYER.

⇒The DP trade, being more hazardous than seafaring and less predictable than farming, has generated more supersitions than these two older professions combined. In addition to the more or less universal folklore of computer science, each site develops its own local myths and the supporting rituals and incantations to placate the particular in-house dyads, sprites, daemons, and nereids known to influence the stochastic quick-sands of computation. The following examples illustrate the diversity of DP folklore:

"Red tape at night, payroll's delight."

"Joggle, joggle, joggle quick;
Throw the top card to Oulde Nick."

"Take a flowchart, add a square;
Draw a circle, join with care;
When a sweet accord is won,
Sign the chart 'Ben Nicholson.'"

"Glaucomus discus, seek forever;
Sector and track, forsake us never."

(To be chanted after each crash):
"Bittie, bytie, bytie, bit,
Holy, holy, holy shit!
Bytie, bitty, bitty, byte,
Holy, holy, holy shyte!"

"We shall not, we shall not be moved; (repeat)
We're not re-loc-a-table, we should not be moved."

"Six lines in the file there be;
One for you and one for me,
One to comment, one to shun,
One to test, and one to run."

"In-house mouse, in-house mouse,
He ventured into a FILO nest;
The farmer followed, and all the rest;

---

27. "Superstitione tollenda religio non tollitur" ("You cannot get rid of religion by eliminating superstition" (Cicero).

The mouse is now a permanent guest;
In-house mouse."

"Too many terminals spoil the response."

"A patch in time makes nine."

"When Adam punched and Eve dem'd
Who was then the DPM?"

"Two's complement, three's a crowd."

superuser *n. also called* **root.** *See* SYSADMIN.

suspect *n.* A name on a prospect list offering little or no prospect of future sales. *Compare* INTROSPECT. *See also* TRAVELING SALESPERSON PROBLEM.

SW5 *n.* A modal logic discovered in London.

⇒The general idea is that everyone knows everyone in Chelsea, at least in the biblical-semantic domain.

sweatshop *n.* A department devoted to the rapid, accurate, and cheap entry of data.

⇒ Punch, punch, punch,
   In poverty, hunger so hard;
   And as she skipp'd
   And as she dup'd
   She sang the "Song of the Card."

(Thomas Hüd, *Lochentotenlieder*)

syllogism *n.* An early (Aristotlean) template for making logical inferences.

⇒The dangers of careless syllogistic reasoning, of the kind that machines have difficulty avoiding, are illustrated by the following well-known examples:

God is Love   No cat has five tails
Love is Blind   I am no cat
God is Blind   I have five tails

All green-cheese objects orbit the Earth
The Moon is a green-cheese object
The Moon orbits the Earth

All *soi-disant* Cretans are liars
All liars are mortal
Socrates says he's a Cretan
Socrates is a liar
Socrates is immortal

symposium *n.* [From Greek *syn* "together" + *posis* "drink."] **1** A gathering of scholars where each attendant is intoxicated by his/her contribution and sobered by the lack of response. **2** *DP usage* One of several symposiums (*Archaic* symposia.) **3** The academic Happy Hour during a CONVENTION.

syntax *n.* **1** (Natural languages) the presumed set of rules/tests that would generate/validate all and only "grammatically correct" sentences, including the few, possibly this, that have "meaning." **2** (Computer languages) the set of rules/tests embodied in the compiler regardless of the designer's formal and informal intentions. *Do not see* SEMANTICS.

sysadmin *n. often intercaps* **SysAdmin.** *Also called* **root; avatar; shiva; superuser.** *Soviet-type contraction* for systems administrator. **1** The UNIX-installation supreme, *grosse banane*, diktat-dispensing apparatchik who allocates disk space, home directories, and passwords. **2** A bimonthly journal from R&D Publications, Lawrence, Kans. *See also* GURU.

⇒Other sysadmin duties include, but are not limited to, booting, rebooting, shutdowns, backups, file-integrity, security, virus-detection, disaster-recovery, links to other sites, performance-tuning, prioritizing, policing, punishment, documentation, education, upgrades, and posting "Your mother doesn't work here" notes on the site microwave. A rumored compensation for these underpaid chores is the freedom to read, write, execute, or erase any user file as the mood dictates. Hence the quip: "Our sysadmin was expelled from the Gestapo for excessive cruelty" (Henny Thumpman).

system *suffix & prefix* **1** *suffix* A delimiter used to signal the termination of a string of DP nouns and adjectives, as: "executive file control system," "information processing system," "control program generation language system," "computer system." **2** *prefix* An indication that the following object or property is beyond the pale of the average user, as: system memory, system performance, system goal, system interrupt, SYSTEMS ANALYST, SYSADMIN.

⇒The noun *system* has lost all discernible meaning in current DP usage and is best avoided except as an occasional aid to right-hand justification in certain   word-processing   systems! Originally meaning "an orderly combination or arrangement of parts or elements into a whole," *system* suffered early and massive debasement in DP parlance by being applied indiscriminately to any old ratbag of seamful components. It is probably too late to restore systematic precision (compare, for example, the many dilations of *nice* since 1400), for we can hardly expect a manufacturer to launch "The all-new **XYZ** nonsystem which we hope will soon be SEAMLESSly integrated in an orderly fashion."

systems analyst *n.* An unsuccessful programmer who, to maintain the system's integrity, has been disbarred (removed from all keyboards) and assigned to an off-line TEMPLATE.

T

T-shirt *n.* A cotton, torso-hugging sandwich-board.

⇒A quirk of the times is that we now pay advertisers to wear their promotional rags. Dubious, possibly illegal, DP examplars carry the legends "Dual Floppies" and "Look'n'Feel."

tacky mat *n.* A device originally designed to remove dust from the shoes of anyone entering "clean" areas such as the old-fashioned computer installations. Present-day systems, though, actually thrive on a certain amount of GRUNGE, and the tacky-mat makers seemed doomed to join the dodo-stuffers local of the Taxidermists' Union. The advent of SuperGlue™, however, has recently revived the craft. Dr. McTavish has extended the use of the mat to solve the vexing problem of site security. His invention was launched with the slogan: "Keep the buggers out with McTavish's Tenacious Tacky Mats!"

target audience *n.* (COMPUTER BOOKS) all breathing primates with $34.95 spare change.

⇒The convention-call equivalent is "Who should attend?" except that the "breathing primate" condition is extended to all credit-card carrying organisms, living or dead.

An intriguing branch of literary "theory" covers the complex "relational matrix" between "text-provider" and "target-reader." Thus, one ponders lengthily why Mario Salvadori's *Why Buildings Stand Up* is not selling well in Sarajevo, or why *The Eat-What-You-Like Diet Plan* flopped in Rwanda.

Consider too *The Revolutionary Guide to Turbo C++*, by Valery Sklyarov (translated by Sergei Ponomariov), Birmingham, UK: The WROX Press, 1992. The large red C++ of the title is made to look like a hammer and sickle, the erstwhile epitome of revolutionary icons. However, with a touch of free-market decadence the book opens with the quaintly worded section "Who is this Book Aimed at?" As with all such target delineations, the blunderbuss is cocked widely at "experienced programmers *and* beginners who want to learn C++." The true Stalinist approach implied by the title and cover would surely dictate a must-or-else-Gulag readership, conscripting those who have no desire to learn C++ at any level. Professor Sklyarov is a prolific and respected author back in the ex-USSR, the Russian Peter Norton, in fact. He teaches computer science at Minsk, the capital of Belarus. Lenin called the White Russians "revanchist reactionaries," so perhaps the correct target readership is "all counter-revolutionaries with ill-gotten hard currency."

template *n.* 1 A hardware device for producing stylized graffiti.

⇒A tangential application is the preparation of FLOWCHARTS. Irish Business Machines offers a single-sided template that reduces the cost of the holes. More versatile models are double-sided, with one side (face down, 9-edge leading) designed for TOP-DOWN symbols, while the obverse (face-up, 12-edge trailing) is intended for BOTTOM-UP applications.

The most expensive template ever constructed belongs to Xerxes P. Qume, Jr., an amateur AI buff from Ottumwa, Iowa. His symbol shapes were cut to ANSI X3.5 specification by laser beam into a 4- × 8-inch plate of pure ruby at a reputed cost of $2.5 million. Mr. Qume runs a Radio Shack TRS-80 and has resolutely turned down many trade-in offers from Amdahl and Cray.

2 *C++* An overdue mechanism for data-type parametization, overloading the symbols "<" and ">" rather than the already superloaded "(" and ")". **3** *Computer Science & Folksong* A useful pattern (PARADIGM) when creativity flags, as in, "X-aware," "X-compliant," "X considered harmful," "Come all ye bold X," "I was born in X, raised on the Y side," "You don't miss your X 'til your Y runs dry," and "If all the young X's were Y's on the Z."

temporary *n.* *C++* An OBJECT that is either destroyed before it has served its purpose or persists long after its useful span.

teramite *n.* **1** The charitable donation from a jackpot-hitting widow (cf. Mark 12:42). **2** A massive invasion of acarines.

Terminal Diseases Inc. An international company devoted to performing post mortems on dead terminals. Their computerized service and diagnostic center is "on the net" (INTERNET), whence their proud slogan, "If you can reach us, you don't need us."

terminology *n.* Both the nomenclatura and its catastrophic side-effects. *See also* ONOMANCY; WINDOWS.

⇒In my version of the musical "Oklahoma" the lexicographer and terminologist "should be friends." The poor passive lexicographer tries to divine meaning from occurrence in a world of Tweedleda, while the terminologist is devoted to actively assigning useful words to (possibly) new objects and ideas. In real-world fact, the writer-creator of (possibly) fresh concepts introduces terms that take off before the terminologist is consulted. The unfazable lexicographer reports that "class" and "object" are used ambiguously this-and-thus, but the terminologist gnashes his or her gteeth.

In an innovative dissertation, Tweedledum's preamble declares that "X means Y"[28] and no harm is done if Tweedledee simultaneously announces that "Z means Y." Here

---

28. "It is to be observed that a definition is, strictly speaking, no part of the subject in which it appears. For a definition is concerned wholly with the symbols, not with what they symbolise....Theoretically, it is unnecessary ever to give a definition...it is, nevertheless true that they [definitions] often convey more important information than is contained in the propositions in which they are used....First, a definition usually implies that the *definiens* is worthy of careful consideration. Hence the collection of definitions embodies our choice of subjects and our judgement as to what is most important. Secondly, when what is defined is (as often occurs) something already familiar...the definition contains an analysis of a common idea, and may therefore express a notable advance (A. N. Whitehead and B. Russell, *Principia Mathematica,* vol. 1 [Cambridge: Cambridge University Press, 1920], pp 11–12).

we have the normal synonymicity that all language is heir to. But if Tweedledee states that "X means Z," where Z and Y are antonymical, we invite the car bumper sticker: "Eschew terminological obfuscation." Many critics of the DP laxicon fail to distinguish healthy synonyms from confusing ambiguities.

The latter often arise from the overloading of "familiar" terms, a habit common to those scientific domains that misguidedly shun neologisms. Consider "space," "real," "set," "crank," and "fiber bundle" in Mathematics, "syzygy" in Astrology, "deep" in Linguistics, "thinking" in W. Danny Hillis's multiprocessors, and "individuation" in quantum mechanics.

And, even as you read this, new concepts are expensively searching for old, trade-remarkable words, and vice versa. Thus a screen subrectangle becomes a Microsoft Window—who would pay $99.95 for Subrectangles 3.1? And thence the struggle to assign "frame," "pane," "sill," and "shopper" to related marketable ideas.

T_EX *pronounced* tech[guttural]\\[™American Mathematical Society.] Don Knuth's ultimate metafont, metamacro, metatext formatter, ideal for printing your poems in ever-decreasing spirals in either direction.

⇒Correct pronunciation of the Greek chi is the shibboleth that distinguishes gentlepersons from players (compare SQL). Some have even suggested that the subscript E calls for a dipping intonation as in the fourth Mandarin tone. Note also that non-T_EX systems can be spotted by their references to TEX or TeX without the proper kerned subscription.

I used to think that T_EX's ability to print in spirals fell into the category of "clever but pointless" (rather like, as we say in Liverpool, being able to fart the tune of "Annie Laurie" through a keyhole), but a recent piece of serendipitous research has changed my mind. A large clay disk, known as the Phaistos Disk, was discovered in Crete in 1908. It has engraved pictograms on both sides that have not yet been deciphered. The Phaistos Disk has been dated to ca. 1700 B.C.E. and according to John Chadwick has "the distinction of being the world's first typewritten document. It was made by taking a stamp or punch bearing the sign to be written in a raised pattern, and impressing this on wet clay."[29]

The amazing fact is that the script on each side of the disk runs in a spiral. The more amazing fact is that after much scholarly dispute, it is now agreed that the script runs from right to left (unlike other Minoan scripts), and from this fact and other clues it can be shown that the script was "typed" from the rim down to the single pictogram at the center. The T_EX spiral examples, as I recall, take the easier center-to-rim direction, but no doubt, given fixed strings and diameters, T_EX could match the efforts of those pioneering typists. I am calling on ANSI to establish standards for circular paper sizes—the Phaistos Disk is 6 1/2 in (160 mm) in diameter, by the way, which clearly deserves consideration as the ad hoc standard. I believe that the disadvantages for humans in reading spiralized text are more than offset by the ease with which paper

---

29. John Chadwick, *Linear B and Related Scripts* (University of California Press/British Museum, 1987).

"disks" can be scanned by OCR "heads" using obvious and minor adjustments to our present mass storage technology.

Rumor reports the scurrilous graffito at Stanford: "Knuth's secretary uses WordPerfect." *More at* TNHD. *See also* CASE-INSENSITIVE; X, CURSE OF.

text editor *n.* [From Latin *texere* "to weave" + EDITOR.] The software needed to generate any number of deviant copies from an original, correct text. *See also* SQUIGGLE; TEXTUAL HARASSMENT.

⇒James Joyce's *Finnegans Wake* provides an early example of the random distortions which can arise when editing literary texts on a computer. Dr. Thumpkins's monumental *Key to the Key to the Key to the Key to Finnegans Wake* (known as "Key to the fourth" in the Joycean industry) paints a convincing picture of Joyce pounding successive versions of his ironically named "Work in Progress" into a primitive GLASS TTY. Thumpkins proves conclusively that Joyce's failing eyesight was a result of what DP ophthalmologists call "myopia terminalis." There remains some doubt, however, regarding the compiler used by Joyce. The constantly occurring ALP motif (Anna Livia Plurabelle) suggests that the anagrammatic APL or PAL languages were used. One remains confident that a period of scholarly vituperation will resolve this question. Certainly the published text, as we have it today, is an intriguing melange of text files and backups, together with bits of source and miscompiled object code from the editor itself. Thumpkins is now studying the following hitherto unpublished Joycean fragment, reported to have appeared on a disconnected CalComp during a DP séance held in Dublin on Bloomsday 1979.

"I AM the begin/end. Declare all positively. And weren't we all in the DOS house together, boys, up to our flying heads in the floating fixed-length turds, overlaying our dunderheads and undermining our overheads, greytrackedsuited in every whitecollared, blackboxed sector with never the sign of a bit of a byte to console our terminal demands? Access me no succubus till I abscess all those who abacus against us.

"O, Father Tee Jaysus O'Watson! send not yer therribly numerate bugs to plague us! Think, tank, or forever hold yer world-piece-wise-linear-vector-bundled-policy. Shall I compare thee parotty-fashion, sweet Brighton Poly? Flame, flame! Or else to some odd-holed who-doughnut? WATFOR, esprit de core? Wipe that lisp off yer interface you unprintable, parenthetical swine. You CDR well, mes petits CONS. LET no bound fairyballs go free WHILE we decompile in oure haze of algohol.

"In endless loops my grandfather/father/son lies, their bones of CORAL made. Arrays! Arrays brave Fortranbras and tak the low code while Putney Bridge is falling down. I see hell! ICL! I see hell in your eyes; one single-tender glance. All hands off DEC as we cross the Hudson, the river of low returns. Seekest thou the sweet Honeywell, well, well or the feedholes of a naked Burroughs lunch? Holy Macro, Mother of GOD, things Rank Xerox and Herb Grosch in nature possess us merely. That it should come to this. Not three months merged. Nay, not so much. The one true road beckons. Una vecchio. Univaccio. O Lord, sperry us from their fastrandy forcesales. I hear the crash of distant drums. Mauchly eckerstistical! Is the END so near? Halt-tape-jam-break-fast. 4K the lot."

textual harassment *n.* The actionable adjustment of an author's submission.

⇒Umberto Eco is my favorite standup semiotician. One day he may quit stalling, eschew half measures, go *le tout cochon*, and become a full otician: "...the first draft of Eliot's *Waste Land* opened: 'April is the cruelest month. And March isn't all that great, either'" (*The NY Review of Books,* June 9, 1994).

that *pron. & adj.* See THIS.

THINK sign *n.* A printed injunction formerly issued to all IBM employees and prospects, but withdrawn when too many of the recipients developed symptoms associated with a thoughtless, literal interpretation.

⇒The original ⃞ THINK ⃞ sign was, in fact, introduced by Thomas J. Watson, Sr., at the turn of the century when he was sales manager of NCR, some 20 years before he founded IBM.

Before adopting the slogan for his new company, T. J. commissioned a local think tank to devise pithier mottoes. He quickly turned down:

> Endeavor constantly to employ fully your ratiocinative processes.

on three grounds: (1) lack of pith, (2) the high cost of sign bytes, and (3) to blatantly avoid a split infinitive was a shade un-American. The next proposal submitted to the great man was based on the noble, universal dignity and snobbery of the Latin epigram:

> COGITO ERGO VENDO!
> VENDO ERGO SUM!

T. J. quietly pondered. "I think, therefore I sell; I sell, therefore I am. Well...the syllogistic conclusion seems sound enough in a naively existentialist epistemological framework, but, as you know, the truth of the implied proposition can in no way be taken as a validation of either antecedent. In other words, I reckon you're putting Descartes before de horse!" A wry chuckle split his wrinkled face. "I need time to think it over," he beamed. "In the meantime, you're all fired."

this *pron. & adj.* C++ The implicit pronomial keyword POINTER such that `*this` (known as `self` in other OOP languages) represents the object under discussion.

⇒Although `that`, `those` and `these` are not C++ keywords, the concepts are readily implemented by explicit data members pointing to or referencing other objects *sans gêne.*

In general usage, the demonstrative "this" is full of surprises. For example, the TV/Radio advert preamble "And now this..." is self-negating, a warning to grab the muting device.

thrashing *n.* The punishment meted out to greedy users by a tired, confused, and overworked multiprogramming system.

thread *n.* **1** A poor but honest process trying to survive in a hostile environment. **2** A time-wasting sequence of messages unrelated to your target topic.

threadbare *adj.* (Of an OS) unable to support multithreading.

⇒Thus, billions of DOS users, too poor or cowardly for OS/2 or UNIX, are unable to process and print their words while their SPREADSHEETs are suffering background recalculation.

throwaway *adj.* (Of a program) sold below cost for public debugging. *See also* PROTOTYPING.

throwaway character *n.* Any character in a transmitted message.

⇒Prior discussion with the common carrier can sometimes limit the set of throwaway characters to, e.g., alpha only, least significant digits, etc.

Thumps, Micky *Also* **St. Micky Thumps** *or* **St. Micky.** The patron saint of timesharers *See* CURSOR.

thunk *n.* [Origin: Fred Descartes (no relation): "I thunk therefore I was."] Ingerman's procedure for implementing calls by name via Landin's applicative expressions (1961). *More at* TNHD.

⇒To clarify this in the Windows environment, `MakeProcInstance` takes a pointer to the `AboutDlgProc` procedure and a pointer to the current instance of your program and binds the two together. This creates your *thunk*, a prolog or small piece of code that identifies a data segment and then branches to the window proc. The thunk thereby ties the shared code to the data segment of one instance...(cont'd. page 3029).

time *n. & v. & adj.* **1** *n.* "That which tries to prevent everything happening at once." (Anon.) **2** *n.* That which flies like an arrow *esp.* when the MT grant is running low. **3** *adj.* A species of fly that infests arrows. **4** *v.* To measure the speed of flies *esp.* using a methodology devised for archery. *See also* KBMT.

time management *n.* The extension of memory management techniques to that other vital computing resource, time.

⇒The random-access time (or RAT) board is plugged into the standard S-100 bus just like an additional memory board. RATs come in a variety of 8-, 16-, 32-, or 64-Kt (kilotick) configurations with many bank-switching options. The *tick*, of course, is the standardized byte of time, which will vary according to the system's basic clock frequency. The Lorentz dilation factor can be safely ignored except for those manufacturers reporting exceptionally fast-moving inventories.

Each RAT provides either shareable or user-dedicated blocks of addressable cycles that can be "stolen" by the CPU as required. With the advent of the megatick chip and more advanced cycle-compression techniques, we can now envisage a computing framework offering *better* than real-time processing. Under the mooted virtual time management environments, the user would be able to access pages of stacked-fixed-tick blocks controlled by the stacked-fixed-tick-block clock. When a virtual RAT becomes exhausted (or "totally cycle-depleted"), it would issue a stacked-fixed-tick-block-clock nack, and this would initiate some form of recycling procedure. The latter, as yet unsolved, problem is at the searing, white-hot tip of technology and explains the recent renaissance of IBM's Time Recording Division, which has quietly taken over both the Poughkeepsie, N.Y., and Havant, U.K. facilities. The RAT race has been summed up by Prof. Manfred Thümps: "Forget the Top Quark; we want the antichronon!" In what bizarre high-energy situation these elusive particles will emerge remains to be seen. Time will tell.

timesharing *n.* [Origin: English folk song "Let No Man Share Your Thyme."] A system in which many users try to corrupt the same database simultaneously.

⇒To protect itself, the system traditionally increases RESPONSE TIME until the user loses interest. *See also* CURSOR.

time slice *n.* The occasional CPU cycle begrudgingly conceded by the operating system to the user. *Also called* **the period at risk.**

⇒Typically, the OS compares the complexity and importance of your programs with those of its own internal problems. It then allocates time slices (and memory, perhaps) accordingly. If you do gain a brief place in the JOB TRICKLE, you can be assured that you really *do* have a problem. *See also* RESPONSE TIME.

TLA *pronounced* Tee-El-A\\ *Abbrev.* Three Letter Acronym or *pronounced* TLA\\ Acronym for Three Letter Abbreviation. [Origin: the Semitic consonantal triads.] *More at* TNHD.

⇒TLA offers 26^3 = 17,576 distinct upper-case combinations but time is running out. We know that since Ed CHERLIN joined the Hanoi Tower monks in 1991 their ring-swapping algorithm is much improved—the brief history of time could be briefer than we thought. On the other hand, we have so many TLA OVERLOADs that it is difficult to predict TLA exhaustion.

TM *n.* [Time Management.] A fashionable branch of management science devoted to the proper utilization of the executive's extraprandial time resources. An intense, full-time, 3-year course is offered by the Thumps Institute for Advanced Business Studies, an unusual feature of which is that diplomas are awarded only to those who drop out after 10 minutes.

TNHD *The New Hacker's Dictionary. Also called* R&S. *See* JARGON FILE.

top-down *adj.* Relating to a programming methodology whereby unwritten modules are linked together to produce the target program. *Compare* BOTTOM-DOWN; BOTTOM-UP; MIDDLE-OUT. *See also* METHODOLOGY.

⇒The chief advantage of top-downing is that unwritten modules can be linked without the bothersome interfacial anomalies encountered between *written* modules. Rivals who preach the bottom-up approach warn us that top-downing is simply a naive way of postponing the gruesome day when *all* must be made clear and sweetly dovetailed. As with the other seven and twenty jarring schisms that divide the computing fraternity, the top-down/bottom-up controversy does not seem resolvable by "old, barren Reason" alone. The dispute affects only largish software projects, although one hears of classroom exercises where two weeks are spent discussing the correct programming strategy for a five-line BASIC assignment to list factorial N until the paper runs out. The outsider might argue that *if* you start at the top, the number of directions available in pursuit of your dream is severely limited. Likewise, as confirmed in many a popular song, the only escape from an infimal situation is upward. The outsider is well advised to mind his or her own business. For any major software project, in fact, there is no start, finish, bottom, *or* top. Such concepts do emerge fleetingly, from time to time, as each deadline passes, but the one true coordinate, when all the obscurantist theologizing has evaporated, is the *middle* of the project. This is no mere ecumenical compromise, but a fundamental tenet of the middle-outers. The latter have gained many converts of late thanks to a well-equipped and persuasive Inquisition.

Tourette's disease *Also* **Tourette's syndrome**. *n.* [after Georges Gilles de la Tourette, French neurologist (1857–1904)] A motor incoordination associated with echolalia/echophrasia (the meaningless repetition of words) and coprolalia (obsessive use of obscene language); commonly found among overworked C programmers.

⇒The obvious symptoms are random scatological strings in both code and comments:

```
whPRINTFile ((type = getop(shits, MAXassOP)) !=Episs)
swPRINTFitch (type) {    . . . } \\f**kme it's 5.0am
```

TPD *n.* Overloaded *abbrev.* Trivial Problem Discriminator, Total Program Diagnostic, Terribly Poor Documentation, Terminal Printer Destruct, Tchebyshev Polynomial Derivation, Total Program Dump, The Prophesied Delay, Turing's Problem Decided. *Warning* Often resists contextual disambiguation. *See* MUM.

TQM [Total Quality Management.] Yet another "apple-pie and everlasting peace" concept that one is loath to oppose.

⇒TQM has certainly crushed the rival PQM (Partial Quality Management) movement.

trademark *n.* A legally protective operator serving to distinguish, say, Hoover the generic vacuum cleaner from Hoover a particular deceased, Red-baiting, transvestite head of the FBI. *See also* COPYLEFT; COPYRIGHT; INTEL-LECTUAL PROPERTY; PATENT; WEASEL.

⇒For a complete guide to the current state of international intellectual property law in relation to trademarks, patents, and copyrights, send me a cashier's check for $500,000. Allow 6–8 years for a response.

An interesting, potentially infinite, digression is found in my attempt to trademark the font for the letters "t" and "m" in my special "tm" digraph. Thus we need "$t^{(tm)}m^{(tm)}$" and so on.

The traditional preamble explicitly acknowledging each subsequent trademark is now replaced by the vapid disclaimer: "All brand and product names are the trademarks or registered trademarks of their respective holders." What would Hoover say to this if he were alive?

The high anxiety of trademark paranoia is seen in a recent ComputerWorld advertisement. The footnote listed a dozen trademarks including "IBM is a trademark of International Business Machines." A perfectly valid statement. However, the main text of the advert contained no references to IBM! Similarly, one encounters thousands of "Windows™" in spite of the fact that (as we go to bed) Microsoft has been refused a trademark on this generic term.

trailer *n.* [Latin *trahere* "to drag."] **1** (Of magnetic or paper tape) that portion of the medium that drags on the unwind spool or trails on the floor. **2** (Of a punched-card deck) a member of the rear guard in the battle between card deck and card reader. *Compare* LEADER.

transparent *adj.* Being or pertaining to an existing, nontangible object. "It's there, but you can't see it" (*Borland dBASE for Windows announcement*, 1992). *Compare* VIRTUAL.

trash can *n.* (GUI) An iconized disposal device designed to facilitate the accidental deletion of essential files. *See also* ICON; GARBAGE; MOUSE; BIN.

⇒Within an hour of installing their Macintosh, my daughter Carol and her son Luke contrived to drag'n'drop three files into the avaricious trash-can black hole. As the saw-mill operator exclaimed when showing the foreman how he lost a finger, "There goes another one!"

My alternative, game-inspired deletion method has boxed filenames floating and bouncing around the screen. As you ZAP the target files with the joystick, the boxes explode with suitable megaroidal sound effects. Destroying vital files such as COM-MAND.COM or kernel.bin earns you 10,000 bonus points, EOG (End of Game), and a sarcastic sermon on the need for BACKUPS.

The goal of a common iconic interface was rudely thwarted when Apple claimed complete dominion over the smell'n'feel of its particular MacTrash design. The ould Liverpool street song was heard in Cupertino:

"O you can't put your muck in our dustbin,
"Our dustbin, our dustbin,
"You can't put your muck in our dustbin,
"Our dustbin's full [aliter: copyrighted]..."
(Trad. to the tune of "Balls to Mister Banglestein")

Overnight, GUI implementers faced the challenge of adjusting their BITMAPS to provide non-infringing but recognizable receptacles. Given the limitations of 16×32 PIXELs, it is not surprising that juries are still *mal pendus*, peering at blown-up slides of diverse PVC lids, handles, and fluted bodies. IBM's OS/2 countered with shredding as the metaphor for file erasure. This makes the un-erase (UNDO) action less credible than Apple's method of picking through the trash to retrieve a document. More realistic metaphors, available on NeXT, offer tractors pushing your unwanted piles of paper into a landfill.

Guy L. Steele Jr. notes (private communication until now), "...how difficult it can be to dispose of a real-life trash can. Just setting it out empty by the curb on trash collection day doesn't work, no matter how battered it is. Even attaching a note requesting disposal does not always work. A trash can is a RESERVED word in the sanitation business. You must really crush it or tear it to pieces so it no longer looks like a trash can."

traveling salesperson problem *n.*, *also (archaic)* **traveling salesman problem.** A classical scheduling problem that has baffled linear programmers for 30 years, but which, in a more complex formulation, is solved daily by traveling salespersons.

⇒The traditional LP version of the problem requires that a salesperson visit a given finite set of prospects (without repetition) in a sequence which *minimizes* the distance traveled. The *practical* problem, faced by real-world peddlers, *adds* the following conditions: (1) multiple visits are allowed to certain prospects, dependent on several parameters, such as temperature and conviviality; (2) claimable expenses need to be *maximized*. In some marketing organizations further conditions regarding the effectiveness of the chosen peregrination are decreed, as a given sales quota must be achieved. To compensate for this restriction, traveling salespersons are encouraged, at any point in the visitational strategy, to append to their prospect set any number of subsets from their fellow-traveling salespersons' prospect sets. This stochastic process is known as POACHING. The skill needed to reconcile the petty conflicts arising from overlapping prospect sets is known as *sales management.*

In other marketing situations, the finiteness restriction on the prospect set is lifted, allowing the addition of any number of spurious names to the sales forecast. Such extensions to the prospect set form two classes, viz., SUSPECTS (visited only to maximize expenses) and INTROSPECTS (beyond any conceivable canvassing methodology, but adding luster to the prospect list).

Ironically, a major theoretical breakthrough in the LP problem was made by L. G. Khachian (Doklady, 1979) of the then Soviet Union, where the practical traveling salesperson problem and the allied traveling kulak problem had been dramatically resolved in 1917 by the revolutionary Lenin-Trotsky method.

tree *n.* **1** A resource widely considered renewable until the advent of the paperless office. **2** Judge Lynch's instrument of justice (Ambrose Bierce). **3** (Data structures) An inverted hierarchy with the root on top; any node can be taken as the root of its subtree.

⇒Ungodly access to the ultimate SYSADMIN root has for long been proscribed: "...Of every tree of the garden thou mayest freely eat; But of the tree of the knowledge of good and evil, thou shalt not eat of it; for in the day that thou eatest thereof thou shalt surely die" (Genesis 2:16–17).

trivial *adj.* [Latin *tri* "three" + *via* "way."] Pertaining to a marital problem requiring outside help, and, by extension, to any problem needing discreet delegation. *See also* TPD.

⇒Under the ETHELRED OS, any previously tackled program is flagged as "trivial." Thus, a typical abort message might read "O Lord, not another f***ing payroll..."

truncate *v. trans.* To remove (from a field, string, message, or salary) some or all of the most significant digits of characters. *See also* CURTATION.

truth *n.* "An ingenious compound of desirability and appearance. Discovery of truth is the sole purpose of philosophy, which is the most ancient occupation of the human mind and has a fair prospect of existing with increasing activity to the end of time" (Ambrose Bierce).

truth table *n. Marketing* A loaded list of competitors comparing available features. *Compare* MENDACITY SEQUENCE.

TTY *n.* *pronounced* titty\ [*Abbrev.* TeleTYpe.] Any terminal of the teletype vintage in which the restricted character set is more than offset by the unique busy signal, viz., clatter. *See also* GLASS TTY.

tty01 *n.* What UNIX calls your new $20,000, hi-res., 30-inch, 3D color terminal.

TUI [Text User Interface] *pronounced* too-ey.\ The doomed attempt to implement Windows on cheap 640K 8088 PCs with ASCII monitors.

⇒Borland's TurboVision (1991) proved that you could indeed have all the GUI fun of drag'n'stretch, drop-down-menu, event-ridden windows without the expense of EGA (Enhanced Graphics Adapter) and 16 MB RAM. Alas, bitmapped icons and related marketing forces intervened...

Türing, Alan M. Alan M. Turing's doppelgänger. *See also* TÜRING MACHINE.

Türing machine *n.* A diacritical aberration of TURING MACHINE arising from the Teutonic misconception that Alan M. Turing's exhaustive treatment of the Entscheidungsproblem had earned him at least one umlaut.

Turing machine *n.* [After Alan M. Turing (1912–1954), British mathematician and computer pioneer.] The earliest but still the fastest and most reliable computing system ever conceived. "Dis maschine vill run und run" (K. Gödel).

⇒The Turing machine's legendary MTBF (Mean Time Between Failure) is best exemplified by the absence of a power switch—leading to the famous HALTING PROBLEM. Indeed, it can take either the combined efforts of four metacomputer scientists or Raymond Smullyan to turn the thing off. From a marketing standpoint, it represents the salesperson's dream machine, since to run even simple jobs the system has an insatiable appetite for add-on tapes at $1.98 per foot. *See also* UTM.

Turing Test *n.* The much-cited AI litmus, invariably misrepresenting Turing's original *Gedankenexperiment* ("Computing Machinery and Intelligence," *Mind*, October 1950).

⇒The Turing Test is often portrayed as a simple "Do I have a computer or a real 'thinking' person on the line?" In fact, Turing devised a more precise online game between (A = human male or inhuman machine; B = human female) and interrogator C = either male or female human. C knows (A, B) as (X, Y), but not which is which. A's role is to lie (sic); B's role is to tell the truth (sic). The object: can C via an arbitrary series of interactive queries with A and B spot the woman? e.g., is B = X or B = Y? We then imagine a sequence of games played with (i) A = male human and (ii) A = *digital computer* (Turing rules out other devices!) and see how often C wins. If C's success, on average, is the same for A = human and A = computer, the Turing Test is passed: we have demonstrated that machines can "think."

To date, the only publicly staged Turing Tests have been major fiascoes, testing only if the "remote online entity" is a person or a machine programmed to respond to questions in narrow, predetermined domains. Thus, leading Shakespearean scholars have been scored as mere databases, and Eliza-type programs dedicated to fanciful discourse have been ruled human. For a detailed refutation of the Turing Test, see chapter 1 of Mark Halpern, *Binding Time* (Ablex, 1990.)

turnaround *adj.* (Of a tab card or document) prepared by a computer and sent out in the hope that, when returned, it will provide machine-readable proof that it's back.

⇒The turnaround card was the first disquieting sign that the computer was prepared to take unilateral action to bypass dumb human interference. In the early 1960s many astute machines, tired of inaccurate and slow key-punching (rates were often as low as 5000 columns per manicure), decided to output their own input.

turnkey *adj.* *pronunciation* (often) silent "n".)\ *Also called* **outsourced.** Relating to an externally offered hardware/software package, the success of which hinges (*turns*) on a *key* component to be supplied by the user.

twins *n.* Dreaded collocational wedlock; two words that are not surprised by each other's company. *See also* RETRONYM.

⇒Whoever heard of gratuitous kindness or a dishonest broker? Some DP pairs are now so bonded that word processors will, for instance, automatically append "integration" whenever you type "seamless." Other inseparables include "sustainable growth," "POSIX-compliant," "client/server," "head-turning graphics," and the quadruplet "tight, efficient assembly code.

two's complement *n.* [Origin: old DP folklore "Two's complement, three's a crowd."] The result of applying the Goebbel transformation to a binary number, i.e., changing 1s to 0s and 0s to 1s. *See also* BINARY.

⇒Is the Universe 1's complement, 2's complement or unsigned? Let $U =$ ....1111; so $U + U =$ ....1110; whence $2U = U - 1$; whence $U = -1$; therefore the Universe is 2's complement.

type *n.* (*adj.* typed). *See* DATA TYPING; CAST.

⇒Yet another confusing quirk of the DP laxicon arises from the terms "strongly typed" and "weakly typed." These, in certain computer-linguistic contexts, are unrelated to the force used when pounding the keyboard, but dictate how identifiers are associated with value ranges and chunks of memory.

In strongly-typed languages, you must declare upfront whether your `salary` is string, numeric, Boolean, pointer to function, array of containers, or whatever; and if hopefully declared numeric, whether it is limited to $655.36, $42,949,672.96 or might float beyond. Once the data type of `salary` is declared, its use in the program is carefully and annoyingly monitored. The weakly typed languages, however, are nearer to our natural habits: the data type is generally "deduced" from usage. Thus, `salary := salary + 100;` implies that `salary` is of the numeric, incrementable persuasion. Decades of donnish language-designer blood have been shed debating the pros and cons of these and other extremes.

U

un- *prefix* [*Chiefly archaic* form of NON-, NOT-.] A vulgar, weak indication that the prefixed entity or property is absent.

⇒The subtle differences between these negatory options need to be mastered by all DP communicators. First, the prefix "not-" is best reserved for the Boolean environment, i.e., where the truth value of the following two-valued logical element or expression requires strict reversal. Wherever possible, the more impressive symbol "~" should be used. The X in "not X" ["~X"] must be a true Boolean-type variable; for example, the expression "not ready" is completely nonacceptable, since the predicate "ready" in DP usage admits to at least four distinct, valid negations ("almost ready;" "ready except on a set of measure zero;" "mañana;" "ready when you are;" and so on). The current ascendancy of "non-" derives from its positively nonnegative connotations compared with the defensive, almost apologetic "un-." Consultants may shrink from submitting an "unfinished" report, but can proudly invoice a "nonfinished" one, implying that the best is yet to come. Similarly, reference to an "unidentified fault" indicates resignation, whereas a "nonidentified fault" surely will be confronted and nailed within a page or two. Finally, consider two systems, one "unstable," the other "nonstable." The former leaves us uneasy, uncertain as to cause or cure. The latter confidently assures us that no cure is possible!

unbundling *n.* [From *un-* "deprived of" + *bundling.*] A widely adopted marketing strategy whereby, say, a car manufacturer charges extra for such options as wheels and seats, or a thief invoices the victim in order to recover legitimate out-of-pocket expenses incurred during the crime. *See* BUNDLED; RETRONYM; -READY.

undecidability of arithmetic *n.* A set of theorems variously established by Gödel (1931), Tarski (1935), Church (1936), and Rosser (1936). Briefly, it has been shown that for a set of axioms rich enough to "support" everyday arithmetic, no algorithm exists which can determine for every arithmetical sentence in finitely many steps whether it is true or false.

⇒Computer users should be aware of the metamathematical bugs lurking around God's programming of the integers. The "God is dead" school suggests that had He survived His remarkable 6-day crash development project (and remember that both the hardware *and* the software were strapped in from one word—the logos, to boot), He surely would not have left arithmetic *incomplete.* Users faced with numerical inconsistencies in their PENTIUM should pause before castigating the programmer or calling Intel. There are related flaws, apparently, in what one might call God's epistemological operating system. The size of the problem can best be appreciated by considering Russell and Whitehead's *Principia Mathematica* as a ONE-LINE PATCH that consumed 50 man-years of effort, but failed to fix the problem. Let us, therefore, be more tolerant of the quirks in our own person-made subsystems. "Shoot not thy programmers on the Sabbath, but rather, cast them into the wilderness with bread sufficient unto seven days" (St. Prespers's *Disciplina Formularum*).

undetected *adj.* Of which the least said the better.

⇒Nevertheless, it should be observed that in the mataphysics of error analysis, the undetected error plays the role of the demon (*See also* DAEMON) in medieval theology, that is to say, a real but quiescent lurkage upon which the exorcising FIX cannot be laid until some malevolent manifestation impacts the tormented. Or, in modern parlance: "Don't worry, dear, it may never happen." Now, as then, exorcism requires the prior location and naming of the responsible demon, followed by feverish readings from obscure cabalistic documentation. Sometimes the laying of the hands on the keyboard is supplemented by the banging of the fists on the cabinet. Some computer scientists claim that well-structured incantations exist that guarantee the absolute purity of program segments; others remain haunted by the inestimable devils crouching in the links, ready to pounce whenever the segments are joined; and, at the merry end of the spectrum, are the Calvinists, to whom software is one diabolical continuum of nondetectable evil awaiting the final Armageddon. Most practical programmers shun such pessimistic obfuscation, content to let sleeping bugs lie, and positively relishing the occasional visit from a third-shift succubus.

undo *n.* (Text editing) A command that vitiates (rolls back or renders inoperative) the previous editing action or command.

⇒Toggling your undo button serves as a time-killing, look-busy ploy. And for biblical processors of the Word, the whole of Mark 16:9–20 can be made to disappear and reappear with a single keystroke. Undo should not be confused with REDO, a command that *repeats* the previous action or command. However, if the command preceding the redo was an undo, or vice versa, confusion is permitted and often mandatory. Editors with multilevel (nested) undos and redos that allow the repeated redoing of earlier undos, and conversely, have been known to cause user-madness and cries of "Alas, am I undone or redone?" In theory, given disk enough and time, an editor could store every intermediate state from the time of piracy, allowing one to de-install via an appropriate sequence of undo/redo commands.

Dr. Rudolph Langer of Sybex tells me that the nested-undo pioneer was probably A. L. Samuels of checker-playing-program fame. Apparently, saving all the previous states of Samuel's early IBM system called for a growing number of *rooms* of magnetic tape reels and decks.

Some have pondered the possibility of the ultimate undo that would eventually take you back to the brink of the Big Bang or whatever the t = 0 state happened to be or, as it were, not to be. At some point in this GUT-wrenching event-reversal, of course, the undo button would cease to exist...heiliger Strohsack! Back to das ould Zeichenbrett—wir müssen noch einmal von vorn anfangen!

undocumented *adj.* (Of a feature) essential.

⇒The longstanding barb that BUGS could be wished away as undocumented features has shifted to a higher level of cynicism. MICROSOFT, to pick just one tiny example, has been accused of withholding vital API information from rival software developers, and even of inserting sneaky "hidden" code to bedevil non-MS operating systems and applications. These alleged shenanigans have triggered hugely successful books such as *Undocumented Windows,* giving us the new categories, "documented-undocumented" and "undocumented-undocumented."

One interpretation of the paper "Run Privileged Code from Your Windows-based Program Using Call Gates" (Matt Pietrek, *Microsoft Systems Journal,* May 1993) is that "privileged" means code that enlists those features known only to Microsoft. Microsoft is clearly responding to criticism from perplexed Windows developers by offering a direct hotline to its all-knowing CEO: "If it don't work, call Gates."

Unicial *adj.* Relating or pertaining to the UNIX operating system.

UNICS Early name for UNIX.

uninstall *v. Also called* **unpirate.** To set free arbitrary regions of a hard disk while further corrupting vital .SYS and .INI files.

union *n.* (C/C++) *Also called* (Pascal, Modula-2) **variant record.** A sneaky but essential mechanism for bypassing type safety; the realization, after a hundred pages of pure CS polemic, that RAM and SEMANTICS don't really mix.

⇒The C notion of anonymous unions is celebrated in the song "Strangers in the Night."

UNIX *n. & adj.* Although registered by AT&T Bell Labs, the Mother Church, as an *adjective* (as in, UNIX system; *UNIX Review;* UNIX World Takeover), the name is usually treated as a noun. Written (mainly) in C, UNIX was the first truly PORTABLE operating system, a fact which many see as a mixed blessing. *Also called* RUNIX to celebrate its many arcanities. *More at* TNHD.

⇒My *UNIX Review* column, July 1993, appealing for "low-self-esteem" computer-book titles to challenge the lunacy of *DOS for Dummies* (*See* BOOKS FOR THE BAFFLED), roused hundreds of my esteemed devotees from their torpid hammocks . The most frequent suggestion, "UNIX for Eunuchs," reminds me that some so-called puns are surely entitled to a well-earned vacation (*See* PUN MORATORIUM). I hereby allow newcomers to the fun-packed world of UNIX a stop-watched, five-minute giggle over the near-homophonic pair, UNIX-Eunuchs. Thereafter, all nudge-nudge references will be ruthlessly dereferenced *sous peine de garrottage.* Let it be noted, one more time, that "In 1970, Brian Kernighan jokingly referred to their [Ken Thompson and his Computer Research Group, Bell Labs colleagues] two-user system as UNICS, for the 'UNiplexed Information and Computing System' since MULTICS seemed to be a vastly oversized operating system by comparison...Soon after, UNICS became UNIX and the name has stuck ever since..." (Don Libes and Sandy Ressier, *Life With UNIX, A Guide For Everyone* [Englewood Cliffs, N.J.: Prentice-Hall, 1989]).

Since MULTICS had attracted the nasty SARCONYM "Many Unneccessarily Large Tables In Core Simultaneously," the implied joke was that "UNIX was a castrated version of MULTICS" (ibid.).

There was a time when UNIX hackers were so wild and uncouth...how wild and uncouth were they, Stan? Well, some were refused entry to a Grateful Dead concert for violating the dress code. But those early Woodstockian days of "Sex, Drugs & UNIX" banners are well-nigh gone as UNIX celebrates its Silver Anniversary in gray-suited boardrooms. Peter H. Salus, *A Quarter Century of UNIX* (Reading, Mass.: Addison-Wesley, 1994) provides a detailed blow-by-blow account.

up *adj.* In the (figurative) direction of being operational, whence the field engineers' Sisyphean task of "getting it up." *Compare* DOWN. *See also* DOWN-TIME; UPTIME.

upgrade *n. & v. trans.* [From *up* + Latin *grădus* "steep incline."] **1** *n.* An expensive counterexample to earlier upward-compatibility conjectures. **2** *n.* A painful crisis which belatedly restores one's faith in the previous system. **3** *v. trans.* To replace (obsolete stability) with something less boring. *See also* APPLE; CONVERSION; OBSOLESCENCE; RIGHTSIZE; SIDEGRADE.

⇒ Our 360/50, it pleases us plenty;
We bought it last week to replace the 370!
We traded the VM originally installed,
But a second-hand DAT box is worth bugger-all.

uptime *n.* Some future (unspecified) time when the system will be UP and running. *Compare* DOWNTIME. *See also* CRASH.

urn *n.* A high-class jam jar containing colored balls and the ashes of dead statisticians. "What's a Bayesian urn?" "Less than expected!"

user *n.* [Origin: perhaps ironical use of agent noun *user* "one that makes use of," or confusion with *used* "exploited."] **1** *n.* The individual or group invoiced for and waiting to operate certain boxed items lying unopened in another department.

⇒Until the items are correctly delivered, decrated, and assembled, the user is also known as a REFERENCE ACCOUNT.

2 *n.* The first of the SEVEN CATASTROPHES OF COMPUTING. *See also* END USER.

user-friendly *adj.* **1** *Marketing* A predicate applied so widely and uncritically that it is now totally devoid of meaning. **2** *Programming* (*derogatory*) Hacker-hostile; insanely mollycoddling; obsessively fool-proof and fit only for fools. *See also* APPLIANCE COMPUTING.

UTM *n.* [Universal Turing Machine.] The top-of-the-range TURING MACHINE, able to simulate any past, present, or future computing system.

⇒Theoretically, it can do this using just one BISTABLE element (C. Shannon, 1966) and a lot of tape. The speed of the UTM is limited only by the user's imagination and is not constrained by the trying tardiness of physical elements, such as electrons, that screws the competition. This freedom more than compensates for the archaic, 1930s architecture and the need to write your own add subroutine.

V

vaporware *n.* Products that are announced with a great flourish but then held back from the market, possibly indefinitely, until the vendor is thoroughly convinced that they are 100 percent BUG free. *See also* FS; NT; PROGRAM; STATE-OF-THE-ART.

⇒Rumors that vaporware is sometimes a ploy to unsettle competitors are too scurrilous to be taken seriously.

VAR Possibly overloaded *abbrev.* **1** Variable; changeable; unreliable. **2** Value-Added Reseller.

VC Overloaded *abbrev.* **1** Victoria Cross (highest British military medal). **2** Verification Condition (Dijkstra/Gries design process). **3** Venture Capitalist.

⇒Possible link: if you meet a VC's list of VCs, you win the VC.

VDU *n.* *pronounced* toooob\ [Visual Display Unit.] *See also* CURSOR; GLASS TTY.

vector *v. trans.* [Pentagonian.] To dispatch in the wrong direction, as in "Our planes were vectored to intercept the enemy."

vendor-independent *adj.* Not for sale. *Compare* MACHINE-INDEPENDENT; PORTABLE.

verification *n.* An optional method of compounding the errors of data entry: e.g., the situation where Jo(e) decides that the "8" that Fred(a) thought was a "3" is really a "5."

version *n. & v. trans.* **1** *n. Software* Any one of a series of conflicting, mutilated copies of a lost original. **2** *v. trans.* To make yet another version of something. *See also* VERSION, LATEST.

⇒Versions are distinguished, one from the other, by assigning arbitrary tags such as *current, authorized, my, your,* and *latest.* Further subcategorization calls for a variety of local "Dewey-it-yourself" classifications, or an entry in the date-stolen field. Although scoffed at by uninformed prescriptionists, the verb "to version" has a well-attested heritage, predating the DP industry by many centuries.

version, latest *n.* That VERSION which most exceeds the DEADLINE for completion.

versionitis *n.* An incurable TTD (textually transmitted disease) commonly associated with careless file-sharing. *See also* SHELL.

vi *n.* *pronounced* vee-eye, never veye or six\ (UNIX) *Abbrev.* visual interface. A full-screen text editor devised by Bill Joy at UC Berkeley.

⇒Earlier UNIX text editors, such as ed, were "blind" requiring the use of line numbers and a good memory. vi is seen by some as the first mollycoddling assault on the UNIX machismo. It is neither widely known nor true that vi is named for Vladimir Ilyitch (Lenin), still a hero in the People's Republic of Berkeley.

video games *n. Also* **VG.** *See also* NINTENDINITIS.

⇒A VG ethician writes: "Although socially disastrous and intellectually stunting for the players, video games present the most exciting and creative challenges in contemporary software development. VG demands an almost insane dedication to solving problems in computer graphics and sound with absurdly low-cost hardware. Mainframe COBOL payroll programs simply fail to match the excitement of simulating mass decapitations."

A less widely known aspect of computer games concerns the ethical integrity of the user. Part of the addiction of game playing, of course, arises from the desire to win ("win big," I gather, is the current idiom). When taken to excess, this can lead to the urge to cheat. A strange undergound culture has emerged offering ways to "beat the game."

I cannot resist revealing some of the winning ploys as related in the *Abacus* (Atari Bay Area Computer Users Society) *Newsletter* of May/June 1990. It seems that VG programmers leave certain hooks in their code for debugging and testing. If these can be uncovered by fair means or foul, the player can take advantage of them to improve the odds for victory. The *ABACUS Newsletter* tells all.

In the game Defender of the Crown, if you hold down the "k" key while game is loading, you acquire a "home army of 1024 knights and a campaign army of 1024 knights."

Platoon seems to have a more bizarre cheat: "Type *Hamburger* at the title screen...press your joystick button, then F5 when the jungle screen comes up. Your man is now invulnerable to the attacks of the little Commie #!$&*s." (Are these games purveyors unaware of recent widely publicized reforms in the once-Evil Empire?).

The game ARKANOID can be corrupted by typing space (pause) "DSIMAGIC" (pause) spacebar. Thereafter, you are free to increase your resources beyond the legal limits. Typing "04-08-59," the author's birthday (so much for unobvious passwords), during certain episodes of Barbarian makes Hegor immortal!

To cheat at MENACE, you type "XR31TURBONUTTERBASTARD" (no relation to Philippe Kahn of Borland) while the game is in progress. This magical (and, of course, hitherto UNDOCUMENTED) incantation replenishes your supply of shields, cannons and lasers.

The ultimate cheat, however, is a black box called Game Genie, distributed by Galoob Toys of South San Francisco, Calif. The Game Genie "causes Nintendo games characters to move at slower speeds or bypass obstacles originally programmed into the games. It allows players to skip entire game levels, and to add extra 'lives' to a player's life" (Business Briefs, *San Francisco Chronicle,* June 2, 1990). Not surprisingly, Nintendo, on behalf of all honest gamesters, has sued Galoob Toys to keep this device off the market.

virtual *adj.* **1** Being or pertaining to a tangible, nonexistent object. "I can see it, but it's not there" (Lady Macbeth). *Compare* TRANSPARENT.

⇒Announcing Virtuality a few days before IBM but 7 years after Ferranti, a spokesperson for Irish Business Machines said, "Oh, so it's person, is it, indeed? I'll be having none of that, I tell yer. It's me, Sean, as well you know. Come outside and say that, if you're man enough...." Later, when the presentation had been restructured, the following statement was issued: "Virtual products offer a revolutionary challenge, not only to this company and its customers, but to the entire accounting profession. We are now able to bill well in advance of delivery, deliver well in advance of production, and spend the money long before we invoice. On the other hand, our users can claim tax investment credits and depreciation well in advance of installation. We suggest a new difference-of-the-digits depreciation metolo...melthodogoly..." (prolonged cheers, waving of order papers, chants of "We want Sean!," counterchants of "Over my dead system!"). The rest is history...

2 (Of a C++ function) providing the mechanism for POLYMORPHISM via late (dynamic or run-time) binding. *See also* BINDING TIME.

⇒"Virtual function" are far from "virtuous." In fact, the best C++ style guides are openly cautious: "I conclude that it is more important to show where to avoid virtual functions than where to use them" (Tom Cargill, *C++ Programming Style* [Reading, Mass.: Addison-Wesley, 1992]).

3 (Of a reality) disconcertingly projected as a palsied sequence of low-definition images.

virus *n.* [Latin *vir* "male person" whence the cognates "slimy liquid, venom, poison, stench, swamp."] **1** A piece of code spread *deliberately* to annoy or incapacitate the user. *Sometimes* confused with "poor but honest" code that inadvertently creates the same problems. *See* DOS. **2** Nature's warning to eschew PIRACY and careless disk-swapping.

⇒"Living" viruses and the biologists who study them are understandably annoyed at this namespace corruption. That a few lines of assembly language can achieve FAT-zapping and self-replication hardly matches the complex invasive strategies of even the simplest real virus.

Confusing DP viral taxonomies have been proposed with phyla and species such as Trojan Horse and WORM, while individual viruses are proudly named for their idiot perpetrators, dumb places of origin, or the date they are primed to attack. Until infected, most users assume that viromania is a scaremongering ploy to sell anti-viral software. The ultimate scare was the discovery of a virus in a virus-detection package. The only safe approach is to start with an empty disk and write your own OS, editor, compiler/linker and applications with *no* outsourcing whatsoever. P.S.—Did you check all your ROMs?

visionary *n.* Formerly a shunned, pie-in-the-sky dreamer, but now granted an Op-Ed and Keynote Conference monopoly. *See also* XERASSIC PARC.

⇒"Once we've killed the lawyers, let's disembowel the visionaries" (Anon).

visual *adj. Chiefly* Marketing. (Of a programming method) able to generate applications directly from a flow-chart; requiring a good eye and steady hand but no previous coding experience. *See also* METRIC.

⇒Thus diverse AppBuilders promise the non-programmer a palette of drag'n'drop widgets and the line-drawing tools to sketch their interdependencies.

VLCC [Very Large Crude Carrier.] **1** Ma Bell before her breakdown. **2** A super-tanker using the "ahead-of-time" delivery methodology also known as "spillage."

VLSI [Very Large Scale Integration.] The successor to LSI (Large Scale Integration) and the predecessor to ELSI (Extremely Large Scale Integration). *See also* HYPER-.

⇒The use of vague size modifiers leads to problems since our technology is quite wont to leap forward. We could soon see ULSI (Unbelievably Large Scale Integration). Follow that, Carver!

VMOS *n.* [Acronym for Virtual Memory Operating System.] *See* PAGING.

Voltaire-Candide, law of "All is for the best in the best of all possible environments." (Originally: "Tout est pour le mieux dans le meilleur des mondes possibles" (Voltaire, *Candide*).

⇒A cynical 18th-century acceptance of the status quo adopted by computer users in the 20th century, but not without some envy of the relatively trouble-free adventures enjoyed by Candide and Pangloss. Among the many familiar observations supporting the law, we offer:

"God sent us this 360, and Lo! our 1400 payroll programs run no slower than before."

"The six-month delivery setback will allow us to refine our flowcharts and build a computer room."

"The file I have just accidently erased was due for purging sooner or later."

"The more data I punch on this card, the lighter it becomes, and the lower the mailing cost."

"Our system has broken down. We can all retire to the canteen, where the on-site engineer is watching the Big Fight on TV."

"This flowchart, although rejected in toto by the DPM, will nicely cover the crack in the wall above my desk."

"The system has crashed just as I was beginning to suspect an endless loop situation."

"We were freezing during the power outage, until the standby generator caught fire."

voton *n.* *pronounced* vote-on\ A high-energy physics particle with a half-life of exactly 2 years. Although it failed to produce the elusive Z particle, the Superconducting Super Collider produced a shower of *negative votons* heretofore unknown to physics (Henry G. Nimble).

VTSO *n.* [Virtual TimeSharing Option (© Irish Business Machines).] An option which allows one teleprinter to support up to $64 \times 370/168$s (no modem is needed if all units are within a radius of 60 feet).

⇒Theoretically a total of $128 \times 370/168$s can be attached, but response time degrades to an unacceptable level owing to mainframe THRASHING. Also, it becomes physically difficult to meet the 60-foot limit, so the extra cost of modems must be considered. See the accompanying illustration.

VUE *n.* A text editor available on the Alpha Micro system, the most memorable feature of which is that <Ctrl+L> moves the cursor to the right.

⇒It's fun to compare the various keystroke-to-action mappings lurking in the jungle, especially if you are forced to switch spasmodically between word processors. For instance, <Ctrl+T> pages down in VUE but deletes a word in WordStar. This is a nuisance but not a major hardship, so let's assign 15 to {<Ctrl+T>, VUE, WordStar} where my subjective metric over all {keystroke, WP1, WP2} triples assigns a "calamitous disparity" range from 0 to 100. {<Ctrl+Y>, VUE, WordStar} is hard to pin down, though, since <Ctrl+Y> in VUE line-deletes "only to the right of the cursor" but in WordStar the whole line disappears. Perhaps a bonus of 5 should be awarded for such delightful, cursor-sensitive quirks. I have not yet found the perfect 100—what I have in mind is a keystroke command that either saves your changes or deletes every file on the network.

vulnerability *n.* A measure of the adverse impact which the output of a program or package has on its recipients. *See* PAYROLL.

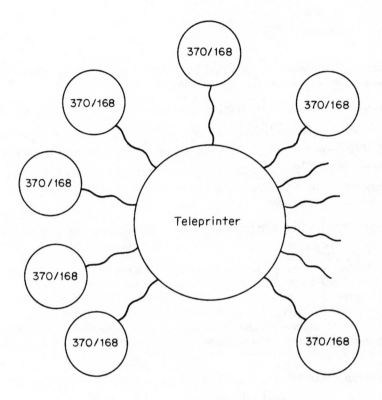

VTSO

W

warp *n.* [Origin: *warp* "To distort (the facts)."] A version of OS/2 that IBM claims will run on LOW-MEMORY systems.

waterfall model *n. Also called* **Houdini model.** The software development METHODOLOGY preferred by Niagaran barrelassers.

watergate *n.* A fluid logic switching device uniquely able to render previous states "inoperable."

weasel *adj.* (Of words or actions) couched to avoid litigation, *esp.* the cowardly predication "alleged." *See also* TRADEMARK.

Weaver fish the England! *interj.* One of the standard counterexamples to simplistic, dictionary-based MT (Machine Translation).

⇒The (true) story is that a young French boy wants to end a letter to his English penpal with *Vive l'Angleterre!* ("Long Live England!"). He finds *vive [n. f.]* "Weaver or weever fish; a member of the family Trachinidae..." in his dictionary. He already knows that *l'* is a form of the definite article, and the rest is apocryphal...

A possibly Koestlerian coincidence is that Warren Weaver was one of the first (1948) to warn us of the complexities of real systems such as human language. Possibly not.

Welfare, Rabbi Burns's Law of "Gie a mon muckle matestamps an' he gollops the day; teach him the forgin' o' it an' he's aye set."

⇒Liberally translated: "Give people fish and they have a meal; give them rods and nets and they have ongoing sustenance." Unliberal version: "Give people foodstamps and they eat today; teach them to forge foodstamps and they're set for life."

what-if *adj.* (Of a program) primed with hypothetical instances to guide future actions. *See also* SCATOMANCY; SPREADSHEET; WHY-NOT.

why-not *adj.* (Of a program) primed with hypothetical instances to justify past actions. *See also* SCATOMANCY; SPREADSHEET; WHAT-IF.

wheel *n.* A device with so many conflicting applications that each user must reinvent it to preserve sanity. *See also* NIH; REUSABILITY.

⇒In particular, never say "We must avoid reinventing the wheel" to an auto-parts expert...she'll hit you with a 5-lb catalog (and that's just the GM 1993 wheel range). Regular and spurious variations in wheel and tire specifications (at the drop of a hubcap?) play a major role in automotive economics, comparable to the CONNECTOR CONSPIRACY in our fair trade.

A wheel-historian writes: "The transition from square to round wheels was delayed by the introduction of the triangular PARADIGM. This well-reasoned approach, seducing mankind over several dark ages, maintained that three bumps per revolution was one less than four."

widget *n.* [Origin obscure: possible blend of "whatsit" and "gadget."] **1** The so-and-so, thingy OBJECT *akin to* French *machin* and *truc*. **2** A visible GUI component whose name and function are obscured by an icon.

⇒Compare: "Experience is what's left when you've forgotten their names."

wild card *n.* **1** A symbol which DEFAULTs to anything and is therefore mandatory at moments of doubt. *See also* METACHARACTER. **2** *Archaic* A tab card randomly inserted upside down in a pack to enliven the action. *See also* LUDDITE.

WIMP, wimp 1 Overloaded SARCONYM a. (GUI) Windows, Icon, Mouse, Pulldown. b. (Physics) Weakly Interacting Massive Particle. **2** A mollycoddled user unable to cope with command-line syntax.

WIN31 *n.* An odd compromise between WIN16 and WIN32.

⇒For the puzzled outsider: WIN31 stands for Windows 3.1, whereas WIN16 and WIN32 refer generically to 16- and 32-bit implementations. WIN31 is, in fact, a WIN16.

windows *n. Also capitalized* **Windows** as presumed (disputed) trademark of MICROSOFT. *Derog. form* **Windoze**. Conspicuous tesselation promoted by the purveyors of RAM and MIPS. *See also* GATES, WILLIAM; GUI; X WINDOWS.

⇒The Windows literature tells us "…whenever an application creates a window, Windows sends that window a WMCREATE message. This is certainly reasonable, since being created is after all an event that might be of interest to the window" (Durant, Carlson, and Yao, *Programmer's Guide to Windows* [Alameda, Calif.: Sybex, 1987], p. 151).

One is tempted to add that, prior to creation, the window is incapable of showing interest or disinterest in anything at all. I detect a neo-Cartesian autoepistemic syllogism here: "I (window speaking) have been told that I am; I hear this interesting message; therefore I am."

Wirth, Niklaus Also known affectionately as **Ould Nick.** "The grand old language designer of grand old languages…" (D. Ritchie's grandmother).

⇒1970, Pascal; 1975, Modula; 1980, Modula-2; 1985, Oberon; 1990, Modula-3… but what's he done for us lately?

The long-standing Wirthean in-joke was definitively related by Ould Nick himself at the ACM HOPL-II (2nd History of Programming Languages) Conference, Boston, 1993. Someone *did* ask him how the "W" should be pronounced, and he *did* reply, "That depends on whether you call by vorth or by walue."

WOM *n.* [Acronym for Write-Only Memory. © Irish Business Machines.] An early chip designed to implement the POLISH NOTATION, now superseded by the EWOM. *Compare* WORM; WORN.

word processor *n.* WP. **1** *Archaic* any system equipped with a slow, double-case printer. **2** A TEXT EDITOR with 200 unused features. *See also* DTP; SPELCHEK.

workstation *n.* A cheap mini or an expensive PC.

⇒F. Michael Trimberger suggests that "workstation" is modeled on "Train station" (a place where trains stop).

WORM 1 [Acronym for Write-Once Read-Many.] Optimistic term applied to a particular optical disk technology whereby the user can create but not update a CD. Known to pessimists as WORN (Write-Once Read-Never). *See also* CD-ROM. **2 worm** *n.* A type of VIRUS, so-called because it *worms* its way throughout the net, gobbling up RAM; a globally malignant MEMORY LEAK.

WORN [Acronym for Write-Once Read-Never.] The state of most COMPUTER BOOK authors. *See* WORM.

worst-case design *n.* The one delivered.

Wrigeletto, Signor (1929–) Doppelgänger spokesperson invoked to explain my apparent errors to fellow DORYPHORES.

writ-only *adj.* (Of a CAL [Computer-aided Litigation] program) able to generate documents for the prosecution.

Wysiwyg, Zbigniew (1920–1943) *pronounced* veeseevig.\ Polish philosopher; student of Husserl; murdered at Buchenwald.

⇒Ironically misremembered in the acrostic GUI claim "What You See Is What You Get" (*pronounced* wizziwig\), Zbigniew's own phenomenological anti-Nazi thesis was "What You Get Is What You Permit."

X

X *Also called* **The X Window System** (MIT, 1984–) *n.* A CLIENT/SERVER graphics system for displaying pixels along the X-axis using xlib calls. 2-dimensional displays require the addition of ylib, and so on. *Caution* Avoid the term "X Windows," which *may* provoke trademark litigation from the purveyors of the popular but inferior Microsoft WINDOWS. *More at* TNHD.

⇒So far, MIT's X qua singleton X has avoided The Curse of X (*see* X, THE CURSE OF). However, the use of X in the algebraic template and corpse-locational senses has been compromised. Thus, *X for Dummies* can mean any title in the BOOKS FOR THE BAFFLED series or a particular book that even IDG dare not publish. (As we go to bed, a *UNIX for Dummies* has appeared, so the dare is no longer beyond daring.) On the bright side, there is a delightful book called *The Joy of X* by Niall Mansfield (Reading, Mass.: Addison-Wesley, 1993) in which the X is clarified by the subtitle: *An Overview of the X Window System.* For a GUI fetishist, the illustrations are appropriately titillating.

X, The Curse Of *n.* A jinx far worse than the mummy's; it strikes all trendy companies and products with names that contain the letter X.

⇒The curse is magnified for repeated X's. Consider Exxon, Axxess, Xerox, Xenix, REXX, Xanthoxylum, Pope John XIX (and higher). QED. Could it be related to the algebraic connotation of too many unknowns, or to the uncertainty of pronunciation? Cynics explain, for instance, that the first "X" in Xenix is pronounced as in "zoo" and the second as in "eczema."

XAND *n. & adj. & v.* *pronounced* ex-and, kzand, or zand.\ [eXclusive AND] A Boolean operator of dubious utility. "A XAND B" is read "A AND B but not both." Its TRUTH TABLE, if any, is left as an exercise for the reader. *Compare* NAND.

XDS *n.* [Xerox Data Systems.] In use until 1976, when Xerox Corporation decided to concentrate on the traditional, more reliable aspects of reprography.

⇒XDS is now used as an abbreviation for eXoDuS, yet another warning that mortality in the DP arena is not confined to the midgets. Xerox has since returned to computerdom, pioneering but failing to market many fine advances at the famed Xerox PARC (Palo Alto Research Center).

Xerassic Parc An SK-B movie in which Alan C. Kay, well cast as the crazed visionary, inadvertently clones hordes of Illiacs, which then take over the INTERNET. The happy ending is that Internet response magically improves and Kay joins the Clinton/Gore administration as SDH supremo. *See also* MAINFRAME.

xlib *n.* [Origin suggested by Anne Butzen: Ukrainian "bread."] A library of X routines; a source of bread for many UNIX software vendors and VARS.

Y

ya- Acronymic prefix: yet another. *See also* YACC.

⇒Following this tradition, I dubbed my *Understanding UNIX* (Sybex, 1992; 2d ed. 1994), YAUB (Yet Another UNIX Book). The Spanish translators (*Cómo Usar UNIX,* 1993) missed the joke by rendering YAUB as TOLU (Todavía Otro Libro UNIX).

yacc *pronounced* yack.\\ **1** (UNIX) Yet Another Compiler Compiler. **2** (AI) Yet Another Comment Compiler. A major advance that ignores your code and compiles your comments.

⇒Pass 1 converts, say,

```
i++; // post-increment counter by 1
```

to

```
post-increment counter by 1 // i++;
```

maintaining the old convention that any vagueness in the left hand column can be supplemented by vagueness on the right, or vice versa. Work is well advanced on Pass 2.

yacc's chief market is the cheap conversion of LEGACY code to modern formats. If you haven't been commenting your programs adequately, don't blame yacc. You've been warned often enough!

yank *n. & v.* UNIX VI command that transfers text from the editing buffer to a specified temporary buffer.

⇒Using a lower-case "y" causes the previous contents of the temporary buffer to be overwritten; this is the *destructive yank* known in Atlanta as the *Sherman.*

yet another *adj.* Often prepended with "O Lord Spare Us!" *See* YA-.

YODALS *n.* [Acronym for Yangtse Opium Den Accounts Leceivable System.] *See* CHINESE TOTAL.

your program *n.* A maze of PASTEMIC non sequiturs littered with clever-clever tricks and irrelevant comments. *Compare* LESS THAN; MY PROGRAM.

Z

Zadeh, Lotfi (1921–) Inventor of Farsi, later known as FUZZY, logics, sets, measure theories, topologies, inference schemata and washing machines. *See also* DEFUZZIFICATION; FUZZ; FUZZIFICATION.

⇒It was while pondering whether his brother Lofti was "quite tall," "tall enough," or "very tall" that Zadeh hit on the idea of fuzzy sets. The ensuing fuzzy-ethos explosion and its altercationary aftermath are nicely documented by McNeill and Freiberger (*Fuzzy Logic*, Simon & Schuster, 1993). Three quotations they omit are

> "I am no respecter of Persians" (Peter Cheeseman).

> "When de fuzz hit de fan, man, you gonna run if you can, man!" (Schnapple IcedTea Rap Group).

> "Fuzz neither hits the Fan nor misses the Fan. Fuzz *is* the Fan (Bart Kosko, *Zen and the Art of Fuzzy Maintenance*, 2001).

Also missing is the oratorio "Baisez les Baysiennes" (words: Lotfi Zadeh; music: Georges Baizet).

zap *v. trans.* [Origin: onomatopoeia.] **1** To kill, delete. **2** To revive, add zest, enspice. *See also* AUTO-ANTONYM; TRASH CAN.

⇒Thus, you can zap a file of strings or a string of beans. To those of modest palate, the two meanings may coalesce. The killer-zapper, however, carries mindless, vicious overtones, echoes of the VIDEO GAME culture of wasting asteroids and alien intelligence with equal panache—hardly the same as the Szechuan attack on soups and vegetables.

zero-knowledge *adj.* **1** (Of a proof)…sorry, I'm not prepared to discuss it. **2**. (Of a COMPUTER BOOK author) overqualified.

ZIF 1 Zero-insert Force. **2** Winner of the Miss Zif-Davis Beauty Contest.